Ad Law

Ad Law

The essential guide to advertising law and regulation

Edited by
Richard Lindsay

KoganPage

An IPA book
Institute of Practitioners in Advertising

London office

Regional offices

44 Belgrave Square
London
SW1X 8QS

Arms Evertyne House
Quay Road
Dun Cow Quay
Blyth
Northumberland
NE24 2AS

Catchpell House
Carpet Lane
Edinburgh
EH6 6SS

www.ipa.co.uk

First published in Great Britain in 2016 by Kogan Page Limited

2nd Floor, 45 Gee Street
London
EC1V 3RS
United Kingdom

1518 Walnut Street, Suite 1100
Philadelphia PA 19102
USA

4737/23 Ansari Road
Daryaganj
New Delhi 110002
India

ISBN   978 0 7494 7289 4
E-ISBN   978 0 7494 7290 0

British Library Cataloguing-in-Publication Data

A CIP record for this book is available from the British Library.

Typeset by Graphicraft Limited, Hong Kong
Print production managed by Jellyfish
Printed and bound by CPI Group (UK) Ltd, Croydon CR0 4YY

CONTENTS

PART THREE   Do I comply? Key challenges and themes in advertising   121

11   Defamation and malicious falsehood 166

Nick Walker and Jonathan Coad

12   The internet and beyond: advertising on the internet and in social media 180

Brinsley Dresden

13   Lotteries and prize promotions 202

Charles Swan

14   Music in advertising 218

Scott McKinlay

PART FOUR   Industry issues: Key challenges for certain business sectors   281

18   Alcohol   283

Paul Jordan, Sally Dunstan and Andy Butcher

19   The advertising of food: Nutrition and health claims   297

Rebecca Chong and Richard Lindsay

23   Smoking and vaping   339

Dan Smith, Mathilda Davidson and George Sevier

Introduction   339
Tobacco   339
Incidental smoking in advertising and smoking paraphernalia   344
Anti-smoking advertising and smoking cessation aids   346
Electronic cigarette advertising   347
Summary   352

PART FIVE   Business affairs   355

24   Client/agency contracts   357

Jo Farmer

Introduction   358
The ISBA/IPA Suggested Terms   358
Term of the appointment: retainers   359
Term of the agreement: projects   360
Exclusivity and non-compete   360
Remuneration and third-party costs   362
Third-party contracts   363
Warranties   363
Limitation of liability   364
Copyright and other intellectual property rights   365
Audit   367
TUPE   367
Summary   368

25   Pitching   369

India Forsyth and Richard Lindsay

Introduction   369
Resources for IPA member agencies   369
Other considerations   371
Summary   373

LIST OF CONTRIBUTORS

BRISTOWS

www.bristows.com

Andy Butcher

Andy advises across the full range of 'soft' IP rights, with advertising and trade mark law being his principal practice areas. He assists clients with domain name and other IP disputes in the High Court and below, while on the non-contentious side he advises on trade mark filing strategy and compliance of advertising copy with UK advertising regulations.

andrew.butcher@bristows.com

Sally Dunstan

Sally is a senior associate, qualified in both Australia and England, advising across all aspects of the development, prosecution and exploitation of brands, including advertising and marketing issues, trade mark and design prosecution and advice, contentious registry proceedings and brand protection. She also drafts and negotiates commercial agreements, including those relating to the development and exploitation of IP.

sally.dunstan@bristows.com

Paul Jordan

Paul is a partner in the Brands group, leading the Advertising and Marketing team. He has significant experience in relation to all aspects of ad law, including the negotiation of all key media contracts, regulatory compliance, campaign clearance and brand protection strategy, multi-jurisdiction promotions and IP enforcement and dispute work.

paul.jordan@bristows.com

BWB

Bates Wells Braithwaite

www.bwbllp.com

Rupert Earle

Rupert Earle is a partner at Bates Wells & Braithwaite, specialising in media and regulatory law. He has long acted for UK advertising regulatory bodies. He has many years of experience in advising other clients on advertising-related disputes (comparative, IP, data processing etc), as well as defending Trading Standards prosecutions. In addition he has defended and prosecuted numerous libel actions, pursued high-profile Freedom of Information Act challenges, and defended and challenged regulatory decisions in judicial review proceedings.

r.earle@bwbllp.com

www.dlapiper.com

John Wilks

John Wilks is a partner in the London office of global law firm DLA Piper. His practice encompasses advertising and marketing, data protection, copyright and trade mark work. While he has acted for a broad range of clients, he has a particular focus on the media, leisure and technology sectors. His data protection work tends to focus on issues relating to advertising and marketing, and he has also advised and litigated extensively in the area of IP rights in data and databases.

john.wilks@dlapiper.com

GOODMAN DERRICK LLP

www.gdlaw.co.uk

Paul Herbert

Paul is a partner at Goodman Derrick LLP and head of the firm's Media, Communications & Technology practice. Paul has practised in the advertising and marketing sectors for most of his 30-year career and has a particular speciality in the areas of Broadcast and VOD advertising, as well as in relation to Programme Sponsorship and Product Placement. Goodman Derrick is a full-service City law firm, recognised for providing high-quality legal advice across a range of practice areas and for its distinctive, client-focused service.

pherbert@gdlaw.co.uk

 # GOWLING WLG

www.gowlingwlg.com

Mathilda Davidson

Mathilda is a senior associate in the Gowling WLG Advertising and Marketing Team. She advises brands on the compliance, IP and contract issues arising from the day-to-day work of marketing and innovation teams. Her experience includes time in-house at Unilever and Premier Foods.

mathilda.davidson@gowlingwlg.com

George Sevier

George is a principal associate in Gowling WLG's Advertising and Marketing Team. He has around 10 years' experience of guiding brand-owners through advertising, marketing and associated IP issues, including in-house at Unilever and Coca-Cola. He has particular expertise in relation to automotive, food and beverage, FMCG and medical device marketing.

george.sevier@gowlingwlg.com

Dan Smith

Dan heads up the UK arm of Gowling WLG's renowned international advertising law group. Grounded in the digital age, he helps brands and agencies to be disruptive and push creative boundaries, while managing legal and PR risk. Acting for clients including Unilever, Volkswagen Group and Carlsberg, Dan advises on everything that touches advertising, whether that's client/agency, ad tech and sponsorship deals, ad clearance or complaints or hot topics such as native ads, vloggers and ad blocking.

dan.smith@gowlingwlg.com

Harbottle & Lewis

www.harbottle.com

Scott McKinlay

Scott McKinlay is an associate at Harbottle & Lewis, working with clients operating in both the advertising and music sectors. The firm frequently advises agencies, brands and individuals operating in the advertising and marketing industries on issues such as digital, broadcast and print advertising, marketing and promotions as well as sponsorship and licensing. Scott combines this with his music work, advising rights-holders and content creators on a variety of matters, including publishing, recording, management, composer and live event agreements.

scott.mckinlay@harbottle.com

www.ipa.co.uk

Rebecca Chong

Rebecca is a qualified solicitor and trade mark attorney, specialising in intellectual property and advertising law. Rebecca joined the IPA in 2010, after practising as a commercial intellectual property lawyer at Morgan Cole (now Blake Morgan). Rebecca is also on the editorial board for the *Journal of Intellectual Property Law & Practice*.

legal@ipa.co.uk

India Forsyth

India Forsyth is a solicitor working in the Legal and Public Affairs team at the IPA. She trained and qualified at Lovells (now Hogan Lovells), specialising in intellectual property law. She first moved into advertising law when working in-house for Cadbury plc, focusing on marketing work.

legal@ipa.co.uk

Kim Knowlton

Kim's experience covers all aspects of commercial production. She has been a head of TV of a major advertising agency, an executive producer at the COI and a production company producer. This wealth of experience across the board, spanning a career of over 30 years, gives Kim a broad perspective of the key production issues facing our industry, and means that she is well placed to help and advise the membership on all areas of production.

kim@ipa.co.uk

Richard Lindsay

Richard trained and qualified as a solicitor at the City law firm Lovell White Durrant (now Hogan Lovells), going on to work for various media organisations, including Granada Television as Head of Legal & Business Affairs for its Enterprises division and the Telegraph Media Group as Group Legal Director. Richard joined the IPA in August 2010 and, as Director of Legal & Public Affairs, represents the IPA on CAP, BCAP and Clearcast's Copy Committee. He is also a director of MediaSmart and chair of the Communications Agencies Lawyers' Forum (CALF).

richard@ipa.co.uk

 **LEWIS SILKIN**

www.lewissilkin.com

Jonathan Coad

Jonathan acts for a wide range of clients, preserving the value of their corporate and individual reputation, and those of their brands when they are threatened by the media, using a full range of legal and regulatory protections available. Jonathan has worked in this area for over 20 years, and works closely with leading PR agencies to craft media strategies when corporate or individual reputation is under threat.

jonathan.coad@lewissilkin.com

Brinsley Dresden

Brinsley leads Lewis Silkin's renowned Advertising & Marketing Law Group and advises on content issues in all media. These issues include advertising clearance, publicity rights, copyright, parodies, comparative advertising, trade mark infringement, sales promotions and gambling laws. He also advises advertising agencies defending claims by production companies, breaches of client/agency agreements and third-party claims of IP infringement. Brinsley is the only lawyer ranked in the *Campaign* 'A List' of leading individuals in media, marketing and advertising.

brinsley.dresden@lewissilkin.com

Jo Farmer

Jo advises a mix of brand-owners, media organisations and marketing communications agencies on their commercial activities, agreements and day-to-day needs. Jo is recommended as a leading individual in the latest edition of the *Chambers* Legal Directory, which states that Jo is a 'very pragmatic and commercially driven advertising and marketing specialist'. Jo lectures regularly on advertising law and commercial agreements, both at external conferences and as part of in-house training programmes developed to meet individual client needs.

jo.farmer@lewissilkin.com

Nick Walker

Nick is a partner in Lewis Silkin's Media, Brands and Technology team. He is currently ranked as a leading individual for intellectual property by *Chambers* UK. Nick's work covers a broad range of commercial disputes, with a particular focus on intellectual property, media and entertainment law. He advises on intellectual property infringement (copyright, trade marks and passing off), breach of confidence, technology disputes, breach of contract, and issues concerning defamation and privacy matters.

nick.walker@lewissilkin.com

OLSWANG

www.olswang.com

David Zeffman

David Zeffman is a senior partner at international law firm Olswang LLP where he is a member of the firm's board. He is also head of Olswang's Gambling Group which acts for many of the leading European online and offline gambling companies. Olswang's full-service legal offering combined with its industry expertise ensures that its gambling industry clients (and clients from other industries who are involved with gambling products and services) receive comprehensive and consistent advice in all areas.

david.zeffman@olswang.com

www.osborneclarke.com

Stephen Groom

Stephen is a consultant at Osborne Clarke LLP and a specialist in advertising law. He co-founded Osborne Clarke's advertising blog www.

ocmarketinglaw.com in 1999 and has edited and curated it ever since. He is also Deputy Chair emeritus of the DMA Governance Committee and was a member of the team that produced the first suggested form of contract for the provision of advertising services published by the IPA, ISBA and CIPS in 1998.

stephen.groom@osborneclarke.com

Nick Johnson

Nick Johnson is an advertising law specialist with over 20 years' experience and leads Osborne Clarke's dedicated ad law team. Directories *The Legal 500* and *Chambers* consistently identify him as a leading individual for advertising law. *Legal 500* and *Super Lawyers* also cite him for gambling and technology, media and communications work. Nick is a board director of the European Sponsorship Association, an editorial board member of *E-Commerce Law and Policy* and a regular blogger on www.ocmarketinglaw.com, which he co-founded.

nick.johnson@osborneclarke.com

www.pillsburylaw.com

Rafi Azim-Khan

Rafi is Head of IP/IT & Data Privacy, Europe. Listed as a 'leader' in advertising law since 1994 and one of the 'digital dozen' UK e-commerce/data specialists, expertise includes global product launches (Red Bull, Coke); comparative advertising (leading ECJ case, global Gillette 'razor wars'); sponsorships; promotions; lotteries; social media; and regulator problems. Rafi has rare 'gamekeeper turned poacher' experience, having previously worked at the ASA's law firm. He is listed in *Chambers World's Leading Lawyers*, *The Legal 500* and *Super Lawyers* guides.

rafi@pillsburylaw.com;

swanturton

www.swanturton.com

Charles Swan

Charles Swan is rated as a leading advertising lawyer by both *Chambers* and *The Legal 500* and rated by Thomson Reuter as a UK Super Lawyer. He is the Honorary President of Adlaw International, a global network of advertising law specialists with members in 23 countries. He advises agencies and advertisers on all aspects of content, on contracts with clients, talent contracts, sales promotions and ASA complaints. Charles is the author of the Advertising Industry section in *Copinger and Skone James on Copyright*, the leading work on copyright law.

charles.swan@swanturton.com

Wedlake Bell

www.wedlakebell.com

Michael Gardner

Michael Gardner is a partner at Wedlake Bell LLP where he heads the firm's Intellectual Property team. He advises clients on all aspects of IP protection with a particular emphasis upon dealing with disputes involving trade marks, passing off, copyright, designs, confidential information, data privacy and domain names. His advertising sector experience includes acting in litigation concerning comparative advertising and advising on complaints to the ASA as well as defending and prosecuting claims arising from advertising and digital marketing activities.

mgardner@wedlakebell.com

EDITOR'S NOTE

Richard Lindsay, Director of Legal & Public Affairs, IPA

Advertising in the UK is heavily regulated, both by the law and by its own self-regulatory system. This book contains 26 chapters divided into five parts. Each chapter is, I think, fundamental to understanding the basics. The book is aimed, primarily, at non-lawyers (though lawyers will, hopefully, find it useful too) – at those who work in the industry and need a practical guide to what they can and can't – or shouldn't – do. It would be wrong to say that it only scratches the surface – and that would not be fair to its contributors – but it is not intended to be an academic textbook. A complete tome on advertising law and regulation would stretch to many more pages than are contained here.

Laws and codes change. The chapters in this book were up to date when written, but readers should bear in mind that some of the information is bound to be out of date soon if not already. It is always advisable to check whether the rules relevant to whichever topic you require information about have been updated.

In particular, the chapters of this book were written before the UK voted to leave the European Union. At the time of publishing, the UK Government has not yet given notice under Article 50 of the Lisbon Treaty of the UK's intention to exit the EU. It follows, then, that the status of law applicable in the UK which is derived, in one way or another, from the EU should remain unchanged for several years until Brexit is complete. The UK advertising industry's self-regulatory CAP and BCAP Codes, which are only partly based on EU law, should also remain unaffected until then.

Editing this book has been a privilege. Each of its contributors is an expert in his or her field and I have benefited far more than they from their labours. I thank them all for their endeavours and hope that my editing efforts do them justice.

Thanks too to Marina Palomba and Chris Hackford for their efforts on the previous edition. Finally, I hope that you will find this book helpful and that it provides answers to some of those tricky questions that crop up so frequently.

FOREWORD

Rt Hon Lord Smith of Finsbury,
Chairman, Advertising Standards Authority

Advertising is one of our most important creative industries. It is worth billions of pounds in turnover and in its contribution to our economy. It helps to oil the wheels of business. It helps to inform the consumer and assist them in making choices. It adds to the brightness, the enjoyment, and the creativity of life. And it's something the UK does supremely well.

And I like to think that the advertising self-regulatory system, which aims to ensure that every UK ad is a responsible ad, helps towards the success of the sector. All advertising, in any medium, has to abide by strict rules laid down by the Committees of Advertising Practice (CAP), after wide consultation and careful consideration. And those rules are then applied and interpreted by the Advertising Standards Authority (ASA), which has been performing this role for well over 50 years. The ASA system is widely respected around the world, regarded as something of a gold standard in helping advertising to be responsible, and therefore to deserve the trust of the public.

But the rules themselves, and the way they have been applied over the years, can be daunting at first sight. The framework of codes and legal requirements, and the way they tie in with consumer protection legislation, can be very confusing. And that's where this up-to-date compendium becomes not only useful but essential. It sets out with real clarity, and in language that we can all understand, and with a host of examples, exactly how to navigate the statutory and regulatory landscape. It offers a range of articles provided from a wealth of experience by leading legal experts. It covers fundamental issues such as copyright and consumer directives and the CAP Codes. It touches on ethics as well as practicality. In other words, it's a must-have guidebook for anyone in the industry.

The rules are there not to stifle creativity, but to help it to express itself as effectively as possible, in as trustworthy and responsible a manner as possible, and with the greatest impact. This guide will, I know, help that to happen.

PREFACE

Paul Bainsfair,
IPA Director General

It's sometimes said that advertising is where commerce and art intersect. It's certainly true that the best advertising uses creative, original and often entertaining ideas to win fame and favour in order to make brands stand apart from their competitors.

This often means that advertising agencies are challenging the status quo, looking for ideas that are different from what has gone before. It might be in their use of the medium. It might be in the creative idea itself.

Although the need to stand out is job no. 1, doing so has to be achieved without falling foul of the rules. The UK advertising market is one of the most sophisticated in the world and is underpinned by the law. However, to ensure that all advertising is legal, decent, honest and truthful, it also has one of the world's most admired and effective self-regulatory systems, complete with its own set of codes for both broadcast and non-broadcast ads. These are constantly under review by the Committee of Advertising Practice in an effort to keep pace with technological and legal developments, most notably, for example, through the extension of the digital remit of the non-broadcast code in 2011.

Navigating the law and the self-regulatory codes is the responsibility of all those involved in the industry – advertisers, agencies and media owners – but since the rules are numerous and complex, they often need professional, legal advice. While our editor has warned me that this book does not constitute legal advice (!), it brings together the best expertise from our own IPA legal team and from specialists at many of the UK's leading law firms in the sector, to whom I would like to extend my thanks.

Edited by Richard Lindsay, Director of the Legal & Public Affairs Department at the IPA, this book is a practical guide. It covers what we consider to be the key legal and regulatory issues facing agencies and their clients, and looks to help answer the sorts of questions that arise on a daily basis.

I hope you find it helpful.

PART ONE
Intellectual property: The law and content rights

Copyright

MICHAEL GARDNER

Wedlake Bell

Introduction

Copyright is so important in the context of advertising that everyone who works in the industry should have at least a basic understanding of the main principles.

Copyright is by far the most widespread of the intellectual property rights covered in this book. For example, everyone reading this chapter will be a copyright owner, whereas relatively few will own trade marks or designs. The penalties for failing to have regard to copyright, whether one's own copyright or a third party's, can be severe. More positively, the benefits of a greater understanding of copyright can be significant.

What is copyright?

Copyright is a legal right which enables its owner to prevent others from copying or dealing with copies of the work that is protected by copyright. It differs from registered trade marks, patents and registered designs in two key respects.

First, in the UK at least, the creation of copyright requires no registration or other formalities. It arises automatically whenever the conditions are met for the creation of a valid copyright work and provided the copyright work is recorded in some permanent form.

Second, it does not create a statutory monopoly over the copyright work. It protects only against the copying, or dealing with infringing copies, of a work.

There are a number of categories of copyright work. These cover virtually every type of creative material likely to be used for advertising – in whatever media – including, for example:

- television or radio commercials;
- pop-up or banner adverts on the internet;
- PowerPoint presentations for new pitches;
- research reports, including charts, tables and supporting databases;
- billboard advertising, posters, signs and point-of-sale materials;
- packaging and promotional material;
- media schedules; and
- photographs and content on social media.

In practice, there will often be different types of copyright work subsisting in the same type of advertising material.

In the UK, copyright law is governed by the Copyright Designs & Patents Act 1988 (CDPA). This statute has been extensively amended over the years, not least to cope with the onset of the internet and the digital age which has almost entirely grown up since the CDPA was enacted.

The CDPA is complex and runs to over 300 sections. Worse still, EU legislation concerning copyright and the involvement of the European Court have made the law even more complex. A detailed examination of all of this law is beyond the scope of this book. Instead, in this chapter, an attempt will be made to summarise the most important points as they relate to those engaged in the advertising industry.

What types of copyright work are there?

The CDPA sets out a number of different types of copyright work that can be protected. Many of these have their own particular rules governing such matters as the length of time the copyright protection will last, how it can be infringed and so on.

The different types of copyright works are:

- original literary works;
- original artistic works;
- original dramatic works;
- original musical works;

- sound recordings;
- films;
- broadcasts; and
- typographical arrangements of published editions.

In addition to these types of copyright, the CDPA also provides protection for two further categories of rights: performers' rights and moral rights.

It is worth exploring in more detail some of the key aspects of the various types of copyright. This will help advertisers recognise the rights they have and avoid infringing the rights of other copyright owners.

Literary, artistic, dramatic and musical works

The CDPA stipulates that, in order to enjoy copyright protection, literary, artistic, dramatic and musical works must be 'original'. What does this mean?

It is important to note that originality for the purposes of copyright law does not have the same meaning as might be thought. In a copyright context it has nothing to do with the literary or artistic *merit* of a particular work. Rather, the concept of originality means that a work must be the product of at least an investment of some independent skill and labour on the part of the author of the work or the author's own intellectual creation. It cannot simply be a slavish copy of something.[1]

Literary works

A literary work means any work (except a dramatic or musical work) which is written, spoken or sung and includes, *inter alia*, a table or compilation, a computer program or a database.[2]

In relation to advertising, a literary work could include the script for a TV or radio advertisement, the text of a brochure, the text of a print advertisement and so on. But it would not cover single words such as a product or brand name – in spite of the fact that considerable research and investment often accompanies the choosing of a new brand identity.[3] Traditionally it has been hard to argue that simple slogans used in advertising can be protected by copyright. But developments in European law may well have made this possible.[4] Where slogans are important, it would be best to try to protect them as registered trade marks (eg Tesco's slogan 'Every little helps').

Artistic works

These would include a graphic work (such as maps, drawings, charts etc), photograph, sculpture or collage (again, irrespective of artistic quality), works of architecture (such as a building or a model for a building) or a work of artistic craftsmanship.[5]

While a brand name in the form of simple words would almost certainly not be protected as a literary work, a stylised version of the brand name in the form of a logo could be protected by copyright as an artistic work (as well as by a trade mark or design).[6]

Dramatic works

A dramatic work is a work of action, with or without words or music, which is capable of being performed before an audience. These include a work of dance or mime or a play. As a result of a case involving a disputed advertisement back in 2001, a film can itself now be treated as a dramatic work as well as being a recording of one.[7]

Musical works

This means a work of music – but excluding any words or action intended to be sung, spoken or performed with the music. So song lyrics, for example, are protected not by musical copyright but by literary copyright.

Sound recordings, films and broadcasts

Unlike with literary, artistic, dramatic and musical works, there is no requirement for originality in the copyright sense in relation to copyright in sound recordings, films and broadcasts. However, no separate copyright subsists in any of these works to the extent that they are merely copies of existing works.

Sound recordings

A sound recording is a recording of sounds from which the sounds may be reproduced, or a recording of the whole or part of a literary, dramatic or musical work – regardless of the medium in which the recording was made.[8]

Obvious examples of sound recordings as copyright works include albums recorded on CD, or recordings of radio programmes.

Films

A film means a recording, on any medium, from which a moving image may, by any means, be produced.[9] (As well as enjoying film copyright, a film can also be a dramatic work.)

Broadcasts

These cover television (including satellite television) broadcasts. Only certain broadcasts over the internet are included within the definition, such as where the broadcast is being made over the internet and via other means at the same time.[10]

Typographical arrangements

This type of copyright protects the appearance of the printed pages of published editions.[11] It subsists irrespective of originality. It is a totally separate copyright to any other form of copyright.

For example, a book will contain literary copyright in the content of the text, but the appearance of the book and its pages will be protected by typographical arrangement copyright.

Moral rights and performers' rights

The CDPA also provides for what are known as moral rights for authors. These are limited rights that are personal to the creator of the copyright work in question. They can be waived or, in certain situations, enforced. This is looked at in more detail later in this chapter.

Performers' rights are another species of right created by the CDPA.[12] They protect the rights of performers and exist independently of other forms of copyright. Thus, a recording of an album by a rock band would have protection as a sound recording for copyright purposes, and the performance of the band itself would attract performers' rights protection for their actual performance.[13]

Overlap of copyright works

In practice, there will often be an overlap between various types of copyright works. For example, a published book will contain material protected by literary copyright, by artistic copyright (if illustrated) and by typographical arrangement copyright.

A typical music CD will have a multitude of different copyrights, including in the cover booklet and in the CD itself.

Duration of copyright

The duration of copyright protection varies according to the type of copyright involved. The following sets out the term of copyright applicable to each type of copyright work.

Literary, dramatic, musical and artistic works

- Life of author, plus 70 years from end of year of death.
- Employer's copyright lasts for the employee's life plus 70 years.
- Assigned copyright lasts for the life of the original author plus 70 years from their death.
- Joint authorship lasts for 70 years from the death of the last joint author to die.

Sound recordings

- Fifty years after making, or 70 years after first release (if released within that time).

Broadcasts

- Fifty years after first transmission.

Films

- Seventy years after death of the last of the principal director, author of screenplay, author of dialogue or composer of soundtrack.

Typographical arrangements of published editions

- Twenty-five years after first publication.

It should be noted that the CDPA came into effect in 1989 and there are various transitional provisions that deal with copyright works that were created prior to that.

Ownership of copyright

Generally speaking, the first owner of copyright in a protected work is the person who created it (ie the author).[14]

This does not apply where the work is created by an employee in the course of his or her employment. In such situations, the ownership of copyright automatically vests in the employer.

However, it is important to note that where a work is commissioned, the general rule is that it is the creator, not the commissioner, who retains ownership of the copyright in that work (though the facts of the particular case can blur this general rule). This is very important and has caused problems in a number of advertising situations where an advertising or design agency has been asked to create something, but has not transferred copyright to the client.[15]

It is crucial, therefore, that in any contract between client and agency or, where work is sub-contracted, in contracts with suppliers or freelancers, the ownership of copyright in the work is clear. Otherwise disputes can easily occur. Typically, transfer of the ownership of the copyright is made by way of an assignment. Alternatively, if the parties agree that the creator should retain ownership, then the creator should allow use of the work by way of a licence. (Hence, the new ISBA/IPA Creative Services Client/Agency Agreement discussed in Chapter 24 provides options for either scenario.)

Joint ownership may apply where more than one person contributes to the creation of a copyright work. This is unlikely to be much of an issue where several employees are involved, since copyright will automatically belong to the employer anyway. But if different, independent contributors are making distinct contributions to the creation of something, care will be needed to ensure that copyright ownership is clearly dealt with.

Copyright infringement

Copyright cannot be infringed by the independent creation of a work that happens to be very similar to an existing protected work. Only if there has been copying or dealing with an infringing copy can the infringement provisions of the CDPA be brought into play.

Copyright is infringed if one of the prohibited acts set out in the CDPA is done in relation to the whole or a substantial part of the copyright work, either directly or indirectly.[16]

What is 'a substantial part'?

In understanding what constitutes infringement, it is crucial to understand what is meant by 'a substantial part'.

Unfortunately, there is no single test by which anyone can assess whether or not something is a copy of the substantial part of a copyright work and so infringes it. This will always be a matter of impression for a judge to form on the available evidence.

Substantiality is, primarily, a *qualitative* rather than a *quantitative* test. The key factor is not the quantity of the copying, but whether what has been copied is a substantial part of the relevant, original skill and labour of the copyright owner.

Things are more complicated where there is altered copying or copying of only various extracts from the protected work or where someone has altered the original wording and tried to disguise the fact that they have copied from it. In each case it is a question of examining what has been taken and determining whether it is a substantial part.

A good illustration of the substantial part rule in action can be found in the High Court judgment in the 'Dr Brown's' case, where the claimant successfully sued for, among other things, copyright infringement in relation to the copying of a substantial part of its logo. The competing logos are shown side by side in the judgment and demonstrate how infringement can occur even in relation to a relatively straightforward logo.[17]

In the advertising industry, as in other creative fields, such as fashion or journalism, there are all sorts of 'rules' which are bandied around about what percentage of someone's copyright work can safely be copied without penalty. These rules have absolutely no foundation in law and should be ignored.

Moreover, there have been some European Court cases on copyright infringement which appear to have tightened up the substantial part test. The English courts have yet to fully reconcile these cases with the CDPA. However, if anything, the net result is that it may be easier than it previously was to infringe copyright.[18]

The CPDA sets out various different ways in which copyright can be infringed. There are, broadly speaking, two categories of copyright infringement: primary infringement and secondary infringement.

Primary infringement

This type of infringement is a strict liability form of infringement. It does not matter whether the person committing the infringement realised that what they were doing was wrong. If they do the act giving rise to the infringement, they will be liable.

There are six categories of primary copyright infringement. These include:

- copying the work;
- issuing copies of the work to the public;
- communicating the work to the public;
- performing, showing or playing the work in public;
- renting or lending the work to the public; and
- making an adaptation of the work or doing any of the above in relation to an adaptation of the work.

It is worth looking briefly at some of these.

Infringement by copying[19]

There are different rules for what type of copying is relevant depending on the type of copyright work involved.

For literary, artistic, dramatic or artistic works, the copying can be in any material form. So, photocopying, writing out by hand, scanning into electronic format, photographing or reading a literary work into a recording device could all infringe – provided either the whole or a substantial part of the original copyright work were to be taken. With an artistic work in two dimensions, the making of a three-dimensional copy could infringe and vice versa.

Copying in relation to a film or broadcast, however, requires a copy of the whole or any part of any actual image of the work and includes taking a photograph of the whole of a substantial part of any image forming part of the film or broadcast.

So, it cannot be an infringement of *film* copyright to shoot a new film incorporating identical subject matter to the original. This is because none of the images of the original film would have been copied.[20]

However, the advent of digital photography has complicated matters when it comes to assessing infringement in relation to photographs. For example, much debate followed the news story about the photograph of a monkey 'selfie' which was allegedly taken by the animal itself. Although much of this centred on whether a monkey (as opposed to a human being) could own copyright, the other point concerned the degree of skill or creativity involved. Can it really be said that merely pressing the button on a digital camera involves any degree of creativity on the part of the photographer?

Another issue arises where a digital image is manipulated after it has been taken, or where someone copies another's work but uses their own photographs and manipulation to achieve a similar result.[21]

Another important area concerns so-called 'cuttings' services where providers, such as PR firms, send their clients a summary of relevant extracts from the press in which they have featured. This used to be done in the form of paper cuttings from newspapers but is now more commonly done in digital form. Care must be taken because the copying of such extracts can easily amount to infringement if performed without a licence.

Infringement by issuing copies to the public[22]

This is known as the 'distribution right'. It prevents anyone but the copyright owner from putting into circulation for the first time, within the European Economic Area (EEA), originals of the copyright work or any copies (or substantial parts of them). This is the provision that enables rights-owners to carve out separate territories in the world for CDs, books and DVDs.

By the same token, once originals or copies of the copyright work have been put on the market in the EEA by the rights-owner, he or she cannot exert any further control over those particular copies, so they can be freely traded. Of course, any subsequent copying of them, or a substantial part of them, will, if done without the rights holder's permission, be an infringement.

Infringement by communicating the work to the public[23]

This form of infringement was introduced, in part, to update the CDPA to cope with the internet age. As more and more content is published and distributed in digital form (whether it be written, photographic or audiovisual content), so this has become one of the most important forms of infringement.

For example, if a company advertised its services over the internet but used the artwork of another company on its website, it could fall foul of this section by communicating the infringing copy to the public.

Merely providing an electronic link to a copyright work that is freely (and lawfully) available on the internet will not infringe copyright.[24]

Infringement by adaptation[25]

If an advertiser were to take a literary work and, without permission, turn it, for example, into a script for a dramatised commercial, that could amount to an infringement by adaptation. Another example of an adaptation would be a translation of a protected work.

Secondary infringement

Secondary infringement is another form of copyright infringement. It differs from primary infringement because the state of mind of the infringer is taken into account. You can only commit an act of secondary infringement where you either know or have reason to believe that you are dealing with an infringing copy. That is why it is always sensible, where possible, to place a copyright notice on a copyright work.

Infringements of moral rights

Advertisers should also be wary of infringing moral rights of authors.[26]

Authors of copyright works have the right to be identified as the author, provided they assert that right.[27]

Authors who have not waived their moral rights also have the right to object to the derogatory treatment or 'mutilation' of their work.[28] This could be an issue where an advertiser tries to make use of a protected work, such as a film or artistic work in, say, a TV commercial, in another form of advertising.

For these purposes, a treatment is 'derogatory' if it amounts to distortion or mutilation of the work or is otherwise prejudicial to the honour or reputation of the author (or director in the case of a film).

Authors also have the right to oppose false attribution of authorship. Again, this is something that could arise in an advertising context.[29]

Infringements of performers' rights

There are various ways of infringing rights in performances. These mirror many of the ordinary copyright infringement provisions. They include primary and secondary infringements.

Advertisers should be aware of performers' rights if they are proposing to make use of recordings of performances, such as musical performances, variety acts, recitations or other live performances.

Defences to copyright infringement

There are a few 'fair dealing' defences by which the CDPA renders lawful what would otherwise be an unlawful infringing act. Traditional fair dealing defences have been available in cases where the copyright work is being copied or used for purposes such as non-commercial research and private study, criticism or review, reporting current events or where the use is by an educational establishment.[30] None of these has been particularly useful for advertisers though.

However, the Copyright and Rights in Performances (Quotation and Parody) Regulations 2014 (the 'Quotation and Parody Regulations') introduced some new fair dealing exceptions which are more relevant to advertising.

Quotation

One of the changes brought in by the Quotation and Parody Regulations extends the existing exception in the CDPA for criticism and review.[31] It provides that copyright in a work is not infringed by the use of a quotation from the work (whether for criticism or review or otherwise) provided that:

(a) the work has been made available to the public;

(b) the use of the quotation is fair dealing with the work;

(c) the extent of the quotation is no more than is required by the specific purpose for which it is used; and

(d) the quotation is accompanied by a sufficient acknowledgement (unless this would be impossible for reasons of practicality or otherwise).

This new exception has yet to be tested in the courts, so its scope is uncertain, particularly since what amounts to fair dealing is not defined. Intellectual Property Office (IPO) guidance explains that whether the use of a work amounts to fair dealing 'will always be a matter of fact, degree and impression in each case'. The guidance continues:

> Factors that have been identified by the courts as relevant in determining whether a particular dealing with a work is fair, include:
>
> - Does using the work affect the market for the original work? If a use of a work acts as a substitute for it, causing the owner to lose revenue, then it is not likely to be fair.
>
> - Is the amount of the work taken reasonable and appropriate? Was it necessary to use the amount that was taken? Usually only part of a work may be used.
>
> The relative importance of any one factor will vary according to the case in hand and the type of dealing in question.

Advertisers wishing to include a quotation from a copyright work in an advertisement will need to ensure that their proposed use complies with each of the four caveats to the exception, giving particular consideration to whether use of the quotation amounts to fair dealing.

Parodies

The world of advertising lends itself readily to using parody, caricature or pastiche.

For example, a few years ago Sony made a well-known television commercial for its BRAVIA televisions. This depicted slow-motion shots of tens of thousands of multicoloured rubber balls bouncing down the hilly streets of San Francisco to the accompaniment of a soothing Jose Gonzales soundtrack. The advertisement was parodied by the makers of the Tango drink.

Sony 'Balls' advert, courtesy of Fallon/Sony

Until the introduction of the new parody fair dealing defence under the Quotation and Parody Regulations, the mere fact that an advertisement may have been intended to be a parody of another work did not imbue it with any special status as far as the law of copyright was concerned. If the parody amounted to copyright infringement, it was unlawful.

Now, the relevant provisions of the CDPA have been amended so that fair dealing with a work for the purposes of caricature, parody or pastiche does not infringe copyright in the work.[32]

However, as with the use of quotations, the boundaries of this new exception have not been tested in the UK courts. Again, the IPO guidance is useful. It explains that

In broad terms:

- parody imitates a work for humorous or satirical effect. It evokes an existing work while being noticeably different from it.

- pastiche is a musical or other composition made up of selections from various sources or one that imitates the style of another artist or period.

- caricature portrays its subject in a simplified or exaggerated way, which may be insulting or complimentary and may serve a political purpose or be solely for entertainment.

It also reiterates that the exception only permits use for the purposes of caricature, parody, or pastiche to the extent that it is 'fair dealing', which allows use of only 'a limited, moderate amount of someone else's work. Anything that is not fair dealing will require a licence or permission from the copyright owner'. (See also Quotation above in respect of fair dealing.)

And the IPO guidance explains that the exception does not affect the law of defamation or an author's moral rights to object to derogatory treatment of a work.

As with the inclusion of a quotation, use of caricature, parody or pastiche in an advertisement should be made with care. Not only will the treatment need to fall squarely within the particular category, but it will also need to amount to fair dealing.[33]

Copyright and comparative advertising

Although there has been considerable litigation involving trade mark law and comparative advertising, there remains very little in the way of guidance as to the interplay between copyright law and comparative advertising. For example, the key legislation introduced by the EU which is supposed to regulate comparative advertising and intellectual property[34] says absolutely nothing about copyright.

Care should therefore be taken when using material that could be protected by copyright in comparative advertisements. Comparative advertising is discussed in Chapter 10.

Consequences of copyright infringement

Copyright infringement is actionable in the High Court in the same way as most other intellectual property rights infringements. A copyright owner can sue for a range of relief, including an injunction to prevent further infringements and mandatory orders of the Court requiring delivery of, or destruction of, infringing materials.

The remedies are discussed in more detail in Chapter 4 dealing with passing off.

Summary

Copyright is a very important intellectual property right in the world of advertising. The breadth of copyright protection for everything from text to sound recordings means that there will be copyright in almost every piece of advertising – in whatever form it takes.

It is vital for those in the industry to understand the importance of ensuring that copyright in the material they create is properly dealt with and that the infringement of other parties' copyright is avoided.

Copyright does not just protect against the act of copying. The distribution right protects against putting copies (and originals) into circulation in the European market without the permission of the copyright owner. Secondary infringement can apply to dealings with infringing copies. Online infringements are also actionable.

Notes

1 Or in European lawspeak, 'it must be the expression of the intellectual creation of the author' (see *Infopaq International A/S* v. *Danske Dagblakdes Forening* C-5/08)

2 Copyright Designs & Patents Act 1988 section 3

3 Although decided under the old legislation that pre-dated the CDPA, the case of *Exxon Corporation* v. *Exxon Insurance Consultants International* [1982] RPC 69 is still regarded as authoritative on this point.

4 For example, in the Infopaq case, it was held that a mere 11 words could be an infringement, and English decisions have since acknowledged that a newspaper headline could attract copyright protection in its own right (*NLA & Ors* v. *Meltwater Holding BV & Ors* [2011] EWCA Civ 890).

5 CDPA section 4

6 See for example the 'Dr Brown's' logo referred to in *Handicraft Company & Anor* v. *B Free World Ltd & Ors* [2007] EWHC B10 (Pat)

7 See *Mehdi Norowzian* v. *Arks Ltd & Ors* [1999] EWCA Civ 3014

8 CDPA section 5A

9 CDPA section 5B

10 CDPA section 6/6A

11 CDPA section 8

12 See CDPA Part II Rights in Performances

13 There is no suggestion in the authorities or textbooks that a studio recording does not qualify for performers' rights protection or that there must be a true 'live' performance.

14 CDPA section 11

15 See for example *Atelier Eighty Two Ltd* v. *Kilnworx Climbing Centre CIC and others* [2015] EWHC 2291 (IPEC), 30 July 2015

16 CDPA section 16(3)

17 *Handicraft Company & Anor* v. *B Free World Ltd & Ors* [2007] EWHC B10 (Pat) – see in particular the appendix to the law report at www.bailii.org/cgi-bin/markup.cgi?doc=/ew/cases/EWHC/Patents/2007/B10.html&query='Dr+Browns'&method=boolean

18 Cases such as *Infopaq* appear to indicate that if what is taken is the 'expression of the intellectual creation of the author', that will represent the reproduction of a sufficient part of the copyright work to infringe.

19 CDPA section 17

20 *Norowzian* v. *Arks Ltd & Ors (No.1)* [1998] EWHC 315 (Ch)

21 See for example *Temple Island Collection Ltd* v. *New English Teas Ltd* [2011] EWPCC 19

22 CDPA section 18

23 CDPA section 20

24 Although providing a hyperlink to something that is not behind a paywall is not in itself an act of copyright infringement, if the link itself reproduces a substantial part of the copyright work (such as a headline or the opening lines of an article), that could be potentially be an infringement!

25 CDPA section 21

26 CDPA Chapter IV

27 CDPA sections 77–78

28 CDPA section 80

29 CDPA section 84 – see also *Clark* v. *Associated Newspapers Ltd*

30 CDPA sections 29–30

31 CDPA section 30 (1ZA)

32 CDPA section 30A

33 See also *Johan Deckmyn & Anor* v. *Helena Vandersteen & Ors* case C-201/13

34 Directive 2006/114/EC

Trade marks 02

MICHAEL GARDNER

Wedlake Bell

Introduction

Trade marks are all around us. They are synonymous with brands and can become highly valuable assets for any business. A product bearing a well-regarded trade mark can, irrespective of its relative quality, generally achieve a higher price than its unbranded competitor.

Trade marks are so important in the commercial world that special national and international systems of registration have grown up to protect them in almost every country in the world. While it is still possible, even without registration, to enforce some trade mark rights in the UK through laws such as passing off, registration is an essential measure for any serious business that wishes to protect its trade marks.

This chapter will focus on the law of registered trade marks. The protection of unregistered trade marks through passing off is dealt with in Chapter 4.

A trade mark is a sign (which can be in the form of a name or word, logo, slogan, sound, colour, shape or combination of such elements) which serves to distinguish the goods or services of one business from those of another.

For example, if you are surfing the internet looking to order a new smartphone, no doubt you will be presented with a choice of phones made by different manufacturers and using different networks. You will naturally use trade marks to distinguish between them.

If you take a trip in your car, you may hear on the radio the telephone dialling tone which accompanies adverts for Direct Line insurance. When you are driving along looking for a filling station, you may see the green colour of the signage denoting a BP garage. When you select a bottle of Coke from the refrigerator in the garage, the distinctive shape of the Coca-Cola bottle will reassure you that you are buying the real thing.

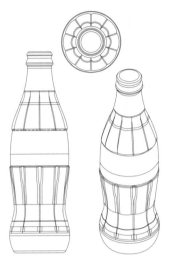

Courtesy of Coca-Cola

What are the relevant registration systems in the UK?

In the UK, the governing law of registered trade marks is derived from an EU Directive,[1] and this is implemented in the UK by the Trade Marks Act 1994 (TMA). The TMA provides a system of national registration under which businesses can file UK trade marks and enforce them within the territory of the UK.

Aside from UK registrations, the other most important type of registered trade mark for UK businesses is what are known as Community trade marks (CTMs).[2] These are marks registered at the Office for the Harmonisation of the Internal Market (OHIM).[3] Once registered as CTMs, they are enforceable in all countries of the EU.[4]

Another system that operates in harmony with the UK and Community trade mark systems is the international system of registration known variously as the Madrid or WIPO system. This enables trade marks filed in other countries to have their protection extended to cover the UK or EU too, as though their trade marks were ordinary UK or Community registered trade marks.[5]

Fortunately, as far as the UK is concerned, the law applicable to UK registered trade marks, CTMs and trade marks registered here through the Madrid/WIPO system is essentially the same.

How does the system of trade mark registration work?

As there are an infinite variety of possible businesses that can exist, it is not necessary for a trader to register for trade mark protection in relation to every possible type of activity in which his or her business is engaged. Instead, trade marks tend to be registered in an appropriate 'class' (or classes) to cover the specific types of activity the business is involved with or is likely to be involved with in the future.

In this way, the same trade marks can actually be filed and used by different companies without conflict.

For example, the trade mark 'Lloyds' is part of the name of the famous Lloyds banking group. However, it is also the trade mark of the famous London insurance market, Lloyds. There is also a large retail chemist's chain called Lloyds Pharmacy. So, there are three, distinct, well-known and quite separate businesses all sharing the same trade mark at the same time. Their registrations cover different classes. A search of the trade marks register will reveal numerous, similar examples.

So, a business planning to file an application to register a trade mark will need to consider carefully what they will be using the trade mark for and tailor the specification of goods/services in the relevant class accordingly.

To discourage 'blocking' or tactical registrations for trade marks, there are various rules which enable challenges to be made to registrations on such grounds as bad faith or non-use.[6]

What can be registered as a trade mark?

As noted above, trade marks are signs which serve to distinguish the goods or services of one business from those of another. It is essential, therefore, that the trade mark can fulfil that basic function. If it cannot act as a 'badge of trade origin' then it cannot function as a trade mark and will generally not be capable of registration.

The TMA contains a list of types of signs that cannot be registered. For example, you cannot register a mark that is descriptive of the characteristics of the goods or services in respect of which it is to be registered. So, for example, you could not register 'Corn Flakes' for a breakfast cereal consisting of pieces of dried corn.[7]

There are other restrictions, such as marks contrary to public policy or morality, national flags and so on. The full details are beyond the scope of this chapter.

It is also an essential rule of registered trade marks under current legislation[8] that in order to be registerable, they must be capable of being represented graphically[9] and in a manner that precisely identifies what they are.

How does the registration procedure work?

In order to obtain a registered trade mark, an application must be filed at the appropriate trade marks registry. This will include a representation of the trade mark itself and a description of the goods or services for which it is to be registered (known as the 'specification'). A filing fee is paid too.[10]

Unless obviously flawed, the application will be advertised by the registry for opposition purposes. This is to enable any other trader who may be affected by the registration to object to it. If formal opposition proceedings are filed then the progress of the registration is halted until the registry has decided whether or not the objections are valid.

If no successful opposition to the application is made, it will eventually achieve registration (within around four to six months in the case of an unopposed UK registration and slightly longer for a CTM).

It is important to note that once registration is achieved, the date on which the trade mark is deemed to have been registered is the date on which the application for it was originally filed.[11]

How long does a registration last?

A registered trade mark will appear on the relevant register of trade marks and lasts for an initial period of 10 years from the date of registration. It can be renewed for further periods of 10 years at a time. In other words, once granted, a registered trade mark can last indefinitely.[12]

Can a trade mark be challenged once registered?

The fact that a trade mark achieves registration is not the end of the matter. It is always possible for another party to challenge the validity of the registration or to seek to revoke it.

If the party challenging it can show that the mark ought not to have been registered in the first place (eg because it describes the characteristics of the goods in question), it can be declared invalid. In those circumstances, it is deemed never to have been registered.[13]

Where the trade mark was validly registered but has since either not been used for a continuous period of five years or, as a result of the neglect of the proprietor, has ceased to function as a trade mark, it can be revoked.[14]

Can trade marks be traded or licensed?

Registered trade marks are items of property. They can be sold (assigned) or licensed by the trade mark owner. It is quite common for companies that hold trade mark rights to license them to third parties to allow them to manufacture, market or distribute goods bearing the relevant marks.

Licensees of trade marks have their own set of rights under the TMA (although these are subject to the terms of their licence agreements).

What does a registered trade mark protect against?

Ordinarily speaking, and subject to possible defences discussed further below, the registered proprietor of a trade mark can sue for infringement in the following circumstances:

- where a party uses an identical sign to the registered trade mark in relation to identical goods or services to those for which the trade mark is registered;[15] or

- where, because a party uses:

  - an identical sign to the registered trade mark in relation to similar goods or services to those for which the mark is registered; or

  - a similar sign to the registered trade mark in relation to identical or similar goods/services to those for which the mark is registered; and

  - there exists a likelihood of confusion on the part of the public.[16]

All trade mark holders are entitled to rely on the above infringement provisions of the TMA.

However, trade mark law is more generous to owners of better-known trade marks. Where the trade mark owner can show that its mark has a 'reputation',[17] there is a third type of infringement available. This occurs where the use of an identical or similar sign is without due cause and takes unfair advantage of, or is detrimental to, the distinctive character or repute of the registered trade mark.[18]

This type of infringement can apply irrespective of whether the goods or services for which the offending sign is being used are identical, similar or completely dissimilar to those for which the trade mark is registered.[19]

It is not necessary to show 'confusion' in order to be able to rely on a claim of unfair advantage. It is enough that the defendant is riding on the coat-tails of the relevant trade mark and reaping the benefits of the investment in that mark made by its proprietor.

Typical infringement scenarios

Where signs identical or similar to registered trade marks are used without the proper consent in relation to goods or services, there may be trade mark infringement.

'Use' for these purposes covers use in advertising, importing or exporting goods under the offending sign, affixing the sign to goods or selling/offering goods for sale by reference to the sign.[20]

There are a variety of scenarios which can lead to trade mark infringement. In assessing whether or not there is infringement, it is necessary to analyse whether the particular circumstances are capable of amounting to infringement and then seeing whether or not any defence applies.

As noted above, there might also be a question mark over the validity of the registered trade mark whose proprietor is concerned about a potential infringement.

Identical sign/identical mark and identical goods

This was always supposed to be the most straightforward type of infringement. However, due to various decisions of the Court of Justice of the European Union, it has become increasingly complicated. It will apply where a sign is being used in the course of trade and that sign is identical to the registered trade mark and is being used in relation to identical goods or services to those for which the mark is registered. There is no need to show confusion, unfair advantage or anything else.

But it must be shown that the use complained of will have an 'adverse effect' on the trade mark. So, for example, where a trade mark is used in a purely descriptive way to identify the trade mark proprietor's goods or services and there is no question of the person using it trying to mislead anyone, that would not infringe.

Another potential scenario is where a business uses keyword advertising such as Google AdWords to try to attract customers to a website. The courts have held that it is not an infringement for a search engine operator such as Google to operate a system whereby advertisers can pay so that searches made against trade-marked words will call up adverts for rival websites. Nor is the advertiser *automatically* liable for having paid the search engine operator for the privilege. So, for example, it was not automatically an infringement for retailer Marks & Spencer to pay Google to have searches against the trade marked word 'Interflora' produce adverts for M&S's own rival flower delivery service. However, if the resulting adverts produced by such searches do not make clear that the advertiser has no association with the relevant trade mark owner, this can potentially lead to infringement. Caution is therefore needed with the wording of such adverts and the case law is still developing in this area.[21] (See also Chapter 12 on advertising and the internet.)

Similar sign/identical goods or identical sign/similar goods or similar sign/similar goods + likelihood of confusion

Sometimes, traders will avoid using an identical sign to a registered trade mark but will instead adopt a sign that is only *similar*.

But for this type of infringement, similarity between the offending sign and the trade mark and between the goods or services for which the mark is registered is not enough. There must be a likelihood of confusion between the sign and the registered trade mark.

Where a sign is used in conjunction with other words, even descriptive words, this can be enough to dispel the likelihood of confusion and so render the sign non-infringing. For example, the use on the internet of the sign 'Reed Business Information' by a well-known publishing company to promote its job search services did not infringe the 'Reed' trade mark registered by the employment company Reed Executive plc.[22]

Although the requirement to show confusion for this type of infringement is similar to one of the requirements of passing off, unlike with passing off, it isn't necessary for the holder of a registered trade mark to show that the mark has been used so as to build up goodwill and reputation. In the case of a registered trade mark (as opposed to one that is unregistered) the court must assume that the mark has been in use and has developed a basic reputation and goodwill for the specification of goods or services.[23]

Unfair advantage/detriment infringement

This type of infringement is only available to those trade marks which have acquired a 'reputation' in the UK (or in the case of a CTM, a reputation in the EU[24]).

In *Spec Savers* v. *Asda*,[25] the claimant successfully argued that Asda's use of the slogan 'Be a real spec-saver at Asda' to promote its own opticians' service took unfair advantage of the Specsavers trade mark and the reputation it had built up.

In *L'Oréal* v. *Bellure*,[26] it was held that a maker of cheap 'smell-alike' perfumes had taken unfair advantage of certain trade marks by stating that their own versions smelt the same as the L'Oréal originals. The use of the well-known brand names in those circumstances was held to be unfair.

In *Tesco* v. *Elogicom*,[27] the supermarket giant successfully argued that a company had taken unfair advantage of the Tesco trade mark. The use complained of was via the registration of domain names incorporating the word 'Tesco' in them, which were then used to route consumers to Tesco's own website via an affiliate marketing scheme.

Tesco Extra, Dover, courtesy of Tesco

Defences

A complete blanket prohibition on the use of trade marks without the permission of the trade mark holder in all situations would be undesirable for a number of reasons. Therefore, the TMA provides that there will be no infringement where certain uses of the trade marks are made – provided that such use is in accordance with honest practices in industrial and commercial matters.

Statutory defences in the TMA

A detailed analysis of all defences would be beyond the scope of this chapter. The most important defences include 'exhaustion of rights' (see further below) and where the use being made of the mark is purely descriptive or to indicate the characteristics of the goods or services involved.[28] However, to qualify for this latter defence, the use made of the mark must be in accordance with 'honest practices in industrial or commercial matters'.

The Court of Appeal allowed a defence by ASOS, the online clothing retailer, to the effect that it had been using its own name as a trade mark (ASOS being an abbreviation for ASOS' original name 'As Seen on Screen').[29]

In the particular circumstances, this operated as a defence to a trade mark claim brought by Assos, the Austrian cyclewear[30] brand.

Comparative advertising

Due to the impact of European law, there are considerably more restrictions on comparative advertisers these days than was formerly the case.

In 1999, Ryanair ran a comparative advert extolling the virtues of its prices against those of British Airways under the strapline 'Expensive BA***DS'. BA sued unsuccessfully for, among other things, trade mark infringement.[31] However, nowadays, such an advert would almost certainly fall foul of the prohibition against the 'denigration' of the person whose goods or services are being compared.

EU legislation in this area has meant that where an advert seeks to make a comparison between the advertiser's own goods or services when compared to those of its competitor, strict rules have to be observed. These are examined in more detail in Chapter 10 on comparative advertising.

Parallel imports

The European Union is supposed to promote the free movement of goods between Member States. Allowing trade mark owners to place restrictions on the onward trade in goods bearing their trade marks within the EU would be at odds with this. So, the TMA provides for a concept known as 'exhaustion of rights'. This means that once goods bearing registered trade marks have been placed on the market in the European Economic Area (EEA) by or with the consent of the trade mark owner, the trade mark rights in those goods are 'exhausted'.[32] In other words, trade mark rights can generally no longer be used to inhibit trade in those particular goods.

So, if a trader from the UK purchases a consignment of Nike T-shirts that have been put on sale by Nike in Germany, there is nothing to stop him or her importing them into the UK and advertising them for sale over here.[33]

From an advertiser's perspective, just as the trader would be entitled to sell those Nike goods in the UK irrespective of whether or not Nike objected, so it would also be entitled to use the Nike trade marks in the ordinary course of trade to advertise the goods for sale.[34]

However, it is important to note that this 'exhaustion' principle applies only to goods placed on the market within the EEA by, or with the consent of, the trade mark owner. It does not apply to goods from outside the EEA, unless the trade mark owner has given clear consent to their importation.[35] This is so even if the goods in question are genuine and exactly the same kind as those normally sold officially in the EEA.[36]

Since such goods from outside the EEA will be infringing if their trade marks are used without consent, any advertising or promotion of those goods using the trade marks will also be infringing.

If, for example, a consignment of Lee jeans is bought in the United States and imported into the UK without the permission of the trade mark holder and advertised under the slogan 'Lee jeans – direct from the US to save you money', that would be an infringement.

An advertising or printing company that prepared such advertising might itself be in danger of committing trade mark infringement along with the trader if it knew, or had reason to believe, that putting the trade mark on the advertising material was not authorised.[37]

Trade marks and legal proceedings

The owner of a registered trade mark is entitled to bring infringement proceedings against those who are infringing, or threatening to infringe, its trade mark.

The scope of relief available for trade mark infringement and the types of injunctions that can be sought are very similar to those available for infringement of other IP rights such as copyright, designs and passing off. They are dealt with in more detail in Chapter 4.

One aspect of the UK law of registered trade marks that is worth noting is the fact that if a party issues unjustified threats of trade mark infringement proceedings, these can themselves be actionable by the party threatened.[38] So, when confronted by a trade mark claim, it is always worth seeing whether a groundless threats response is appropriate.

Summary

Registered trade marks can be powerful and invaluable business assets. They have a number of advantages over trade marks that are unregistered. These are:

- Because they show up on searches at official registers, it is easier for other traders to avoid clashing with them and this may deter other traders from adopting the same or similar trade marks.

- They make it easier to monitor attempts to register marks that could be in conflict with the registered mark and so make it easier to prevent them being adopted in the first place.

- They are items of property whose ownership is certain, and that can be transferred or licensed to others.

- They can be enforced more easily and cheaply (in relative terms) than unregistered trade marks in some circumstances.

- In some scenarios, passing off will not be available at all (eg where there is no goodwill or trading history), but registered trade marks can still be enforced.

- The Community trade mark and the Madrid/WIPO systems enable protection to be obtained in other territories far more easily than with unregistered trade marks.

- There are limits to the effect of registered trade marks due to statutory defences and issues such as comparative advertising or parallel imports.

Notes

1 EU Directive 2008/95 (although at the time of writing this is due to be replaced with an updated Directive)

2 These may soon be renamed 'European Union trade marks' under plans to introduce new EU trade marks legislation.

3 OHIM will become the 'European Union Intellectual Property Office' under the same legislation.

4 Council Regulation 207/2009/EEC (at the time of writing this is due to be replaced by an updated Regulation)

5 Section 35 TMA

6 See for example Section 46 of the TMA

7 Section 3 TMA

8 The requirement for graphical registration is due to be abolished under proposed new trade mark laws from Europe.

9 Section 1(1) TMA

10 Section 32 TMA

11 Section 40(3) TMA

12 Section 42 TMA

13 Section 47 TMA

14 Section 46 TMA

15 Section 10(1) TMA

16 Section 10(2) TMA

17 Or in the EU in the case of a CTM

18 Section 10(3) TMA

19 *Adidas Salomon AG & Anor* v. *Fitnessworld Trading Ltd* C-408/01

20 Section 10(4) TMA

21 A long-running case involving Interflora and Marks & Spencer is still going through the courts.

22 *Reed Executive & Anor* v. *Reed Business Information Ltd & Ors* [2004] EWCA Civ 159

23 This is an another advantage of having a registered trade mark rather than having to rely purely on passing off, where the claimant must prove they have acquired the necessary goodwill and reputation through use of the mark.

24 See *The Sofa Workshop Ltd* v. *Sofaworks* [2015] EWHC 1773 (IPEC)

25 *Specsavers International Healthcare Ltd & Ors* v. *Asda Stores Ltd* [2012] EWCA Civ 24

26 *[2006] EWHC 2355 (Ch)*

27 *Tesco Stores Ltd* v. *Elogicom Ltd & Anor* [2006] EWHC 403 Ch

28 Section 11(2) TMA

29 *Roger Maier & Anor* v. *ASOS plc & Anor* [2015] EWCA Civ 220

30 Under current EU proposals the 'own name' defence is due to be abolished for corporate entities and will henceforth apply only to individuals.

31 *British Airways plc* v. *Ryanair Ltd* [2000] EWHC Ch 55

32 Article 7(1) of Directive 2008/95/ s12(1) TMA

33 There are exceptions to this rule, such as where there is repackaging or other changes made to the goods before they are resold. These exceptions are beyond the scope of this work.

34 *Parfums Christian Dior & Anor* v. *Evora BV* C-337/95

35 *Zino Davidoff SA* v. *A&G Imports Ltd* C-414/99

36 *Case C-173/98Sebago and Maison Dubois*

37 Section 10(5) TMA

38 See Section 21 TMA or, in relation to CTMs, reg 2 of the Community Trade Mark Regulations 2005

Design rights 03

MICHAEL GARDNER

Wedlake Bell

Introduction

Design law can be relevant in the context of advertising. It can apply to the products which are the subject of advertisements but also to the advertising itself. Design laws are no longer concerned exclusively with three-dimensional objects; they can cover graphics, packaging, logos and a host of other features, and it is worth being aware of them.

In the same way that trade marks are capable of enjoying protection with, or in some cases without, registration, so the same applies to designs.

As a result of EU Community design laws introduced in 2002,[1] designs are nowadays capable of protecting a much larger variety of designs than was formerly the case, including two-dimensional designs. One area, for example, where they have made a significant difference is in relation to the world of clothing and fashion.

Unfortunately, the design regime in the UK is now rather complicated. There are four different types of design protection:

- registered Community designs;
- registered UK designs;
- unregistered Community designs; and
- unregistered UK designs.

Mercifully, there is a considerable degree of overlap between the rules applicable to the first three in this list. Unregistered UK designs is the odd one out.

In addition to these specific design laws, it should also be borne in mind that copyright law can also be relevant, particularly where artistic works are involved. It is also possible to register trade marks for shapes.

Community designs

What is the scope of Community design protection?

Community registered designs and Community unregistered designs protect the following:

> the appearance of the whole or a part of a product resulting from the features of, in particular, the lines, contours, colours, shape, texture and/or materials of the product itself and/or its ornamentation.[2]

'Product', for these purposes, is very widely defined indeed and includes 'any industrial or handicraft item, packaging, get-up, graphic symbols and typographic typefaces'.[3]

It follows, then, that the scope of what can be protected by these design laws is also very wide. For example, the following products have been held to enjoy protection: the shape of an air freshener canister,[4] the mesh of a bag for fishing bait,[5] a poncho,[6] the zip and piping for the expander of travel luggage and a designer handbag.[7]

However, it is not just three-dimensional objects that are relevant. The wide definition of 'design' includes surface decoration and colours. This means that two-dimensional designs can also be protected. Thus a logo or some artwork for packaging can attract protection as a UK or Community registered design and as a Community unregistered design.

A Community design protects against any other design that does not produce on the informed user a 'different overall impression' compared to the protected design.[8]

The design owner has the exclusive right to use the design and to prevent any third party from using it (or a design that doesn't create a different overall impression) without his or her consent.[9]

'Use', for these purposes, covers making, offering, putting on the market, importing, exporting or using a product in which the design is incorporated, or to which it is applied, or stocking such a product for those purposes.[10]

However, it should be noted that, in the case of *unregistered* Community designs, the design owner can only prevent such use if it is the result of the copying of the protected design. So, it is only a registered Community design that gives the design owner a true monopoly on the design in question.

Community designs cannot protect features of appearance of products which are solely dictated by their technical function, or which are contrary to public policy, or immoral.[11]

Designs must be 'new' and have 'individual character'

In order to qualify for protection, designs must be 'new' (ie they must not be identical to any earlier designs) and they must be of what is termed 'individual character'.

In assessing whether or not a design has individual character, the test that is applied is essentially whether the new design creates a different overall impression on the informed user when compared to previous designs made available to the public prior to the relevant date.[12]

Some important points need to be made here.

First, the previous designs against which novelty and individual character must be assessed *exclude* designs that could not reasonably have become known in the normal course of business to the circles specialised in the sector concerned, operating within the EU.[13]

In other words, if someone were to challenge the validity of a Community design on the basis that it lacked novelty or individual character, they would have to produce evidence of a prior design (ie 'prior art') that could reasonably have become known to the relevant sector operating in the EU.

Second, although an application for a Community design registration will specify the product to which the design has been applied, the protection of that design is not limited only to products of that type or in that design sector. If, for example, you register a Community design for the handle of an umbrella and a third party later uses the same design in a handle on a piece of office furniture, the latter will infringe the design. The fact that the defendant has applied the design to a different product in a different sector is irrelevant.

Third, as is noted above, in assessing whether or not a design is new or has individual character, one must ignore designs that 'could not reasonably have become known in the normal course of business to the circles specialised in the sector concerned, operating in the EU'. However, when assessing novelty and individual character, the 'sector concerned' is the sector of the prior art, which may not be the same as the sector in which the design owner is using the design.

For example, company A claims Community design protection for the appearance of spiky balls which are sold as accessories to help improve the performance of tumble dryers. However, it turns out that before A's new design application was filed, another company, B, had been marketing very similar spiky balls for use in massage therapy. Also, B's design could have been known about in EU design circles specialising in the health/massage products sector.

In that scenario, even though A's Community design was being applied to products in a different sector from B's prior design (ie the laundry products sector as opposed to the health/massage sector), and was new in that sector, if A's design does not have individual character when compared to B's design, the design will be invalid.[14]

How are Community designs protected?

In the case of a Community unregistered design, as with copyright, the protection is automatic.

If the designer wishes to protect his or her design as a registered Community design, he or she must file an application at the Office for Harmonisation of the Internal Market (OHIM).[15] The filing procedure is fairly simple. The application must include a graphic representation of the design and a relatively modest fee must be paid.

Applications for registration are not subjected to particular scrutiny by OHIM at the time of filing. So the mere fact that an application has been accepted for registration does not mean that it will necessarily survive if challenged.

How long do Community designs last?

Unregistered Community design protection lasts for three years from the date on which the design was made available to the public.[16]

Registered Community design protection lasts for five years from initial filing and can be extended for further periods of five years up to a maximum of 25 years in total.[17]

Who owns title to Community designs?

As with copyright, the first owner of the Community design is the creator (ie the designer) unless the design was created by an employee in the course of his or her employment, in which case title to the design automatically belongs to the employer.[18]

The governing legislation is silent as to what happens where a Community design is commissioned, so it must be assumed that ownership remains with the designer.

Those commissioning advertising or design agencies should therefore take note.

Can Community designs be challenged – even after registration?

In the same way that registered trade marks or other registered rights such as patents can be challenged, so too can Community designs.

It is common in design infringement cases for the defendant party to deny that its design creates the same overall impression compared to the claimant's design, and at the same time to argue that the claimant's design ought never to have been registered.

This is what happened in the important *Procter & Gamble* v. *Reckitt Benckiser* case. This concerned allegations of Community registered design infringement in relation to the design of two competing air freshener spray canisters.[19] P&G accused Reckitt Benckiser of infringing its design for the Air Wick air freshener. Reckitt counterclaimed for P&G's registered design to be declared invalid.

At the original trial, the judge rejected the attack on the registered design, but held that there was infringement. However, on appeal, although the court agreed that the design was valid, it overturned the finding of infringement. The appeal court held that the Reckitt design did not create the same overall impression on the informed user as the P&G design.

How is infringement assessed?

The overall impression test is conducted through the eyes of the 'informed user'. This mythical person is not a technical expert, but nor is he or she an ordinary consumer. Rather, they are someone in between, a person who is familiar with the designs of products in the area concerned. So, it is important to bear in mind that the standard against which a design infringement case is judged is different from a trade mark infringement case.

When comparing two conflicting designs, the correct approach is to consider them carefully, having regard to their various features. The court will not do this by considering the overall impression that is left in the mind after they have been viewed. A more careful scrutiny of the competing designs is needed. One must continue to look at them in deciding whether or not the disputed design infringes, because it is the impression given to the informed user when the design is viewed that matters. The concept of 'imperfect recollection' that is used in trade mark cases does not apply.

Another relevant factor is the freedom of the designer. This must be taken into account when assessing infringement[20] (ie the more freedom there is to design a product, the more importance the court is likely to attach to design features which are very similar in the disputed design).

What remedies are available in infringement cases?

In effect, the same remedies are available in Community design cases as in other intellectual property rights cases. These include injunctions, delivery up/destruction of infringing materials, damages (or an account of profits) and orders for costs.

These remedies are looked at more closely in Chapter 4.

UK registered designs

The legislation covering UK registered designs was significantly amended at the same time as the introduction of the new Community design regulation. Much of the relevant law is now the same for both design regimes.

Further changes have been made more recently so that, generally speaking, for UK registered designs created after 1 October 2014, it is no longer the case that, where a design is commissioned by someone, the title to the design vests in the commissioner, rather than the designer.[21]

Some quirks in the UK regime remain. For example, if a UK registered design is infringed, an infringer may not need to pay damages if they can prove that, at the date of the infringement, they were not aware, and had no reasonable ground for supposing, that the design was registered. This contrasts with the position with Community designs where there is no such get-out for innocent infringers.[22]

It is also worth noting that UK registered designs, as their title suggests, apply only to the UK. Applications for filing such designs have to be made to the UK Intellectual Property Office, not to OHIM.

UK unregistered designs

What are the main features of UK unregistered designs?

Otherwise known as 'design right', UK unregistered design protection is available under the Copyright Designs & Patents Act 1988 (CDPA). It arises automatically without the need for registration.

UK unregistered design protection lasts for up to 15 years from the end of the year in which the design was first recorded in a design document, or an article was first made to the design. However, where a product design is made available for sale or hire, the term lasts for 10 years from the end of the year in which that first occurred.[23]

The scope of what can be protected by a UK unregistered design is more restrictive than for a Community or UK registered design. UK unregistered designs protect the original designs of 'the shape or configuration (whether internal or external) of the whole or part of an article'.[24]

Such rights do not apply to methods or principles of construction or features of a shape or configuration of an article which enable it to be fitted to another article (ie like spare parts).[25]

Also, and very significantly, 'surface decoration' is excluded from protection. So again this is much narrower than Community designs, which extend protection to colours and ornamentation.

Designs must be original to qualify for protection. They will not be original for this purpose if they were commonplace in the relevant design field at the time of creation in a qualifying country.[26]

As a result of recent legislation, as with UK registered designs, the person commissioning such a design no longer becomes the first owner of design right in the design. The position is the same as for copyright, where it is the person who created the design who is the first owner of that design right. However, this aspect of the law was only changed in 2014 and designs put on the market earlier than that will still be governed by the old law.[27]

One final point of interest is that with UK unregistered designs, in the last five years of the term of protection, the designer is obliged to grant a licence to anyone who wants to use the design. If the licence fee cannot be agreed, there is a mechanism in the CDPA for the fee to be determined by an independent party.[28]

How are UK unregistered designs infringed?

The owner of a UK unregistered design has the exclusive right to reproduce the design (or a document embodying the design) for commercial purposes.

Reproduction covers reproduction of articles exactly or substantially to the design. As with copyright, infringement of UK unregistered designs is divided up into:

- primary infringement (ie copying the design for commercial purposes so as to produce articles exactly or substantially to that design);[29] and

- secondary infringement (ie importing or possessing for commercial purposes or selling, letting for hire, advertising for sale or hire, an article which the infringer knows, or has reason to believe, is an infringing article).[30]

In the same way that UK registered design law allows an innocent infringer to avoid paying damages or an account of profits, so too does UK unregistered design law. Again, this differs from Community designs.[31]

The same remedies are available to owners of UK unregistered designs as per any other intellectual property right.

Groundless threats

As with registered trade marks, the legislation governing designs includes provisions which enable a party aggrieved by threats of design infringement proceedings to launch legal action if those threats are unjustified. This applies to threats made in respect of either form of Community design,[32] UK registered designs[33] and UK unregistered designs.[34]

Relief for groundless threats includes injunctions and damages. Accordingly, again as with registered trade marks, care should be taken before issuing any communication that could be construed as a threat. There are some exceptions to the situations under which the groundless threats provisions will apply. If framed correctly, it may be safe to make a threat of design infringement proceedings without risking a groundless threats counterclaim.[35]

Designs and comparative advertising

As is noted in Chapter 1 dealing with copyright, the extent to which designs can be used in comparative advertisements remains unclear. In the same way that the relevant part of the Comparative Advertising Directive[36] says nothing about copyright, neither does it mention designs. Yet it is perfectly possible that a logo or other sign used in a comparative advertisement could be a Community design rather than a registered trade mark.

Summary

UK design law is complicated by the existence of a number of different types of design protection regimes. These are Community registered and unregistered designs and UK registered and unregistered designs. Copyright and trade mark laws may also overlap in part.

Unregistered design protection arises automatically and, in some cases, a design can attract protection under both the UK and Community design regimes. Registered design protection requires registration within specified time limits.

Registered designs can be more straightforward to protect since registrations are proof of the design and there should be no need to delve into the background and design history when taking cases to court. However, like many patent cases, where design infringement is relied upon, the party threatened by proceedings will very often seek to attack the validity of the claimant's design.

Notes

1   Council Regulation 2/2002/EC ('the Regulation')

2   Article 3 (a) of the Regulation

3   Article 3 (b)

4   *The Proctor & Gamble Company* v. *Reckitt Benckiser (UK) Ltd* [2007] EWCA Civ 936

5   *Reginald John Bailey & Ors* v. *Graham Haynes & Ors* [2006] EWPCC 5

6   *Walton* v. *Zap Ltd, Designs Registry*, 22 January 2007

7   *Landor & Hawa International Ltd* v. *Azure Designs Ltd* [2006] EWCA Civ 1285

8   Article 10 of the Regulation

9   Subject to the usual EU exhaustion of rights principles – see Article 21 of the Regulation and the parallel imports section of Chapter 2 in this book on trade marks (see page 32)

10   Article 19 of the Regulation

11   Articles 8 and 9 of the Regulation

12   For registered designs the date is the date of filing or priority date; for unregistered designs it is the date on which the design was first made available to the public (see Article 6(1) of the Regulation).

13   Article 7(1) of the Regulation

14   *Green Lane Products Ltd* v. *PMS International Group plc & Ors* [2008] EWCA Civ 358

15   OHIM will probably be renamed soon as a result of EU reforms.

16   Article 11 of the Regulation

17   Article 12 of the Regulation

18   Article 14 of the Regulation

19   [2007] EWCA Civ 936

20   Article 10(2) of the Regulation

21   See the Intellectual Property Act 2014 and SI 2014/2330

22   See *J Choo (Jersey) Ltd* v. *Towerstone Ltd & Ors* [2008] EWHC 346 (Ch)

23   Section 216 CDPA

24   Section 213(2) CDPA

25   Section 213(3) CDPA

26   Section 213(4) CDPA – and 'qualifying country' includes, *inter alia*, the UK and all countries of the EU

27   Section 215 CDPA as amended

28   See section 237 CDPA

29 Section 226 CDPA

30 Section 227 CDPA

31 Section 233 CDPA

32 Regulation 2 of the Community Design Regulations SI 2005/696

33 Section 26 of the Registered Designs Act 1949

34 Section 253 of the CDPA

35 See for example, in the case of UK unregistered designs, section 253(3) & (4).

36 Directive 2006/114/EC

Passing off

04

MICHAEL GARDNER

Wedlake Bell

Introduction

The law of passing off protects the goodwill and reputation of a business against unfair exploitation by others. It often overlaps with other intellectual property rights, especially registered trade marks, although it can be relied on in its own right. Passing off is not the product of any statute – hence it is often referred to as a 'common law' right (ie it has been evolved over the years by the courts rather than through an Act of Parliament).

This chapter examines the elements that are required to bring a successful passing-off claim and looks at the different variants of passing off. It also deals with the remedies that are available against those who have engaged in passing off.

The ability of a trader to bring a passing-off claim does not depend on registration or any other formalities. However, it is not always the most straightforward way of protecting a brand from unfair competition. Wherever possible, therefore, traders should look to bolster their protection through the registration of their trade marks and designs.

It should also be noted that ignorance of the law is no defence to a claim of passing off. It doesn't matter whether the infringer knows, or has reason to know, that their activities amount to passing off. Also, even where a party tries consciously to avoid passing off, judges can still be influenced by the degree to which that party has been prepared to sail deliberately close to the wind in promoting itself or its products with similar branding or get-up to an established competitor.

Advertisers must be particularly wary of passing off since, by its nature, it often occurs in the context of the advertising, promotion or marketing of goods and services.

How does the law of passing off work?

Each passing-off case will depend on its own particular facts, but there are three basic requirements to every passing-off claim.[1] Generally speaking, unless all three of these elements are established on the facts, the claim will fail. In basic summary, for a claimant to bring a successful passing-off case, it must show that:

- it has sufficient goodwill and reputation in the UK by reference to a relevant identifying feature, such as a name, logo or 'get-up'; and

- that there has been, or will be, a misrepresentation by another trader using the same identifying name, logo or get-up (or something confusingly similar) which deceives, or threatens to deceive, the relevant public; and

- that damage has resulted, or will result, from that misrepresentation.

These three, core elements of passing off are explained in more detail below.

Goodwill and reputation

In order for a passing-off case to reach the starting block, the claimant must first be able to show that it has sufficient goodwill and reputation in the UK. There are two important points to note about the goodwill and reputation requirement.

First, there must be goodwill and reputation in the *UK market*. It is no good if the claimant has goodwill and reputation in a foreign territory. Some kind of trading record in the UK – with UK-based customers – is essential.

Secondly, there must be a relevant 'identifier' by which the public knows the claimant or its business. That could be a company's corporate or trading name, the name of a particular product or service it promotes, the get-up of a product or its packaging, or a logo. Whatever it is, the identifier must itself be so distinctive that it has a trade origin significance in the minds of the relevant trade or public.

Famous, well-established brands such as Apple or BMW will have no difficulty demonstrating that they have sufficient goodwill and reputation by reference to their trading names and logos. Most people have heard of those brand names.

Similarly, given their big-budget marketing and sales operations, they will quickly build up goodwill and reputation by reference to other identifiers such as product names. For example, Apple has extensively advertised, promoted and sold its iPad product. As a result, the term 'iPad' has become an identifier for that type of product.

However, suppose that an entrepreneur is about to launch a new business start-up under a carefully chosen name. Before it has begun using the name, the business will have no protectable goodwill or reputation in the UK by reference to that name. Therefore, it cannot use passing off to protect itself against a rival trader adopting the same or a similar name. By contrast, if it had registered a UK or Community trade mark for the name, it would have rights from day one – irrespective of whether it had traded or built a reputation in that name.

The same would be true of a successful, foreign company with a brand that is well known in its home country, but which has yet to be introduced to the UK. Absent any UK goodwill and reputation, there would be no chance of successfully bringing a passing-off claim here.

In practice, many instances of passing off involve neither iconic brands, like Apple, nor pure start-ups that no-one has heard of. Instead, they tend to involve ordinary companies which, though perhaps not household names, have nevertheless been trading and promoting their businesses sufficiently to have the necessary goodwill and reputation for passing-off purposes.

Misrepresentation

The second element of passing off requires that a third party be making (or threatening to make) a misrepresentation involving the use of something identical or confusingly similar to the claimant's own identifier (ie logo, name, get-up etc).

By way of a simple example, suppose that a clothing retailer decides to advertise its summer sale on a local radio station. To promote the sale, it announces in the advertisement that it is cutting the price of its Fred Perry polo shirts by 20 per cent. In fact, unbeknown to the retailer, the Fred Perry polo shirts it is selling are actually counterfeit.

The result? The retailer is making a misrepresentation to consumers that it is selling Fred Perry clothing when in fact the clothing is fake. For passing-off purposes, it does not matter whether the retailer knew they were fake or not. The result is the same: the retailer is engaged in passing off.

Instances involving counterfeiting are very obvious forms of misrepresentation. By their very nature, such cases involve the use of identifiers that are identical to those of the goodwill owner (eg the name Fred Perry as per the example above). However, misrepresentations for passing-off purposes can take many other forms and be more subtle.

Use of confusingly similar identifiers

Most passing-off cases occur where one party believes that the other has been using branding that is too similar to theirs in order to promote their business.

In the *United Biscuits* v. *Asda* case, the makers of the well-known Penguin chocolate biscuits sued supermarket retailer Asda for passing off when the latter began marketing a chocolate biscuit of its own under the name of another seabird, Puffin. The judge held that the name and packaging of the Puffin products were deceptive and likely to cause sufficient confusion among consumers. While he did not think the public were likely to mistake the Puffin biscuits for Penguin biscuits, he did think that they would mistakenly conclude that the two were products of the same manufacturer.[2]

So, it isn't necessary that people be deceived into thinking that a particular product is product A when in fact it is product B. It is enough that they are deceived into thinking that product A, though different from product B, is made by the same company.

Also, although it is not necessary in passing-off cases to show that the defendant intended to pass off its goods as those of the claimant, the state of mind of the defendant can nevertheless be an influential factor. If the defendant deliberately chooses something that is quite close to the claimant's identifier, that might be a factor taken into account by the court, as indeed it was in the *United Biscuits* case.

False endorsement

It is not necessary that a trader should hold its products or services out as actually being those of someone else or made under licence from them. In some cases, a trader will seek to gain commercial advantage by wrongly claiming that it, or its products/services, are *endorsed* or *recommended* by the goodwill owner.

For example, suppose that a manufacturer of dishwasher tablets claims on its packaging that its products are recommended by Bosch, a well-known dishwasher brand, when that is not the case. Although no misrepresentation is being made as to who makes the dishwasher tablets, the goodwill associated with Bosch's name as a dishwasher brand is being exploited by the tablet manufacturer. This is passing off.

Celebrity endorsement is another fertile area for passing-off claims. In 2003, the then Formula 1 driver, Eddie Irvine, successfully sued the radio station, TalkRadio, over an advert that made it look as though he was endorsing their TalkSport radio show.[3] More recently, the retailer, Top Shop, was held to have been passing off by selling T-shirts with a photo of the pop singer Rihanna on them.[4] On the particular facts, the court was satisfied that customers would mistakenly believe that the T-shirts were official Rihanna merchandise when they were not.

Instruments of fraud

Internet domain names are the addresses used to access websites. They have become extremely valuable commodities. Even now, the activities of so-called 'cyber-squatters' continue to pose a major headache for brand-owners. The continued release of new domain name extensions has only exacerbated the problem.

Cyber-squatters register internet domain names incorporating others' brand names and trade marks in the hope that they can sell them on at a profit. This kind of activity is another form of passing off (and in some cases, trade mark infringement).

The courts have held that, in the case of famous brand names, such as BT, Virgin or Marks & Spencer, internet domain names incorporating those brand names will invariably give rise to passing off if they are ever used by a third party without permission. Such domain names are, in effect, 'instruments of fraud' in the hands of anyone but the brand-owners themselves, and an injunction can be granted to stop anyone from engaging in this type of practice. Even registering domain names without making any active use of them can still amount to passing off.[5]

It would also be passing off to use well-known trade marks in domain names to earn 'affiliate' income on the internet by routing customers to the websites of the trade mark owners themselves.[6]

The Champagne and other geographical origin cases

As most people know, Champagne is the name given to sparkling wine produced in the Champagne region of France. There are many producers of Champagne and many brands on the market. No single producer has a monopoly on the use of the word 'Champagne'. However, the courts have adopted a flexible approach to the law of passing off and held that it prevents anyone but a wine grower from the Champagne region from describing their wine by reference to the mark Champagne.

So, an attempt by a UK drinks company to market a sparkling drink under the name 'Elderflower Champagne' was prevented by an action for passing off.[7]

It is not merely Champagne that is the beneficiary of this variant of passing off. The English courts have applied similar principles to other classes of goods having particular geographical origin. In one case, the court granted an injunction to certain Swiss chocolate manufacturers to prevent Cadbury from marketing chocolate under the name 'Swiss Chalet'. As with the Champagne case, the courts were persuaded that Swiss chocolate had goodwill and a reputation in the UK that needed to be protected, and that allowing non-Swiss chocolate to be called Swiss Chalet risked damaging that goodwill and reputation.[8]

False attribution

Although comparatively rare, there is a form of passing off that arises where an attempt is made to use another's goodwill to attract interest in a product or service. This type of passing off overlaps with copyright law. It is known as 'false attribution of authorship'.

A classic case of this type of passing off occurred when the *Evening Standard* newspaper was successfully sued by a Tory MP, the late Alan Clark.

Alan Clark MP had achieved considerable commercial success with the publication of his colourful and entertaining political diaries. The *Evening Standard* started running a regular 'Alan Clark Diaries' column, written by one of their journalists in Mr Clark's style. They claimed it was intended to be a parody of Alan Clark's diaries.

Clark, however, sued the publishers of the *Evening Standard* for passing off. He claimed – successfully – that they were unfairly profiting from his success by making readers think that their 'Alan Clark Diaries' were really being written by him.[9]

Reverse passing off

Where a party falsely presents the goods, or pictures of goods, belonging to another party in order to promote their own goods, this is known as 'reverse passing off'.

An example would be a company that sells conservatories producing a brochure showing pictures of newly built conservatories which, in fact, had been built by a rival company. In this example, the court held that this amounted to passing off – even though potential customers had no idea about the identity of the real builder of the conservatories.[10]

Damage

The third and final element that must be proved in order to win a passing-off case is that there is, or will be, damage caused to the goodwill owner by the activity complained of.

In the vast majority of cases, it will not be necessary to produce much evidence of actual damage, since damage will naturally be inferred as an inevitable consequence of the passing-off activity.

A word about disclaimers

Some traders believe that they can avoid the consequences of passing off by using disclaimers in advertisements, on packaging, on websites or on point-of-sale materials. These disclaimers might say, for example: 'Please note that we have no connection with company X or any of its products'.

There are three problems with such disclaimers:

1 They may be ineffectual because many customers may simply not read them at all.

2 They may even be counterproductive by causing confusion that would not otherwise have occurred. This will happen if consumers do not read them fully or catch only a fleeting glimpse of them. Very often, consumers will only notice the presence of the brand name being disclaimed and will come away thinking that there is actually a commercial link between the brand featured in the disclaimer and the advertiser.

3 If legal action is taken for passing off, the fact that a disclaimer was thought necessary can actually damage the defendant's case. After all, why was a disclaimer thought necessary? The obvious answer is that the advertiser must have thought that, without it, there was a risk of customers being misled.

So, disclaimers should be approached with care. They are not, necessarily, going to protect an advertiser against a passing-off claim. To be effective, they may have to be far more prominent than most advertisers would wish. Small-print disclaimers can be counterproductive.

What are the consequences of passing off?[11]

Legal action

If passing off occurs, or is about to occur, the goodwill owner can take legal action against the party at fault. It can issue legal proceedings, seeking a range of remedies. These can be draconian and can include similar relief to that available in a copyright or trade mark case. Potential relief would include:

- a permanent injunction to prevent further acts of passing off from occurring again in the future;
- an order that the party committing the passing off deliver up or destroy all materials and/or products which, if used, would cause passing off to occur (eg unsold stocks of products, marketing and advertising materials);
- an order requiring the defendant to disclose the identity of the entity that supplied it with the offending goods;
- financial compensation for the damage caused by the passing-off activity, or an enquiry into the profits made by the party from the activity complained of; or
- an order that the defendant pay the claimant's legal costs.

Finally, it is worth noting that, in some cases, the Court can now order the losing party to publish the result of the legal proceedings – at its own expense – in newspapers or on its website.

Injunctive relief should not be ignored, because breaching an injunction can amount to a contempt of court which can result in serious fines or even imprisonment.

Interim injunctions

In some cases, the claimant will wish to stop the passing off in its tracks, or even prevent it occurring before the party concerned can start its passing-off activities. This may lead to an application being made for an urgent interim injunction so that the status quo can be protected until the court is able to rule finally on the case at trial. (It may take many months to bring the case to a full trial.)

Interim injunctions can be granted at very short notice by the courts, depending on the circumstances. They also put third parties on the spot.

Where a third party is made aware of an interim injunction, they must be careful not to do anything that would impede the administration of justice.[12] So, if an advertising agency were made aware of an interim injunction under which its client was ordered not to use, or promote itself by reference to, a particular brand name, the agency would be potentially at risk of being in contempt of court if it were actively to help its injuncted client to frustrate the interim injunction.

Interim injunctions and human rights

It might seem surprising, but commercial advertisers are now entitled to rely on parts of the Human Rights Act 1998 (HRA) to help resist interim injunction applications. Under the HRA, where the court is being asked to make an interim order that could affect a party's 'right to freedom of expression' under Article 10 of the European Convention on Human Rights, the court must impose a higher hurdle on the party applying for the injunction.

The courts have held that advertising is a form of freedom of expression for these purposes. Accordingly, a party seeking an interim injunction in a passing-off case to prevent a piece of advertising must show that it is likely to succeed at trial, rather than showing only that it has a real prospect of success.[13]

Evidence

In any legal action, the court will need to see evidence to prove that the three elements of passing off are present (ie goodwill and reputation, misrepresentation and damage).

The claimant will be expected to show that it has engaged in sufficient promotional and trading activities to build up sufficient goodwill and reputation by reference to the appropriate identifier. Examples of advertising and details of promotional spends are often cited. Sales figures are also important.

Companies should, therefore, wherever possible, keep a dossier containing examples of advertisements, exposure in the media and other marketing activities.

The best evidence of misrepresentation is the unsolicited and spontaneous evidence from members of the trade or public who have been confused or deceived by the defendant's activities. However, this is very often in short supply, especially where the offending activity may only recently have started.

Sometimes it will be necessary to undertake surveys by market research companies to help convince the court. However, surveys are expensive and are often treated with scepticism by the court. They should be approached with great care. Sometimes, survey evidence will be undermined in court.[14]

Summary

The right to sue for passing off can be a valuable tool for businesses to use against competitors and others who may try to exploit their success. However, there are situations where it will not be of any assistance, including, for example, situations where no goodwill and reputation has yet been acquired, such as with new businesses and start-ups and where competitors spike rivals' new product launches.

Trade mark and/or design registration should always be considered whenever businesses want to protect their goodwill. Passing off should be seen as a supplement to, not a replacement for, such registered rights.

Advertisers should remember that there are a number of different ways in which passing off can occur: straight passing off of one party's products for those of another, false endorsements/recommendations, instruments of fraud, geographical indications of origin such as the Champagne case, false attribution and reverse passing off.

The consequences of passing off can be serious because the court has wide powers to grant relief against the infringing party in the form of injunctions and orders for delivery up and damages. Finally, neither innocence nor ignorance is any defence.

Notes

1 See for example *Reckitt & Coleman Products Ltd* v. *Borden Inc.* [1990] RPC 341
2 *United Biscuits (UK) Ltd* v. *Asda Stores Ltd* [1997] R.P.C 513
3 *Irvine & Ors* v. *TalkSport Ltd [EWCA] Civ 423*
4 *Robyn Rihanna Fenty & Ors* v. *Arcadia Group Brands Ltd & Anor* [2015] EWCA Civ 3
5 *British Telecommunications plc & Ors* v. *One in a Million Ltd & Ors* [1998] 4 All ER 476
6 *Tesco Stores Ltd* v. *Elogicom Ltd & Anor* [2006] EWHC 403
7 *Tattinger SA* v. *Albev Ltd 1993 FSR 641*

8 Chocosuisse Union des Fabricants Suisses de Chocolat & Ors v. Cadbury Ltd. [1999] EWCA Civ 856

9 *Clark* v. *Associated Newspapers* [1998] EWHC Patents 345

10 *Bristol Conservatories Ltd* v. *Conservatories Custom Built Ltd* [1989] RPC 455

11 The remedies for passing off are pretty much the same as those applicable to other IP rights.

12 *Attorney General* v. *Times Newspapers Ltd* [1992] 1 A.C. 191

13 *Boehringer Ingelheim & Ors* v. *Vetplus Ltd* [2007] EWCA Civ 583

14 See for example *Weight Watchers UK Ltd & Ors* v. *Tesco Stores Ltd* [2003] EWHC 1109

PART TWO
The regulatory system: Key legal and self-regulatory frameworks

The self-regulatory system

05

RUPERT EARLE

Bates Wells Braithwaite

Introduction

The nuts and bolts of advertising regulation in the UK rely not just on the law, but on self- or co-regulation on the basis of codes drawn up by the advertising industry itself through the Committee of Advertising Practice (CAP) and Broadcast Committee of Advertising Practice (BCAP), administered by the Advertising Standards Authority (ASA).

Why self/co-regulation?

Advertisers and the media sometimes question the need for CAP and the ASA, particularly given that there is now so much law governing advertising. Most advertisers, however, recognise that self-regulation maintains higher standards in advertising in the UK than the law alone could. If consumers grow too cynical about claims made in advertising they will pay less attention to it. There are some areas better suited to self-regulation, such as matters of taste and decency. The law is a blunt instrument, and less swiftly adaptable to changing moral and cultural standards, and changing technology. The current editions of the CAP and BCAP Codes date from 2010, but several separate amendments, significant ones being subject to consultation, have been made since. Statutory regulators (primarily Trading Standards authorities) are insufficiently resourced to enforce the huge range of laws that exist. The EU recognises the benefits of self-/co-regulation (it is referred to in consumer protection directives), and self-regulatory systems inspired by the ASA have been set up in many other jurisdictions. The ASA has entered into Memoranda of Understanding with other regulatory bodies to assist consistency of regulation and reduce duplication of regulatory action.[1]

Should the UK vote to leave the EU, it is unlikely that Brexit would have any immediate effect on the self-/co-regulatory system or the Codes.

Non-broadcast structure: CAP/ASA

CAP draws up and revises the UK Code of Advertising, Sales Promotion and Direct Marketing (CAP Code). It provides copy advice to advertisers and publishes AdviceOnline and Advertising Guidance on various areas on which the industry needs particular guidance. CAP member organisations, including the IPA, agree to comply, and members of these organisations in turn agree to comply. This covers much of the UK advertising industry and media through which advertisers place their advertising. Newspapers, magazines and other publishers will ordinarily include in their terms and conditions a requirement that the advertising complies with the CAP Code. It is a requirement of signing up to a mail-sort contract with the Royal Mail that direct marketing complies with the Code, and the other licensed postal operators have a similar arrangement. Internet service providers require compliance with local regulatory requirements (so, for example, Google AdWords advertisers must warrant that the advertised web pages will not violate the CAP Code). One way or another, the majority of advertisements published in the UK should be under a requirement, often contractually binding, to comply with the Code.

The ASA applies the CAP Code, both by considering complaints about breaches of the Code and through proactive regulatory projects. Many complaints are resolved informally, but those requiring formal investigation are ruled on by a Council made up of (currently) 12 members, two-thirds of whom are independent of the advertising industry, headed by an independent chair. ASA Council rulings are published on the ASA's website. ASA decisions are subject to review by an independent reviewer (who can refer matters back to the Council for reconsideration on certain grounds), and ultimately by the courts on judicial review (see later in this chapter).

Note that the ASA administers the rules in Appendix 2 of the CAP Code on advertising on video-on-demand services notified to Ofcom, having been designated by Ofcom in 2010 under the Communications Act 2003.[2]

The ASA and CAP are funded by a levy on non-broadcast advertising (a percentage levy on the cost of space in paid-for media, including online, and on Royal Mail mail-sort contracts) collected by the Advertising Standards Board of Finance (ASBOF).

Enforcement of ASA decisions

The ASA asks an advertiser against whom a complaint has been upheld to sign an assurance that the relevant claim will be changed and not repeated, and the ASA and CAP monitor to ensure compliance. In addition, CAP seeks to ensure that other advertisers abandon similar contentious claims, so ensuring a level playing field. But the ASA has no power to fine advertisers, unlike, for example, the Financial Conduct Authority, Phonepay Plus or the Information Commissioner. So why, apart from peer pressure, do advertisers comply with the Code and ASA decisions?

- ASA decisions may attract significant adverse publicity, which may affect turnover and reverse the beneficial impact of any campaign. Recalcitrant online advertisers may be placed on a name and shame part of the ASA website, and the ASA may take paid-for Google ad space to ensure that search listings against an advertiser's name show the adverse ruling. Agencies may be named in rulings.

- Media and other carriers will not usually publish an advertisement against which complaints have been upheld, although advertisements already booked for publication may be allowed to run their course. They may be reluctant to publish future similar advertisements unless CAP Copy Advice has approved them, so delaying publication for an advertiser.

- CAP may require an advertiser to refer copy to CAP Copy Advice for vetting prior to publication where an advertiser has a history of non-compliance. This applies particularly in the case of posters where poster-site owners do not want disputes about liability for lost revenue when a poster is pulled down.

- Regulators and others on whose goodwill the advertiser may rely may have regard to ASA rulings. Thus the Charity Commission's Guidance on Campaigning and Political Activity by Charities[3] states that a serious or persistent breach of the Codes by a charity might be an indicator of underlying mismanagement or maladministration of the charity's affairs, such as to require the Charity Commission to take regulatory action.

- In the case of misleading advertising or impermissible comparative advertising, an advertiser can be referred to Trading Standards or the Competition and Markets Authority for action under the Consumer Protection from Unfair Trading Regulations 2008 or the Business Protection from Misleading Marketing Regulations 2008. Recent referrals have included Ryanair (for failure to make clear in advertisements significant limitations on advertised offers) and Groupon (for persistent issues with misleading offers in their 'daily deal' promotions).

Broadcast structure: BCAP and ASAB

BCAP exercises duties contracted out to it by Ofcom. The primary such duty is to set and revise codes containing rules which set standards for broadcast advertising, under Sections 319 and 324 of the Communications Act 2003. The most relevant standards are that: 'the inclusion of advertising which may be misleading, harmful or offensive in television and radio services is prevented', that 'persons under the age of eighteen are protected' and that 'the international obligations of the UK with respect to advertising included in television and radio services are complied with'. These obligations include the advertising and scheduling requirements of the Audiovisual Media Services Directive[4] (AVMS Directive). BCAP is required to consult interested parties if it reviews any standards. The Code is the UK Code of Broadcast Advertising (BCAP Code).

Ofcom retains direct responsibility for rules on the amount and scheduling of advertising through its Code on the Scheduling of Television Advertising, and the Ofcom Broadcasting Code includes rules on commercial references, including sponsorship and product placement. The BCAP Code does not apply to commercial references within a television programme, but it does to commercial communications within radio programmes. However, although Ofcom requires adherence to the BCAP Code for the content of programme sponsorship credits, the ASA refers complaints about those, and about product placement, undue prominence and commercial communications within radio programmes, to Ofcom.[5]

Ofcom standard form licences for television and radio services require licensed broadcasters to comply with the BCAP Code. Because it is the broadcasters (as opposed to advertisers) who will be sanctioned by Ofcom for non-compliance, and because of the commercial problems caused if an advertisement has to be taken off air mid-booking, the major broadcasters require advertisements to be cleared as compliant, prior to acceptance, by Clearcast in respect of television, and Radiocentre in respect of radio.

The Advertising Standards Authority (Broadcast) (ASAB) mirrors the ASA. There is a Council of (currently) 12 members, of whom two-thirds are independent of the advertising industry. To assist with consistency, all but one of the ASAB Council members also sit on the ASA (non-broadcast) Council and vice versa. Like BCAP, ASAB derives its powers from Ofcom.

ASAB and BCAP are funded by a levy on broadcast advertising collected by the Broadcast Advertising Standards Board of Finance (BASBOF).

Enforcement of ASAB decisions

ASAB has the power under the Communications Act to give a direction to broadcasters with respect to: (a) the exclusion from a licensed service of a particular advertisement or its exclusion in particular circumstances; and (b) in respect of misleading advertisements, the descriptions of advertisements and methods of advertising to be excluded from the service. Broadcasters are required by their licences to comply with ASAB directions. If a broadcaster fails to comply, or if the breach of the BCAP Code is a particularly bad one, the broadcaster can be referred to Ofcom for further sanctions. Ofcom has the power to levy fines and, *in extremis*, withdraw a broadcasting licence. Ofcom threatened Auctionworld, a teleshopping channel, with withdrawal of its licence and fined it £450,000 in 2004 following numerous complaints about misleading guide prices for jewellery, delays in delivery and poor customer service. The company subsequently went into liquidation.

Remit: what do the advertising codes cover?

In the case of broadcasting, remit is determined by the Communications Act, to which all television, radio and text services licensed by Ofcom are subject. This includes teleshopping and interactive TV.

Television advertising is that which takes place in advertising slots distinct from other parts of programming, as required by the AVMS Directive. It defines television advertising as:

> any form of announcement broadcast whether in return for payment or for
> similar consideration or broadcast for self-promotional purposes by a public
> or private undertaking or natural person in connection with a trade, business,
> craft or profession in order to promote the supply of goods or services including
> immovable property, rights and obligations, in return for payment.[6]

(TV advertisements broadcast from other EU Member States should generally be subject to home authority control in their country of origin.)

In the case of non-broadcast advertising, remit is governed by the wording of the CAP Code, which does not define precisely what constitutes advertising, and leaves a degree of discretion to the ASA.[7] The CAP Code covers advertising appearing in UK media (plus the Channel Islands and Isle of Man) in:

- newspapers, magazines, brochures, leaflets, mailings, e-mails, text messages;
- posters, including digital;
- cinema and video commercials;
- sales promotions;
- video on demand services (see Appendix 2 of the CAP Code);[8] and
- electronic media, including online advertisements in paid-for space (eg banners and pop-ups), paid-for search listings, viral ads, in-game ads, and (since 2011) ads by organisations on their own websites or in other non-paid-for space online under their control that are directly connected with the supply or transfer of goods, services, opportunities and gifts, or which consist of direct solicitations of donations as part of their fund-raising activities.

So a website promoting an advertiser's own goods or services will be caught, while a website promoting a charity or cause will not, as long as it is not fundraising. CAP concluded in 2014 that the Code should continue to cover advertisements in paid-for space which were promoting a cause or campaign rather than goods or services (see Chapter 22 on political advertising).[9]

The following are outside the remit of the Codes:

- advertisements in foreign media, although direct marketing from outside the UK may be subject to the Code if no appropriate cross-border complaint system operates;
- classified private advertisements;
- statutory/public notices (but other ads by public authorities are within the Codes);
- private correspondence, including between organisations and their customers about existing relationships or past purchases;
- live oral communications, including telephone calls;
- press releases and other PR material not caught above, and investor relations;
- editorial content (regulated by Ofcom and for non-broadcast media partly by the Independent Press Standards Organisation);
- flyposting;
- packaging and price lists unless they advertise another product or a sales promotion or are visible in an ad;

- point-of-sale displays, including in shop windows except sales promotions and advertisements in paid-for space;
- website content not covered above, including natural listings on a search engine or price comparison site, and archived heritage advertising;
- sponsorship; and
- advertisements in non-broadcast media whose principal function is to influence voters in a local, regional, national or international election or referendum. Note that advertising by central and local government is still subject to the CAP Code.

Complaints

In general, the ASA acts on complaints, although it may take regulatory action of its own volition.

In 2015 the ASA received some 28,000 complaints, and considered some 16,000 marketing communications. Competitor complainants are identified in any formal investigation. Consumer complainants are not.

A typical complaint investigation in relation to a broadcast or non-broadcast advertisement runs as follows:[10]

1 Complaints received are assessed against the Codes. A complaint should ordinarily be made within three months of appearance of the advertisement.

2 If there is a case to answer, an approach is made to the advertiser.

3 If necessary (because the advertiser disputes the issue, or the complaint raises a matter which is not minor and clear-cut) a formal investigation is launched.

4 The ASA asks for written evidence to substantiate claims. In the case of broadcast advertisements, the clearance centre (Clearcast or Radiocentre) is also involved, given the broadcasters' responsibility as licensees.

5 On receipt of the advertiser's response, ASA staff draft a recommendation that goes to the advertiser and to the complainant for comment. The ASA may take advice from an independent expert, or from another regulator with expertise in that area.

6 The draft recommendation may be amended in the light of comments received, and goes to the ASA Council who may adopt it as their ruling, or come to a different decision.

7 Council's decision is published online on the ASA's website (usually on Wednesdays).

In cases where significant harm is likely to result from continued appearance of the advertisement, ASA procedures may be truncated or the ASA may take interim action, for example requiring suspension of publication of the advertisement pending the outcome of an investigation.

Code rules and how the ASA adjudicates

Guiding principles

Free speech

Advertising should not be restricted unless there are good grounds for doing so, and then only in a proportionate manner. So, for example, 'puffing', or claims that would not be taken seriously, is generally acceptable.

Context

Conformity with the Codes is assessed according to the advertisement's probable impact when viewed as a whole and in context. So, in the case of non-broadcast media, an advertisement featuring a near-naked woman is more likely to offend if placed on a poster near a school than if featured on the inside pages of a glossy magazine. The advertisement in 2000 for Opium perfume featuring Sophie Dahl attracted three complaints about its appearance in women's magazines (which were not upheld) and 730 about the posters (which were upheld). Similarly, a contentious claim for a product may require more detailed explanation of the product characteristics if featured in a consumer magazine than if featured in a trade magazine. In the case of broadcast media, the likely expectation of the audience as to an advertisement's content will change depending on the nature of the surrounding programmes, and time of day.

Substantiation

The CAP Code provides that 'before distributing a marketing communication, marketers must hold documentary evidence to prove all claims, whether indirect or implied, that are capable of objective substantiation'.[11] This is common sense. The regulatory system would quickly break down if the ASA had to prove challenged claims to be untrue. The rule mirrors the language of EU Directives.[12] The advertiser has the specialist knowledge on which it based the claim, and should be in a position to prove it. There is a similar provision in the BCAP Code,[13] and the Broadcasting Acts 1990 and 1996 give ASAB the power to require from the advertiser evidence relating to the factual accuracy of any claim, and to deem a factual claim inaccurate if such evidence is not provided. The Dyson, Enzymatica and Minerva Research cases (referred to below) are examples of an advertiser having inadequate evidence to substantiate the claims actually made (which may not be those intended to be made).

Legality

The Codes require that the advertisements and the products which they advertise should be lawful. The ASA does not generally make findings in relation to the law, but in some cases it may do so if the appropriate regulator is not taking action.

Prohibitions

In addition to products the advertising of which is prohibited by law, the BCAP Code prohibits the advertising of certain categories where harm is thought likely because of the impact of broadcast advertising, including: escort agencies; pornography; political advertising (see Chapter 22); and services offering individual advice on personal or consumer problems unless the advertiser has provided the broadcaster with evidence of suitable and relevant credentials.

Misleading advertising

About 70 per cent of all complaints to the ASA about advertising in 2014 concerned misleading advertising, particularly on the internet. Advertising should not mislead, or be likely to mislead, by inaccuracy, ambiguity, exaggeration, omission or otherwise.

The Codes take into account the provisions of Directive 2005/29/EC on unfair business-to-consumer commercial practices, implemented in the UK by means of the Consumer Protection from Unfair Trading Regulations 2008 (CPRs) (see Chapter 6 on consumer protection).

Prohibited practices

Certain advertising practices are regarded under the CPRs as prohibited without the need to assess their impact on consumers, and these prohibitions are reflected in the Codes' rules. For example:

Clear separation of advertising and editorial

Readers/viewers must not be misled into thinking that praise for a product is the exercise of independent individual or journalistic judgment rather than paid for and controlled by the producer. The BCAP Code requires that 'advertisements must be obviously distinguishable from editorial content, especially if they use a situation, performance or style reminiscent of editorial content, to prevent the audience being confused between the two',[14] and as noted above, the Ofcom Code on the Scheduling of Television Advertising and the Ofcom Broadcasting Code contain rules for sponsorship and commercial references. For non-broadcast advertising, the CAP Code requires that 'Marketing communications must be obviously identifiable as such.' (See Chapter 12 on the internet and beyond for examples in the non-broadcast, online space, including in relation to native advertising and also the use of celebrities to promote products through vlogs.)

Prize draws featuring illusory or costly prizes[15]

A direct mailing by JDM Marketing Ltd (a New York state entity) trading as Bright-Life UK, referred to 'Money due... to you' with a 'Warning' that it would be forfeited if a claim and minimum catalogue order were not placed within 14 days, and the main body of the mailing, which detailed how any award might be calculated, referred to a sum of £2,072.58 and to £25,000 and £135,000. The small print concerning how an award would be calculated referred to a minimum gift value of 31 pence for all those placing orders, once a certain level of orders had been received, but on investigation by the ASA there was little evidence that even this had been paid out.[16]

'Buy one get one free' offers may not be prohibited, but an advertisement which involves payment for more than the legitimate and unavoidable cost of participation in a promotion, or otherwise overstates what is 'free', will be (see Chapter 15 on price claims and indications).

Misleading by action or omission: the average consumer

Other potentially misleading business-to-consumer advertising practices require a case-by-case analysis, the issue being whether they are likely to cause the average consumer to take a transactional decision which he or she would not have taken otherwise. These concepts are considered further in Chapter 6. For example:

UK Services & Support Ltd (UKSS) offered a passport application service from the website www.ukpassportoffices.co.uk. UKSS contended that the use of numerous disclaimers meant that the consumer would have to be particularly careless and unobservant to be misled into thinking that UKSS was, or was associated with, Her Majesty's Passport Office (HMPO). However, the ASA took the view that the average consumer would be unlikely to be a regular visitor to passport websites, might need to obtain a passport rapidly, and/or might be obtaining their first passport and/or might not have English as their first language. He or she was likely to infer that a website providing application services for a government-issued document, such as a passport, was official unless it made clear that was not the case. The URL, and features such as citing the locations of the UK government's official passport offices, prominent pictures of passports in front of a Union flag and the hands of someone apparently checking forms, and of a passport application form, were likely to convey the initial impression to visitors of an official website for passport services. The disclaimers, that UK Passport Offices were independent from HMPO and that any fees paid directly to them were separate from the fee for the passport, could easily be overlooked given the volume of text, 'URGENT' stamps and calls to action such as 'Apply Online Here' and 'BEGIN PROCESS'.[17]

Advertisements may be misleading by action, or by omission of material information.[18] For example:

A press advertisement by Telefonica UK Ltd trading as O_2 featured colourful images of iPhones and was headed 'Pick the winner iPhone 5c at a price you'll love ... £32 tariff, no upfront cost ... Includes £12 Airtime Plan'. A modest box at the foot of the advertisement made it clear that the price would rise by 31 pence within a month of publication, and would be adjusted in accordance with RPI (most likely upwards) a year thereafter. The ASA considered that even though the increase in price would be small, the consumer telecoms market was highly competitive and the advertisement focused on price. The box was insufficiently prominent and transparent to dispel the misleading impression created by the headline claim.[19]

Opodo Limited's website provided a facility for consumers to search for and purchase flights. Its search results for the 'cheapest method' returned prices for payment with Entropay, a virtual Visa card for which consumers were required to register, providing their personal data, and onto which funds had to be loaded (at a fee of at least 3.85 per cent) before it could be used. Only much later in the process did that become clear, and the ASA concluded that the web pages were misleading by omission.[20]

Comparative advertising

The legal and self-regulatory conditions for permissible comparative advertising are covered in Chapter 10.[21] Disputes about comparative advertising are more often resolved through the ASA than through court action, given the costs and evidential difficulties of a legal claim. Set out below are some examples of how the ASA has applied the most relevant of the eight conditions.

The comparison must not be misleading

The principles are the same as those set out above.

In press and YouTube advertisements, Dyson compared its DC59 cordless vacuum cleaner with the Gtech AirRam, claiming '10x the suction' and 'better at picking up across all floor surfaces'. Having taken expert advice, the ASA noted that there was a recognised standard set by the International Electrotechnical Commission (IEC) for vacuum cleaner testing, and that while Dyson had tested both machines, it had not done so at the same time in the same laboratory, as the IEC standard advised, to avoid environmental, operator, test material and other variations. Nor had it demonstrated superiority across all surfaces, as the advertisement suggested, and misleadingly equated suction with cleaning ability.[22]

The comparison must be of goods or services meeting the same needs or intended for the same purpose

This requires interchangeability, but is not a difficult condition to meet.

A mailing for Aldi compared the prices of a selection of its branded products with premium branded products from its competitors before stating 'SWAP & SAVE OVER 40%'. The ASA accepted that exclusive own-brand products could meet the same functional needs as premium-brand products and were therefore sufficiently interchangeable to meet the same-needs condition, but the comparison failed the misleadingness condition for having not made clear that its competitors' exclusive own brands had not been chosen for the comparison.[23]

A regional press advertisement for Tesco's Price Promise stated 'if your comparable grocery shopping is cheaper at Asda, Sainsbury's or Morrisons, we'll give you a voucher for the difference at the checkout or online'. Sainsbury's complained that many of the 'own-brand' comparisons were not valid as Sainsbury's products were certified to have been sourced to superior ethical or environmental standards (eg Fairtrade tea, MSC certified fish) or were of UK rather than overseas provenance (eg 100 per cent British chicken rather than EU-sourced chicken). The ASA disagreed, deciding that the products compared met the same fundamental needs, and Tesco had excluded products from the comparison where differences in origin were likely to be significant to the consumer.[24] The Independent Reviewer of ASA Rulings declined to ask the ASA to reconsider, and Sainsbury's attempt to have his decision quashed on judicial review failed.[25]

The comparison must objectively compare one or more material, relevant, verifiable and representative features of those goods and services, which may include price

The requirement that a comparison be objective rules out expressions of opinion. The requirement that a comparison be verifiable means that it should be verifiable by consumers and competitors based on information in the advertisement or accessible relatively easily from it.

A TV advertisement featuring Ant and Dec publicised Morrison's 'Match & More Card' which gave consumers the facility to earn points if they could have purchased their shopping for a lower price at a competing supermarket. An explanation of how the points total had been calculated was available through a part of the company's website. The ASA rejected the argument that there was no comparison (on the basis that no comparative prices were given) because a number of competitors were expressly identified. And the lack of a clearly labelled, direct link on the 'Match & More' homepage meant that the advertiser had failed to provide a sufficiently well-signposted means for customers who had shopped with them to obtain, readily, specific details of what products had been compared, and at what prices, to verify how the points total had been calculated.[26]

The comparison must not discredit or denigrate the trade marks etc, activities or circumstances of the competitor

Comparisons can be robust, but should not include potentially damaging, untrue information about the competitor or its products, or gratuitous abuse or an attack on the competitor's trading practices.

A national press advertisement for the Sky Talk service stated:

Despite advertising price cuts, BT are giving 11 million customers a price rise today. Are you one of them? At Sky, we believe in real value and fair and honest pricing – that's why Sky customers can get call packages with Sky Talk that are a lot cheaper than either BT or Virgin Media, with no funny business. To join one of the UK's fastest growing phone services, call us ....

The ASA decided that in referring to 'honest pricing' and 'no funny business', Sky had gone beyond highlighting differences objectively through a robust price comparison and had impugned BT's honesty in a manner that was denigratory.[27]

Harm and offence

The rule in both Codes is that advertisements must not cause serious or widespread offence. This can be to the public generally or to a particular group, including on grounds of religion, race, sex, sexual orientation or disability. There are also rules on causing fear or distress and on condemning or encouraging violence or irresponsible behaviour.

The use of a shocking message to grab attention for a commercial product is unlikely to be acceptable.

An advertisement by Paddy Power in *The Sun on Sunday* in 2014 attracted 5,525 complaints, the most that the ASA had ever received, partly fuelled by an online petition on Change.org. It appeared on the eve of the trial of athlete Oscar Pistorius, for the alleged premeditated murder of his girlfriend. It featured an image similar to an Oscar statuette, which had the face of Pistorius. Text stated: 'it's Oscar time', 'money back if he walks' and 'we will refund all losing bets on the Oscar Pistorius trial if he is found not guilty'. The ASA decided that the ad was likely to cause serious or widespread offence by trivialising the sensitive issues surrounding the murder trial, the girlfriend's death, and disability, and had brought advertising into disrepute.[28]

However, a more low-key message, for example, with double entendre word play, may be acceptable. The ASA is not an arbiter of taste.

A 2015 TV and cinema advertisement for online accommodation booking website booking.com, which featured a voiceover that appeared to replace a swear word with the word 'booking' (eg 'It doesn't get any booking better than this. Look at the view, look at the booking view...Booking dot com, booking dot yeah.'), attracted 683 complaints. But it was held not to be offensive. The word 'booking' was clearly enunciated, and was directly relevant to the advertiser's brand name. It was viewed as a light-hearted play on words, which would not encourage children to use expletives.[29]

Advertisements that depict children in an adult context may be problematic.

An online advertisement by American Apparel for a skirt that was part of their 'School Days' range depicted a model bending over to touch the ground with her buttocks and crotch visible. The ASA found the advertisement to be offensive because it objectified women by focusing on the model's body parts rather than the advertised clothes. As the face of the (30-year-old) model was not visible, the advertisement had the effect (given the title of the range) of inappropriately sexualising school-age girls.[30] The ruling was in line with the ASA's positive response to the recommendations of the Bailey Report on the Commercialisation and Sexualisation of Childhood.[31]

There is more scope for a potentially offensive treatment in advertising by government or a charity or campaigning group seeking to communicate an important message, but even here there are limits.

A poster for the Crimestoppers Trust depicted bloodied hands holding a heart with wording that stated, 'BREAK YOUR SILENCE Don't let drugs and violence rip the heart out of your community.' The ASA acknowledged the positive intention behind the campaign but noted that it implied the notion of the heart being ripped out of an individual's chest in an unnecessarily gruesome fashion. Given the untargeted medium used and the fact that some, particularly children, might not understand the rationale behind the image, it was considered that the advertisement was likely to cause unjustifiable distress.[32]

An advertisement by the Department of Health in 2007 to encourage smokers to stop smoking showed people being dragged along with hooks in their faces, to symbolise addiction. It attracted 774 complaints. Complaints that the advertisements were likely to cause fear and distress to children were upheld in respect of the TV and poster advertisements, but rejected in the case of press, magazine and internet advertisements. An 'ex-kids' restriction (not transmitted during or either side of children's programmes or between 4 pm and 5.45 pm) had been imposed for the TV advertisements, but they were likely to distress older children too, so there was a breach of the TV scheduling rules. And although the posters had not been placed near schools, they were otherwise untargeted and were likely to be seen by children. On the other hand, all the complaints about offensiveness were rejected, because adults would understand the seriousness of the message, which justified the otherwise unsettling content. And 181 complaints about an anti-smoking advertisement by Public Health England on TV and VOD in 2015, which featured a man rolling a cigarette with blood and flesh inside, were not formally investigated for similar reasons.

Context and medium are crucial. TV, posters and direct mail advertisements, being more intrusive and less avoidable, are more likely to cause concern than internet, press or magazine publication.

A trenchant full-page Belfast free newspaper advertisement for the Sandown Free Presbyterian Church was headed 'The Word of God Against Sodomy', and quoted Leviticus. It attracted several complaints which the ASA upheld on the grounds that the ad was homophobic and likely to cause serious offence, although it would not provoke violence. However, the ASA's decision was quashed by the High Court in Belfast, which found that, in context, the decision constituted a disproportionate restriction on Sandown's freedom of expression to stand up for its religious beliefs by calling for a peaceful demonstration in response to the annual Gay Pride march.[33]

A similar advertisement on a poster or on the side of a bus would probably not be acceptable.[34]

Social responsibility

Both Codes require that advertisements be prepared with a sense of responsibility to consumers and society. The rule has recently been relied on more than in the past, to regulate advertising that is not in keeping with the spirit of the Codes, but does not fit neatly under other rules. For example:

> An advertisement by Yves St Laurent in *Elle* magazine in 2015 featuring a model who appeared to be unhealthily underweight was found to be irresponsible.[35]

> An e-mail from CashEuroNet LLC trading as Pounds to Pocket in 2014 to those on its mailing list who had shown previous interest in its products and who were celebrating a birthday, offering them a 20 per cent discount on their first scheduled payment if they took out a loan that day, for (financially) 'worry free' birthday celebrations. The ASA decided that the mailing was irresponsible because it encouraged taking a short-term loan for frivolous spending and promoted the process of borrowing as trivial and without responsibility.[36]

On the other hand:

> A poster for Protein World's slimming product on the London Underground network, featuring a toned and athletic woman wearing a bikini, and stating 'Are you beach body ready?', was not thought to be socially irresponsible (or offensive). It invited readers to think about their figures, but would not shame women who had different body shapes into believing they needed to take a slimming supplement to feel confident wearing swimwear in public.[37]

Courtesy of Protein World

Environmental claims

Unsubstantiated, misleading, green claims for products and policies will be in breach of the Codes.

> A regional press advertisement for Transport for London promoting an 'Ultra Low Emissions Zone' in Central London was misleading in claiming that the policy 'will encourage the use of newer, cleaner vehicles to reduce vehicle pollution by half' when the reduction was in fact only for nitrogen oxide and dioxide emissions, the predicted reductions for CO_2 and particulate matter being much lower.[38]

Conversely, the ASA has on occasion upheld complaints against green campaigning groups for exaggerating the risks to the environment of certain conduct.

Both the BCAP Code and the video on demand (VOD) rules under the CAP Code contain a rule that 'advertising must not encourage behaviour grossly prejudicial to protection of the environment',[39] but this has hardly, if ever, been invoked.

Car advertisements may raise issues under the environment or misleadingness sections of the Codes, and have been in the spotlight recently because of the accuracy of mandatory fuel efficiency and CO_2 emissions figures carried out under an EU standard testing regime.[40] New car advertisements are required to include fuel and emissions information and, if based on the standard testing regime, to make that clear.

Volkswagen Group UK Ltd

An advertisement on the website of Volkswagen Group UK Ltd for Audi claimed that the A3 16 TDI was the most fuel-efficient Audi ever, 'returning a quite remarkable 68.9 mpg on a combined cycle'. The ASA noted that the website had given the correct figure for the model advertised and that the fuel consumption figure was (like that for CO_2 emissions) derived from test-drive cycles for urban and extra-urban scenarios conducted under controlled conditions in accordance with EU legislation intended to enable consumers to make a comparison of vehicles on a like-for-like basis, and was required to be included in advertising. However, the ASA said that the average consumer would be unlikely to realise that the figure quoted was based on a standardised test and was not necessarily representative of what they would achieve when driving the car themselves. VW should have qualified the figure to make clear that it was based on a standardised European test for comparative purposes and may not reflect real driving results. The ASA concluded that the claim was misleading.

Another recent example relevant to the application of the average consumer test and car emissions concerns whether claims for electric cars need to take into account upstream pollution.

Renault UK Ltd

A national press ad for the '100% electric' Renault ZOE listed in the small print (as legislation required) its CO_2 emissions as zero, but did not take into account the production of the electricity needed to power the vehicle. The ASA considered that the average consumer was likely to be familiar with the idea that emissions figures for vehicles related only to the emissions generated while the car was in motion (eg from the combustion of fuel) and did not take into account the emissions generated during production (eg refining of petrol/diesel or generation of electricity). There was no particular emphasis on the CO_2 emissions figure, and the ad was not misleading.

ZOE advert, courtesy of Renault

Food (including drink)

The rules in both Codes to a large extent reflect relevant EU law, in particular Regulation EC 1924/2006 on health and nutrition claims on foods[41] (see Chapter 19 on the advertising of food: nutrition and health claims). The rules in the Codes thus provide that health claims for foods may only be made if the claim appears on an EU Register of such claims approved by the EU Commission; and that nutrition claims may be made only if they fall within a list of permitted claims and conditions attached to them in the Annex to the Regulation.

Health claims that refer to the recommendation of an individual health professional are not acceptable.[42] There are complex rules on comparative claims, and even more complex transitional provisions, including one in respect of pre-2005 trade marks and brand names which lasts until 19 January 2022.

Additional restrictions seek to ensure that advertisements do not condone or encourage poor nutritional habits or unhealthy lifestyles in children. There are differences between the Codes. The BCAP Code has scheduling restrictions whereas the CAP Code is solely a set of content restrictions. The BCAP Code adopts the Food Standards Agency's Nutrient Profiling Model to restrict products assessed as HFSS (high in fat, salt or sugar) from being advertised to children, while the CAP Code applies to advertisements for all foods except fresh fruit and vegetables. There are restrictions on the use of licensed characters and celebrities popular with children, and rules to curb advertisements that prompt excessive consumption of food or drink. (See Chapter 20 on the advertising of food to children.)

Medicinal products and health

Prescription-only medicines may not be advertised to the general public. Other medicines should have a marketing authorisation from the Medicines and Healthcare products Regulatory Agency (MHRA) before they can be marketed, and claims must conform with the authorisation. The Codes contain a number of rules about the advertising of medicines which reflect those in the Human Medicines Regulations 2012.[43]

All claims about the efficacy of health-related products must be backed by proper evidence, which will often need to include full reports of proper trials on humans, including a control/placebo, accepted for publication in peer-reviewed journals. Breakthrough claims will require particularly robust evidence.

A 2014 poster ad by Enzymatica was headed 'Help shorten your cold with Coldzyme', but went further in the text and product image (eg 'forms a protective barrier … helps shield you'). Similar claims were made on the Boots website. Enzymatica relied on the Swedish regulator's approval of the product under the Medical Devices Directive 93/42/EEC, *in vitro* data and trials on humans. The ASA was not bound by the Swedish regulator's view, and having taken expert advice, the ASA concluded that the primary study, although randomised, double blind and placebo controlled, did not relate to shortening a cold once infected, and contained insufficient information to support the prevention claim. Other studies produced by the advertiser contained methodological flaws.[44]

The more stark, categorical or absolute the claim, the greater the evidence required.

Poster and magazine advertisements by SmithKline Beecham for Ribena Toothkind in 1999 were headed 'There is only one soft drink accredited by the British Dental Association' and showed bottles of Ribena as bristles on a toothbrush. The magazine advertisement described the dangers of dental erosion from soft-drink consumption, and stated that in a study by a leading university dental school, Ribena Toothkind was found to be almost as kind for teeth as water. A trade press advertisement also stated that 'Ribena Toothkind does not encourage tooth decay'. The ASA concluded, on the basis of its own and SKB's expert evidence, that the carbohydrate content of the drink had been lowered but not eliminated. The product did appear to be less damaging to teeth than other soft drinks, but the poster was misleading in implying that the product actively benefited oral health, and the magazine advertisement was misleading in claiming that the drink did not encourage tooth decay, because this was an absolute claim whereas the evidence justified only a comparative claim. SKB's challenge to the ASA's decision in judicial review proceedings failed.[45]

Claims for complementary and alternative medicine also require substantiation.[46]

Claims in respect of serious conditions for which medical treatment or supervision should be sought should not discourage such treatment or supervision.[47]

The average reader of a health claim may often be more vulnerable than the average consumer, and more susceptible to exaggerated claims, and advertisers need to remember that when creating advertisements for products for slimming, baldness, arthritis and so on. The first case to be referred by the ASA to the OFT under the legislation dealing with misleading advertising concerned unsubstantiated slimming claims.[48]

Alcohol and gambling

The aim of the sector-specific rules is to prevent harm arising from excessive alcohol consumption or gambling. (See Chapter 18 on alcohol and Chapter 21 on gambling.)

A Co-op radio advertisement in 2015 stated:

> *Sun's out, garden chair, drinks. In-laws, great, drinks. Cricket, wicket, drinks. At your local Co-op selected spirits are just £13 each. Little, often, Co-op. Participating stores, subject to availability. 70cl, ends 1st September. Please drink responsibly.*
>
> The ASA decided that the three scenarios, spoken by the same person, and the 'Little. Often' slogan condoned or encouraged immoderate drinking, and was irresponsible.

The rules seek to protect the vulnerable, particularly children and young people, by ensuring that advertising does not make alcohol or gambling particularly attractive to them.

> A website for a gambling service featured a cartoon pirate with sunglasses and a gem-studded beard and a goat with gold teeth and a gold chain around its neck. It was found to be in breach, as the common occurrence of such animated characters in children's programming and culture would make them likely to appeal particularly to under-18s.[49]

Under-25s must not play a significant role in alcohol or gambling advertising.

> A tweet from the Twitter account of Totesport (the trading name of Petfre Gibraltar Limited) was in breach for including a picture of professional golfer Jordan Speith playing golf and encouraging consumers to bet on him. Speith was under the age of 25. Note that the ad would have been acceptable under the Code rule if Mr Speith had appeared in a place where a bet could be placed directly through a transactional facility such as Tote's own website.[50]

Children

Children are generally defined in the Codes as those under 16. Many of the Codes' rules are directed at protecting children from harm. (See, for example, Chapter 9 on advertising and children and Chapter 20 on the advertising of food to children.)

There is a general requirement that advertisements should not make a direct appeal to children to buy advertised products or persuade their parents or other adults to buy advertised products for them, which reflects a prohibited practice in the CPRs, and in the AVMS Directive (in respect of television).

> The ASA upheld a complaint by the Competition and Markets Authority about advertisements within Mind Candy Ltd's online Moshi Monsters game, in which players were urged with statements such as 'The Super Moshis need YOU' and 'Members are going to be super popular' to participate in a paid membership system to obtain extra more desirable content.[51]

Many complaints concern the use of inappropriate media. In the case of television, 'ex-kids' (see 'Harm and offence' above) and 9 pm watershed restrictions are enforced by Clearcast and the ASA, along with other scheduling restrictions. TV companies have a system of indexing audience composition, with an index of 120 meaning that a programme is substantially more popular with children (see also Chapter 20 on the advertising of food to children).

Privacy

The BCAP Code requires (with a few exceptions) advertisers to have the written permission of a living person before broadcasting an advertisement that features, caricatures or refers to that person. The CAP Code simply urges advertisers to obtain permission, and complaints will only be upheld if the individual is featured in an adverse or offensive way. (See also Chapter 8 on celebrities in advertising.)

> On its website, building company Hansen & Co (UK) Ltd included in its 'Case Studies' pictures of the interior and exterior of a property, and its address. The ASA noted that there was no evidence permission had been obtained and considered that the ad falsely implied that the owner (the complainant) had personally approved of the work carried out and the advertised service.[52]

Another important area is the privacy of individuals in relation to databases and direct marketing. There are detailed rules in the CAP Code, reflecting the requirements of the Data Protection Act 1998 and Privacy and Electronic Communications Regulations 2003 (see Chapter 7 on privacy and data protection).[53]

There are also rules in Appendix 3 of the CAP Code relating to online behavioural advertising. Other legislators and regulators are grappling with that (as well as the civil courts), and at the time of writing the ASA had yet to make any formal rulings.

Tobacco and e-cigarettes

The direct or indirect advertising of tobacco is prohibited by law. The advertising of e-cigarettes has similarly now been prohibited, effective from 20 May 2016[54] save for purely local media, and for e-cigarettes registered as a medicine or medical device. Advertisements for such products will still also need to comply with additional rules in the Codes to prevent the encourage-ment of people to take up smoking, portraying e-cigarettes as safe, appealing to children and so on. (See Chapter 23 on smoking and vaping.)

Financial services

The ASA and ASAB will deal with complaints about non-technical aspects of financial advertising, including consumer credit, but more technical issues are referred to the Financial Conduct Authority.

Sales promotions

The rules in the CAP Code comprise a useful checklist for anyone putting together a product promotion. (Lotteries, competitions and prize promotions are covered in Chapter 13.)

Code compliance

Copy advice and clearance

As noted above, copy clearance is required by broadcasters for TV advertise-ments. Most TV advertisements are cleared by Clearcast, although regional advertisements may be cleared locally (eg for ITV). For Clearcast clearance, the advertiser will need to provide at the outset the evidence to substantiate factual claims. A substantive response is likely within a few days, but actual clearance will take longer if expert input is required. Certain categories of radio advertisement must be cleared by the Radiocentre; others are cleared locally by the radio stations. Note that advertisements may be cleared only for a limited time period.

In the case of non-broadcast advertisements, the media may insist on clearance if the ASA Council or CAP advise it, where the advertisements are contentious or the advertiser has a troublesome history. CAP Copy Advice is advisable if the campaign involves high-risk areas such as children, com-parisons, alcohol, food or health. It is generally prompt (within 24 hours), and free. Note that copy clearance does not bind the ASA Council, mean that the advertisement is lawful, or that it might not be refused by the relevant media on other grounds. There is no general right to force a private media outlet to carry a particular advertisement if it breaches their own policies or terms for acceptance of advertising.

Other hints for Code compliance

1 Know the Codes.

2 Open and maintain a dialogue between the marketing department and compliance/regulatory/legal.

3 Explore commercial issues, particularly in sales promotions, to ensure that, for example, demand can be fulfilled.

4 Assess the content of the advertisement as though you were an ordinary, reasonable reader of it – are the key messages included so that it does not mislead?

5 Is the artwork included likely to cause any difficulties? (NB the Codes do not cover intellectual property issues such as trade marks, copyright and passing off.)

6 Check ASA Council decisions, but remember that each case depends on the facts.

7 Check Clearcast Guidance, CAP Advertising Guidance and AdviceOnline (CAP's database of advice, with links to appropriate Code clauses, and the more significant rulings) but remember that this does not bind the ASA Council.

8 If the advertisement is likely to be contentious, is alternative copy available if it has to be pulled quickly?

9 Can the advertiser substantiate all claims, if necessary with expert evidence? Do not make absolute claims for a product if experts disagree or an expert's report says that test results are positive but further research is required.

Complaints

Responding to complaints

If the advertiser has a good previous record and the issue is minor and clear-cut, can the ASA be persuaded to deal with the matter informally if the advertiser puts its hands up quickly and is not going to be publishing the advertisement further?

The sort of arguments that will/will not work include the following:

'*Look at my disclaimer*': In general it is no good making a misleading claim and then trying to put matters right in the small print.

'*We give a money-potential claimback guarantee*': This does not excuse misleading claims.

'*I am just repeating what someone else said*': If testimonials give the impression that a product has been found to work, the advertiser will be required to produce proper evidence that the product does actually work.

'*It would be contrary to the free movement of goods and services under the EU Treaty to stop me advertising*': This will generally only work where an EU Directive or Regulation has harmonised the relevant law such that Member States cannot prevent advertising in a form which meets the requirements of the relevant EU law, or where there is some discrimination against advertising by an (ex UK) EU-based advertiser.

'*You are infringing my right to free speech*': All adverse ASA rulings may do that, but free speech can be subject to limitations, including for the protection of rights of others.

'*I do not believe anyone could possibly complain about my advertisement – the complainant must be a competitor. I want to see the letter of complaint*': The identity of members of the public who complain is kept confidential, the outcome of an investigation rarely depends on any disputed factual evidence from such complainants, and the ASA is experienced in spotting obvious competitor complaints.

'*My substantiation evidence is too confidential to disclose*': ASA procedures provide for substantiation evidence to be treated in confidence by the ASA (and any expert instructed) where it is genuinely confidential, but if an advertiser is going to make claims to the world he or she needs to anticipate that such claims may be subject to external scrutiny.

'*I must have an oral hearing*': The ASA Council does not provide oral hearings, and the law does not require that it should.

'*Council must see all my substantiation material*': This is impractical. Council has delegated the investigation of complaints to the ASA executive, and all that is required to be put to the Council is a fair summary of the advertiser's position and the advertisement. In exceptional cases, the Council may consider additional material.

'*Your expert is biased*': In a relatively narrow field or in relation to a controversial subject, it may be very difficult to find an expert that does not have an existing opinion, but that does not mean that the expert cannot seek to approach the matter afresh, or that the expert's alleged bias will render any subsequent ASA decision unfair.[55]

'*There has only been one complaint*': This is relevant, but is particularly unlikely to be persuasive in the case of misleading advertising. As one judge put it: 'It is in the very nature of a misleading or deceptive advertisement that the consumer is left unaware of the true facts. Further, many consumers, even though aware of the deception, and even though aggrieved, may not have the time, ability, personality or inclination to make a complaint.'[56] Conversely, a large number of complaints, particularly that an ad is offensive, does not mean that the complaints will be upheld.[57]

'*My competitor makes similar claims*': The ASA must seek to ensure a level playing field, but the fact that one advertiser is publishing advertisements in breach of the Code does not justify any other advertiser doing it.

'*I've been doing it for years*': This may be relevant, but not determinative.

'*It works on mice*': Generally not good enough.

'*F... off you toothless watchdog*': Behaving like an outlaw may work for certain advertisers for a while, but in the end the advertiser is likely to encounter difficulties with the media, other regulators and the public.

Complaining about competitor campaigns

The ASA generally treats competitor complaints in the same way as complaints from members of the public, save that the competitor will be identified, and should be able to demonstrate that they have sought, in writing, to resolve their complaint with the competitor first. In addition, competitors will be asked to confirm that they are not intending to litigate the same issue. It is worth noting that competitor complaints are often hard fought and can take longer to determine than consumer complaints; and that once a formal investigation has commenced, the ASA will not generally allow withdrawal of a complaint simply because it looks as though the complaint is likely to be not upheld.

Contesting an ASA decision

Independent Reviewer

The advertiser (or complainant) may use the Independent Review Procedure which is in similar terms for both broadcast and non-broadcast. A request for a review of a decision by the ASA Council can be made to the Independent Reviewer of ASA rulings, either:

- where additional relevant evidence becomes available (and an explanation is provided as to why it was not submitted previously); or

- where it is alleged that there is a substantial flaw in the Council's ruling or in the process by which it was made.

An application for an independent review should be made within 21 days of the date on the ASA's notification of a ruling. The ASA will not delay publication of the ruling pending the outcome of a review, save in exceptional circumstances.

> Debt Free Direct plc sought to obtain an injunction against publication of an ASA decision in May 2007, pending the outcome of its application for permission to bring proceedings for a judicial review of a decision by the ASA upholding complaints about DFD's TV advertising for debt management services offering individual voluntary arrangements. Mr Justice Sullivan ruled[58] that it would require the most compelling reasons to prevent a regulatory body such as the ASA from publishing its adjudications, and that DFD should exhaust its available remedies (ie the Independent Review Procedure) before seeking to involve the court.

If the Independent Reviewer accepts the review request, he or she may reopen the investigation and/or refer the case back to the Council with a recommendation to reverse or revise its previous decision.

Judicial review

If the party seeking the review still does not like the outcome, they may be able to seek permission to bring proceedings for a judicial review of the decision of the Council or Independent Reviewer, seeking an order quashing the disputed decision. An application for judicial review must be made promptly and at most within three months of notification of the decision in question. Any application should be preceded by a letter before action complying with the Pre-Action Protocol for judicial review, setting out the potential claimant's case, in a final attempt to resolve matters without litigation. The court will not substitute its own views for that of the decision maker. Generally, damages are not claimed or awarded even if a judicial review challenge is successful.

The courts will generally be reluctant to overturn the views of a long-established regulator acting within its field of expertise. Generally, the advertiser will be better off seeking to work with the regulator, rather than battling with it in the courts.

Notes

1 Eg with the Financial Conduct Authority, PhonepayPlus, the Medicines and Healthcare products Regulatory Agency, the Gambling Commission, Scottish local authorities, the Department of Trade and Investment in Northern Ireland, the Food Standards Agency and Department of Health.

2 Part 4A, implementing the provisions of Directive 2010/13/EU on the coordination of certain provisions laid down by law, regulation or administrative action in Member States concerning the provision of audiovisual media services (AVMS). The AVMS rules are very high level, and all VOD cases to date have been amply covered by the existing BCAP and CAP Code rules – see eg the ASA's ruling on BUPA, A14-287260.

3 Charity Commission's Guidance on Campaigning and Political Activity by Charities (CC9, March 2008)

4 Directive 2010/13/EU on the coordination of certain provisions laid down by law, regulation or administrative action in Member States concerning the provision of audiovisual media services

5 See Introduction to BCAP Code

6 Article 1(1)(i). See *Komm Austria* v. *ORF* [2007] in which the ECJ ruled that a prize game offered by means of dialling a premium-rate phone number in a television broadcast of ostensibly editorial content could constitute teleshopping or advertising.

7 In respect of which the courts will not interfere unless the decision is manifestly unreasonable – *R* v. *ASA ex p Charles Robertson (Developments) Ltd* [1999].

8 Pursuant to designation by Ofcom of the ASA under the Communications Act 2003

9 CAP Regulatory Statement on the marketing of causes and ideas

10 Details may be found in the ASA's Broadcast and Non-Broadcast Complaint Handling Procedures on the ASA's website.

11 CAP Code (2010 edition) Clause 3.7

12 Article 12 of Directive 2005/29/EC on Unfair Commercial Practices provides for courts or administrative authorities to require a trader to furnish evidence as to the accuracy of factual claims, and to consider such claims inaccurate if the evidence is not forthcoming or is inadequate. See also Enterprise Act 2002 Section 218A.

13 BCAP Code rule 3.9

14 BCAP Code rule 2.1

15 CAP Code rule 8.21.1

16 A15-296396. A more sophisticated newspaper offering in Churchcastle Ltd trading as Spencer & Mayfair involved calling a premium-rate number with correct answers to a word search puzzle to claim a 'lucky clover emerald brooch', which was presented as an award. In fact the premium-rate call cost a minimum of £8.80, and the advertiser did not properly substantiate the cost (to them) and value of the brooch – A11-152661.

17 A14-273276. The High Court refused an application for permission to bring proceedings for judicial review of the decision.

18 CAP Code rules 3.1 and 3.3, and BCAP Code rules 3.1 and 3.2 respectively

19 A14-258322

20 A15-291574

21 They are set out in Business Protection from Misleading Marketing Regulation 2008 (implementing Directive 2006/114/EC, which is maximum harmonisation in respect of comparative advertising).

22 A14-263921

23 A11-147951

24 A13-224516

25 *R (Sainsbury's Supermarkets Limited)* v. *Independent Reviewer of the Advertising Standards Authority* [2014] EWHC 3680 (Admin)

26 A14-283348

27 A07-36773. See a more recent Sky case, involving a comparison with Virgin broadband speeds, A13-231567.

28 A14-261396

29 A14-289781

30 A14-275883

31 'Letting Children be Children: Report on an Independent Review of the Commercialisation and Sexualisation of Childhood', Department of Education, June 2011: https://www.gov.uk/government/uploads/system/uploads/attachment_data/file/175418/Bailey_Review.pdf

32 A15-317339

33 *Kirk Session of Sandown Free Presbyterian Church* v. *ASA* [2011]

34 See the decision of the Court of Appeal in *R (oao Core Issues Trust)* v. *Transport for London* [2014], declining to quash a decision by TfL to refuse to carry on London buses (on grounds of likely offence) a Christian charity's advertisement 'Not Gay, Ex-Gay, Post Gay and Proud, Get Over It!' prepared in response to a Stonewall ad: 'Some People are Gay. Get Over It!'

35 A15-292161

36 A14-261543

37 A15-300099

38 A14-286861

39 Reflecting Article 9 (1)(c)(iv) of Directive 2010/13/EU on audiovisual media services.

40 Passenger Car (Fuel Consumption and CO_2 Emissions Information) Regulations 2001, implementing Directive 1999/94/EC (both as amended)

41 Regulation 1924/2006 on Nutrition and Health Claims made on Foods is a directly effective maximum harmonisation measure. See also Regulation EU 1161/2011 on the provision of food information to consumers, and Regulation EU 609/2013 on food intended for infants and young children, food for special medical purposes, and total diet replacement for weight control.

42 Eg 'Developed with pioneering British scientist Professor Arnold Beckett' accompanying health claims for Vitabiotics' Wellman and Wellwoman vitamin supplements, A13-246039

43 Which in turn reflects the provisions of maximum harmonisation EU legislation: Directive 2001/83/EC on the Community Code relating to medicinal products for human use, as amended (see further *Gintec International* v. *Verband Sozialer Weltbewerb* [2007] ECJ).

44 A14-289509. Note that for medical devices the EU has not harmonised advertising rules, unlike for medicines, although Member States must not create an obstacle to placing approved devices on the market.

45 *R* v. *ASA ex p SmithKline Beecham plc* [2001]

46 See for example A11-157043 in respect of claims on Twitter and its web page by Society of Homeopaths in respect of depression, bronchitis, osteoarthritis etc.

47 Ibid

48 *Director General of Fair Trading* v. *Tobyward* [1989]

49 A15-311328

50 A15-308914

51 A15-305018

52   A14-256671

53   Note this area is likely to be subject to a new EU data protection Regulation shortly, effective from 2018.

54   Again an EU Directive – Article 20(5) of the Tobacco Products Directive 2014/40/EC.

55   See *R (oao Smithkline Beecham)* v. *ASA* [2000]

56   Etherton J in *Office of Fair Trading* v. *The Officers Club* [2005]

57   See eg the Booking.com ad referred to above.

58   *R (oao Debt Free Direct Ltd)* v. *ASA* [2007]. See also *R* v. *ASA ex p. Vernons Organisation Ltd* [1992], *R* v. *ASA ex p. Matthias Rath BV* [2001] and *R (oao Jamba Gmbh)* v. *ASA* [2005]

Consumer protection

06

RUPERT EARLE

BWB
Bates Wells Braithwaite

Introduction

The courts and state have gradually encroached on the maxim 'buyer beware', including in respect of advertising. Some advertising is mere marketing puff or brand building, but in general terms advertising aims to help persuade consumers to buy particular goods or services. The latter may, if false, give rise to claims of misrepresentation, entitling the consumer to sue for damages, or even be treated as a contractual term enforceable by the consumer. Thus in *Carlill v. Carbolic Smoke Ball Company* (1892) the Company promised to pay £100 to any customer who purchased the advertised smoke ball and still caught a cold or influenza. The Court of Appeal held that the offer was specific enough to comprise a contractual offer which Mrs Carlill had accepted when she bought the product. She was able to recover £100, having caught the flu.

Online trading has increasingly blurred the line between representations and contractual terms. Statute law now provides for certain practices, preparatory to entering into a contact, to be treated as unfair, that claims in advertising may, in certain circumstances, be treated as terms of a consumer contract, and for the provision of clear information prior to entering into a contract. This chapter seeks to cover these issues, but does not touch the vast array of legislation that seeks to regulate advertising in specific sectors – dealt with elsewhere in this book. Nor does it address business-to-business advertising. The advertising of prices is considered separately in Chapter 15. Most cases are dealt with in the county court or magistrates' court, so there is a dearth of reported cases.

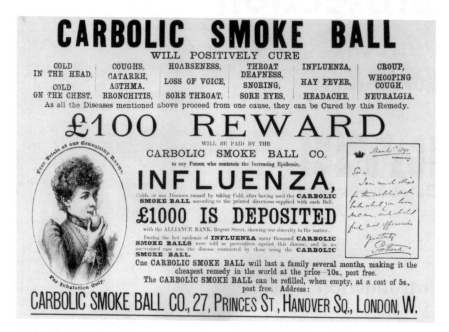

Photo: *Illustrated London* News, 1892. Hulton Archive / Getty Images

Unfair commercial practices

Misleading advertising is now regulated primarily by the Consumer Protection from Unfair Trading Regulations 2008 (CPRs), which implement the Unfair Commercial Practices Directive 2005/29/EC on unfair business-to-consumer commercial practices (UCPD).[1]

Practices prohibited outright

Thirty-one practices listed in Schedule 1 CPRs are prohibited outright.[2] Those relevant to advertising are (by paragraph number in the schedule):

1 Claiming to be a signatory to a code of conduct when the trader is not (eg the Direct Marketing Association's Code).

2 Displaying a quality mark or equivalent without authorisation.

3 Claiming that a code of conduct has an endorsement from a public or other body which it does not have.

4 Claiming that a trader's practices have been approved, endorsed or authorised by a public or other body when it does not, or without complying with its terms.

5 Making an invitation to purchase products at a specified price without disclosing the existence of any reasonable grounds for not being able to do so – 'bait advertising'.

6 Bait advertising with the intention of promoting a different product (bait and switch).

7 Falsely stating that a product will be available for a very limited time in order to elicit an immediate decision, and deprive consumers of sufficient opportunity or time to make an informed choice.

9 Stating or creating the impression that a product can legally be sold when it cannot.

10 Presenting rights given to consumers in law as a distinctive feature of the trader's offer (eg Consumer Rights Act 2015 implied terms, see below).

11 Using editorial content in the media to promote a product where a trader has paid for the promotion without making that clear (see Chapter 5 on the self-regulatory system and Chapter 12 on the internet and beyond).

12 Making a materially inaccurate claim concerning the risk to the personal security of the consumer or their family if they do not purchase the product (eg a CCTV security system).

13 Promoting a product similar to a product made by a particular manufacturer so as to deliberately mislead the consumer into believing that the product is made by that same manufacturer.

15 Claiming that the trader is about to cease trading or move premises when they are not.

16 Claiming products are able to facilitate winning in games of chance.

17 Falsely claiming that a product is able to cure illnesses, dysfunction or malformations.

18 Passing on materially inaccurate information on market conditions or on the possibility of finding the product with the intention of inducing the consumer to acquire the product at conditions less favourable than normal market conditions.

19 Claiming in a commercial practice to offer a competition or prize promotion without awarding the prizes described or a reasonable equivalent.

20 Describing a product as 'gratis', 'free', 'without charge' or similar if the consumer has to pay anything other than the unavoidable cost of responding and collecting or paying for delivery ('buy one get one free' offers are acceptable as long as the consumer's liability is clear and there is no reduction in quality or inflation in price to pay for the free element).

21 Including in marketing material an invoice or similar document seeking payment which gives the consumer the impression that they have already ordered the marketed product when they have not.

22 Falsely claiming or creating the impression that the trader is not acting for purposes relating to their trade, business, craft or profession, or falsely representing oneself as a consumer (see Chapter 12 on the internet and beyond).

26 Making persistent and unwanted solicitations by telephone, e-mail etc except to the extent justified to enforce a contractual obligation.

28 Including in an advertisement a direct exhortation to children to buy advertised products or persuade their parents or other adults to buy them for them.

30 Explicitly informing a consumer that if he or she does not buy the product or service, the trader's job or livelihood will be in jeopardy.

31 Creating the false impression that the consumer has already won, will win, or will on doing a particular act win a prize, when in fact there is no prize or other equivalent benefit or they are required to pay money or incur a cost to claim it or equivalent benefit.

The decision of the Court of Justice of the European Union in *OFT* v. *Purely Creative Ltd and others* indicates that the prohibited practices are likely to be interpreted relatively strictly against traders, with little scope for examination of the circumstances. Thus the Court held that the wording of prohibited practice 31 prevents the trader from requiring the consumer to 'bear the slightest cost... such as the cost of a stamp', and that 'false impression' did not require proof that the advertiser intended to mislead consumers, or that they were misled.[3]

Misleading actions and omissions

If a commercial practice is not on the list in Schedule 1 CPRs, it will still be unlawful if it is misleading.

A commercial practice is *misleading by action* if it:

- contains false information[4] and is therefore untruthful, or if it or its overall presentation in any way deceives or is likely to deceive the *average consumer* in relation to that information, even if factually correct; or

- breaches a code of conduct that the trader has undertaken to comply with; or

- creates confusion with a competitor

so as to cause the *average consumer* to take a *transactional decision* that they would not otherwise have taken.[5]

A commercial practice is *misleading by omission* if it:

- omits, hides or provides in an unclear, unintelligible, ambiguous or untimely manner *material information*; or

- fails to identify the commercial intent of the practice

so as to cause the *average consumer* to take a *transactional decision* that they would not otherwise have taken.[6]

'Material information'[7] means 'information which the average consumer needs, according to the context, to take an informed transactional decision'[8] as well as any information requirement imposed by specific EU legislation.[9] Where an advertisement 'indicates characteristics of the product and price... and thereby enables the consumer to make a purchase'[10] (eg a direct response advertisement on a website or in a direct mailing), this constitutes an 'invitation to purchase' and material information includes:

- the main characteristics of the product;

- identity (eg trading name) and geographical address of the trader;

- price (including any taxes and additional charges) or where the price cannot reasonably be calculated in advance, the manner in which it is calculated;

- right of withdrawal or cancellation where relevant; and

- arrangements for payment, delivery, performance and complaints-handling policy, where they depart from what the consumer would reasonably expect.[11]

However, the material information requirement is not wholly inflexible, in that regard may be had to limitations of time and space in the medium used, and any measures taken by the trader to make information available by other means.[12]

Who is the 'average consumer'? According to the CPRs, in a test derived from the UCPD and EU trade mark cases, the average consumer is 'reasonably well informed and reasonably observant and circumspect'. So in assessing whether an advertisement is likely to mislead, one need not focus on 'the ignorant, careless or over-hasty consumer',[13] but: (i) nor is the average consumer drawn from the brightest or most cynical quartile of consumers; and (ii) the average consumer may be deemed to have been misled by an advertisement if a significant proportion of the public is likely to be misled even if the majority of consumers would not have been misled.[14] In addition, (iii) if a practice is directed at a particular group of consumers, the practice should be assessed from the standpoint of members of that group; and (iv) if the practice is directed at a clearly identifiable group which is particularly vulnerable to the practice or product because of their mental or physical infirmity, age or credulity, in a way in which the trader could be expected to foresee, the practice should be assessed from their perspective.[15]

A 'transactional decision' is a decision to act or refrain from acting concerning whether, how and on what terms to purchase, make payment in whole or in part for, retain or dispose of a product or whether, how and on what terms to exercise a contractual right. Mere advertising puffery is not caught, but a decision to make a phone call, enter a shop[16] or go online to make a purchase is. Although doubted by Briggs J in *OFT* v. *Purely Creative*, guidance from the European Commission and the OFT suggests that progressing through a website with an interest in making a purchase would also be caught; that seems right.[17]

Aggressive practices

A commercial practice is also prohibited if it significantly impairs or is likely significantly to impair the average consumer's freedom of choice or conduct in relation to the product, through the use of harassment, coercion or undue influence, and it thereby causes or is likely to cause the consumer to take a decision they otherwise would not have taken.

Breach of requirement of professional diligence

A practice that is not outright prohibited (under Schedule 1), misleading (by action or omission) or aggressive may nevertheless still be unfair and therefore prohibited if it contravenes the requirements of professional diligence and materially distorts or is likely to materially distort the economic behaviour of the average consumer with regard to the product.[18] Professional diligence means the standard of special skill and care which a trader may reasonably be expected to exercise towards consumers which is commensurate with either (a) honest market practice in the trader's field of activity, or (b) the general principle of good faith in the trader's field of activity. Non-compliance with industry codes of practice in advertising may indicate lack of professional diligence.

Enforcement

The primary enforcement authorities for the CPRs are local authority Trading Standards departments or the Competition and Markets Authority (CMA) (in respect of practices likely to harm the collective interests of consumers). These bodies are required to have regard to the desirability of encouraging control of unfair commercial practices by such 'established means' as they consider appropriate in the circumstances; and in guidance, the government has made it clear that in respect of advertising, the established means is the Advertising Standards Authority (ASA) and, for premium-rate services, PhonepayPlus.[19]

If the ASA cannot resolve the matter or it requires more serious sanctions, Trading Standards (or the CMA) may seek undertakings, or seek an injunction in the civil courts,[20] or bring a criminal prosecution. Breach of all of the CPRs provisions is a criminal offence, save for breach of code commitments under Regulation 5(3)(b) and banned practices under Schedule 1 paragraphs 11 and 28. Officers of a company may also be prosecuted. The maximum penalties on conviction are an unlimited fine and (on indictment) imprisonment for up to two years.[21] There is a defence of due diligence, and of innocent publication of an advertisement (eg by a newspaper or internet service provider).[22]

Before undertaking enforcement action, a Trading Standards authority is required to check that the trader in question does not have a relationship with another authority (its 'primary authority'), and that enforcement action would not be inconsistent with advice already given concerning the commercial practice in question.[23]

Most CMA and Trading Standards action has focused on misleading pricing.[24] Much is left to the ASA (see Chapter 5 on the self-regulatory system). A breach of the CAP or BCAP Codes does not necessarily equate to a breach of the CPRs.

Consumers' right to redress

Part 4A of the CPRs, which came into force on 1 October 2014 through the Consumer Protection (Amendment) Regulations 2014, provides consumers who have entered into a contract with a right of redress where the trader has engaged in a misleading action under Regulation 5 or an aggressive action under Regulation 7 of the CPRs (but not a misleading omission or a specific prohibited practice), and that action was a significant factor in the transactional decision.[25] The consumer is entitled to unwind the contract to get their money back and to refuse to pay any money that is not yet due. The consumer must indicate to the trader that they are rejecting the goods within 90 days of entering into the contract or when the goods are delivered/performance of the service begins etc, whichever is later. This must be done before the goods are fully consumed or the service is fully performed.[26]

Where the consumer has not exercised the right to unwind, there is a right to a discount ranging from 25 to 100 per cent depending on the seriousness of the misleading or aggressive action (providing it is more than merely minor).[27] Where over £5,000 is payable and there is a difference between the amount payable and the market price, the discount is the difference between the market price of the product and the amount payable.

Finally, the consumer may sue for damages for *either* financial loss incurred by the prohibited practice *or* alarm, distress or physical inconvenience or discomfort caused.[28] This is limited to loss that was reasonably foreseeable at the time and the trader has a defence if it can be shown, among other things, that the practice in question occurred by mistake or was beyond their control, or that they took all reasonable precautions and exercised all due diligence to avoid it.

Consumer rights

Information requirements for contracts at a distance

The Consumer Contracts (Information, Cancellation and Additional Charges) Regulations 2013 (CCRs) apply to contracts entered into after 13 June 2014.

They require the provision of certain information to the consumer in a clear and comprehensible manner before the consumer is bound by a contract, failing which it may not be binding. This will be relevant to advertising where an advertisement seeks a direct response by way of a purchase – eg a web page or direct marketing material. The information required includes, for example:

- the main characteristics of the goods or services, to the extent appropriate to the medium of communication and to the goods or services;
- identity of trader (such as trading name);
- geographical and e-mail address and telephone number;
- total price, inclusive of taxes and additional charges, or, if this cannot reasonably be done in advance, how the price will be calculated;
- information about any right to cancel within 14 days of supply of goods, or 14 days after the contract is entered into for intangible digital content or (unless agreed otherwise) services;
- in the case of a sales contract, a reminder that the trader is under a legal duty to supply goods that are in conformity with the contract;
- the existence and the conditions of after-sales services and commercial guarantees (where applicable);
- the duration of the contract, where applicable, or, if the contract is of indeterminate duration or is to be extended automatically, the conditions for terminating the contract;
- the functionality (including applicable technical protection measures) of digital content, where applicable;
- any relevant compatibility of digital content with hardware and software that the trader is aware of or can reasonably be expected to have been aware of; and
- the existence of relevant codes of conduct and where they may be found.

Trading Standards are under a duty to enforce the CCRs, which they can do by seeking an undertaking or injunction.[29] Failure to notify consumers of their right to cancel is also a criminal offence.[30]

Terms implied into consumer contracts

The Consumer Rights Act 2015 came into force on 1 October 2015 and implies into consumer contracts terms as to satisfactory quality, fitness for purpose and description (in respect of goods and digital content) and performance with reasonable skill and care, for a reasonable price and within a reasonable time (in respect of services). Such terms cannot generally be excluded.[31]

Of particular relevance to advertising is that:

- The quality of goods and digital content is satisfactory if the goods meet the standards that a reasonable person would consider satisfactory, taking into account any description, the price, description and 'all other relevant circumstances'. These circumstances include 'any public statement [including, in particular, made in advertising or labelling] about the specific characteristics of the goods made by the trader, producer or any representative of the trader or producer'.[32] A retailer may, therefore, be bound not only by statements made in their own advertising, but also in that of their supplier and the manufacturer, unless they can show that they were not and could not reasonably have been aware of the statement or it had been publicly withdrawn or corrected before the contract with the consumer was made, or the consumer's decision to contract could not have been influenced by it.[33] Note that even freedom from minor defects may be an aspect of quality, unless the defect is specifically drawn to the consumer's attention before the contract is made.

- Goods and digital content must be as described, including in marketing materials to the extent that these become part of the contract. In particular, they must conform to the description of the main characteristics of the product provided in accordance with the Consumer Contracts Regulations 2013 referred to above.[34]

- Services must be performed in conformity with information provided about the trader or service,[35] including anything said or provided in writing to the consumer (eg in advertising) if taken into account when deciding whether to enter into a contract or when making a decision about the service once a contract has been made.

Failure to comply with these terms may allow a consumer to rely on various statutory remedies, including the right to reject[36] (or refund, for digital products),[37] a right to repair or a replacement[38] (or repeat performance, in the case of services),[39] or a right to a reduction in price.[40]

Competition law

Advertising practices which involve an agreement that prevents, restricts or distorts competition or conduct that is an abuse of a dominant market position may attract the scrutiny of the Competition and Markets Authority under the Competition Act 1998. The CMA imposed penalties of over £735,000 on an association of estate agents and a local newspaper publisher in Hampshire which were found to have colluded to not advertise the association's fees or discounts in order to reduce competitive pressure.[41]

While US-style consumer class actions are not (yet) part of the UK consumer protection landscape, notwithstanding an EU Collective Redress Recommendation,[42] the Consumer Rights Act does provide for 'collective proceedings' to be brought before the Competition Appeal Tribunal in competition law cases.[43]

Fraud

Finally, an in-house lawyer battling with a marketing department which appears to have lost its moral compass may, as a last resort, need to draw to colleagues' attention the Fraud Act 2006, which provides for a maximum penalty on conviction of 10 years' imprisonment. Offences under the Act include a person dishonestly making a false representation (express or implied); or dishonestly failing to disclose information which they are under a legal duty to disclose; in either case, with a view to making a gain for themselves or another, or causing loss to another or exposing another to risk of loss.[44]

Notes

1 The EU Commission was due to publish revised guidance on UCPD in 2016. The Competition and Markets Authority has adopted BERR/OFT's guidance on CPUTRs. Note that business-to-business marketing is regulated separately by the Business Protection from Misleading Marketing Regulations 2008 (BPMMRs), which implement the Misleading and Comparative Advertising Directive 2006/114/EC (UCPD).

2 CPUTRs Regulation 3 and Schedule 1

3 Case C-428/11. It involved prize promotions in which (unknown to the consumer) in many cases the cost of claiming the 'prizes' was at least equivalent to their value.

4 False information may be as to the nature or existence of a product, its main characteristics, any relevant sponsorship or approval, price, the rights of the consumer and so on. 'Main characteristics' includes a product's availability, nature, benefits, risks and geographical or commercial origins etc.

5 Regulation 5

6 Regulation 6(1)

7 Regulation 6(3)

8 For example, that cars sold by an internet car brokerage were not properly registered in the consumer's name, exposing them to potential prosecution and insurance difficulties – *R (House of Cars)* v. *Derby Car and Van Contracts*, unreported, 2012, a private prosecution.

9 As implemented into UK law these include the Consumer Contracts (Information, Cancellation and Additional Charges) Regulations 2013, The Package Travel, Package Holidays and Package Tours Regulations 1992, The Timeshare, Holiday Products, Resale and Exchange Contracts Regulations 2010, The Price Marking Order 2004, The Human Medicines Regulations 2012, The Electronic Commerce (EC Directive) Regulations 2002, The Consumer Credit (Advertisements) Regulations 2010, The Financial Conduct Authority's Consumer Credit sourcebook, Chapter 3 (CONC 3) and the Air Services Regulation (EC) No 1008/2008.

10 Regulation 2(1)

11 Regulation 6(4)

12 For example, concerning transatlantic flights, *Konsumentombudsmannen* v. *Ving Sverige AB* [C-122/10]

13 Briggs J in *OFT* v. *Purely Creative* [2011]

14 *Interflora Inc* v. *Marks and Spencer plc (No 5)*, Court of Appeal (2014), paras 107–130

15 Regulation 2

16 *Trento* Case C-281/12

17 Studies of consumer behaviour (eg by the OFT in respect of pricing) may be helpful in understanding the genesis of a transactional decision.

18 Regulation 3(3)

19 Joint BERR/OFT Guidance, as adopted by the CMA, p52

20 Under the Enterprise Act 2002 Part 8

21 CPRUT Regulations 8-13

22 Regulations 17–18

23 The primary authority scheme is provided for in the Regulatory Enforcement and Sanctions Act 2008.

24 See CMA report on the Groceries super-complaint from Which?, and undertakings secured by the CMA in its secondary ticketing investigation.

25 See BIS August 2014 Guidance on the Consumer Protection (Amendment) Regulations 2014

26 Regulation 27E. See by way of example consumers' use of their right to redress to resist county court claims for payment by UK Services & Support, against which the ASA ruled in 2015 (see Chapter 5 on the self-regulatory system and also the Legal Beagles website).

27 Regulation 27I

28 Regulation 27J

29 CCICACR, Regulations 44–46

30 CCICACR, Regulations 19–23

31 CRA section 31 for goods and digital content, section 57 for services

32 CRA section 9 (and section 34 for digital content)

33 See *Webster* v. *Liddington* [2014] CA for an example of clinics which carried out cosmetic surgery using a skin-rejuvenator product being bound by statements made by the product's supplier in brochures which the clinics distributed to prospective patients.

34 CRA sections 11, 12 (and for digital content)

35 CRA section 50

36 CRA 2015 section 20

37 CRA 2015 section 45

38 CRA 2015 section 23 (goods), section 43 (digital content)

39 CRA 2015 section 55

40 CRA 2015 section 24 (goods), section 44 (digital content), section 56 (services)

41 CMA Property sales and lettings infringement decision (2015)

42 2013/396/EU

43 Section 81 and Schedule 8, amending the Competition Act 1998

44 Fraud Act 2006, sections 2 and 3. Dishonesty is assessed by reference to the ordinary standards of reasonable and honest people, *R* v. *Ghosh* [1982].

Privacy and data protection

07

JOHN WILKS AND LORETTA MARSHALL

Introduction

Advertisers and marketers are becoming ever more dependent on data, including, in particular, personal data relating to those to whom advertising is being directed, whether via e-mail, social media, online behavioural advertising or more traditional channels. Personal data must be used in accordance with applicable legislation, guidance and codes, which, on the whole, are becoming stricter and more regularly enforced. This chapter explores some of the most significant data protection and privacy issues that advertisers and marketers in the UK should consider, focusing, in particular, on:

- the sending of direct marketing communications;
- the collation of databases for marketing and advertising purposes, including the use of Big Data;
- the use of cookies for marketing purposes; and
- online behavioural advertising.

Regardless of the medium, advertisers and marketers in the UK must comply with the Data Protection Act 1998 (DPA) in relation to any personal data, such as names and e-mail addresses, that they process. A detailed analysis of the DPA is beyond the scope of this chapter. However, one of the main principles in the DPA is that marketers must process personal data fairly and lawfully and in compliance with at least one of a list of conditions. Broadly speaking, and in a direct marketing context, this means that the DPA requires a marketer to ensure that recipients know the marketer's identity and the purposes for which their personal data are being processed, and the marketer should either: obtain the consent of the recipient to be sent direct marketing material; or be able to demonstrate that use of the recipient's data is necessary for the marketer's legitimate interests, and that such use is not unwarranted by reason of prejudice to the rights and freedoms or legitimate interests of the recipient.

Other principles include that personal data must not be retained for longer than necessary, must be kept up to date and secure, and must not be used for purposes which are incompatible with the purpose for which it was obtained. In addition, the DPA expressly provides individuals with the right, at any time, by written notice to ask for their personal data not to be used for the purposes of direct marketing.

It should be noted that a new legal framework for protecting personal data in Europe, the EU General Data Protection Regulation (the 'Regulation'), was approved by the EU legislative institutions at the end of 2015 and should enter into force across the EU on 25 May 2018. At the time of writing, the UK is due to vote on the EU Referendum. Even if the UK votes to leave, there will still be an interim period of at least two years from the Government notifying the EU of the UK's decision to leave until the exit process is complete. Only then will we know whether the Regulation will apply to the UK or whether the UK will adopt an alternative data protection regime. Assuming the former, the Regulation will necessitate dramatic changes within organisations. All organisations involved in the processing of personal data should – bearing in mind the broader scope as to what will amount to personal data under the Regulation – consider what work they need to do in order to comply.

The Regulation, which will replace EU Member State legislation (such as the UK's DPA) in this field, will introduce new obligations for data controllers (ie persons who (either alone or jointly or in common with other persons) determine the purposes for which and the means by which any personal data are, or are to be, processed) and (for the first time) data processors (ie persons who process personal data on behalf of a data controller), and new rights for individuals. There will be a right to object to automated profiling which produces legal effects concerning the relevant individual or which similarly significantly affects them. Maximum sanctions for breach of the

Regulation will be significantly higher (up to 4 per cent of the annual world-wide turnover of an organisation). Parental approval will be required to obtain consent from under-16s (national governments can lower this to 13, which the UK is expected to do), and individuals will have an express right to have their personal data erased in certain situations, including when it is no longer necessary for the purpose for which it was collected.

Applicable legislation and codes

The considerations regarding data protection in the UK at the time of writing derive mainly (but not exclusively) from the provisions of the DPA and the guidance issued by the UK privacy regulator, the Information Commissioner's Office (ICO), the Privacy and Electronic Communications (EC Directive) Regulations 2003 (the 'Privacy Regulations') as amended and the British Code of Advertising, Sales Promotion and Direct Marketing (CAP Code). In addition, marketers should be aware of the Direct Marketing Association's Code of Practice, the Electronic Commerce (EC Directive) Regulations 2002, the Consumer Contracts (Information, Cancellation and Additional Charges) Regulations 2013 and the Consumer Protection from Unfair Trading Regulations 2008 (CPRs). This chapter is not intended to provide a detailed analysis of all of the relevant legislation, guidance and codes but, rather, it highlights the main, practical considerations that advertisers and marketers should bear in mind when planning direct marketing and targeted online advertising.

Information Commissioner's Office

Direct marketing communications

The Privacy Regulations are the main legislative constraint on the use of unsolicited, electronic direct marketing. By 'direct marketing' we mean advertising or marketing material which is directed to particular individuals. We consider below first the preliminary considerations of campaign medium, target audience and the concept of consent, and then the rules applying to: (i) electronic mail; and (ii) telephone marketing. Separate rules apply to marketing by post and fax but are beyond the scope of this chapter. In addition to the obligations in the Privacy Regulations, Section 11 DPA provides all individuals with the right to prevent their data being used for direct marketing. ICO guidance indicates that e-mail and SMS marketing should stop within 28 days of receiving such a request. Once the recipient has opted out, their details should be suppressed from marketing lists within the above timeframe. It is important not to delete their details entirely, to ensure that they are not contacted again.

Campaign medium

Different considerations apply to different media of unsolicited direct marketing campaigns. We look at the considerations applicable to marketing by e-mail and SMS, social media, and telephone marketing in turn. There is a summary later in this chapter as a quick reference guide.

Target audience

The considerations for some of the media listed above differ according to whether the campaign is targeted towards individuals in their personal/private capacity ('individual subscribers') as opposed to individuals in their business capacity ('corporate subscribers').

The term 'subscriber' refers to the individual/entity that pays the bill for the use of their line for the supply of their internet/telephone service. The term 'individual subscriber' includes sole traders, self-employed individuals and non-limited liability partnerships, as well as private individuals. 'Corporate subscribers' includes employees of companies (eg name@companynamelimited.com would be the e-mail address of a corporate subscriber).

Consent

Both the DPA and the Privacy Regulations refer to the important concept of consent. The ICO has produced substantial guidance on methods of obtaining consent[1] and the type of wording to be used. Although neither the DPA nor the Privacy Regulations provide a definition of 'consent', the EU Data Protection Directive 1995 defines consent as any freely given, specific and informed indication of the data subject's wishes. There must also be some form of communication or positive action whereby consent is knowingly indicated. While the ICO does not prescribe a particular approach, it considers the clearest way to obtain consent is to invite customers to tick an opt-in box confirming that they wish to receive marketing messages.

Although methods of obtaining explicit, active consent, such as opt-in tick boxes, provide the most unambiguous evidence of consent, these are not the only effective methods. Implied consent may also be effective, for example by providing a clear statement and an opt-out box. The following example is an illustration of this:

> By submitting this registration form, you will be indicating your consent
> to receiving e-mail marketing messages from us unless you have indicated
> an objection to receiving such messages by ticking this box   ☐.

A key criterion in determining the acceptability of this technique concerns the clarity of the statement. Even implied consent must be freely given, specific and informed so the individual must have understood what they were consenting to.

Under the Regulation, consent will be required to be 'unambiguous' and to involve clear, affirmative action, as well as being specific and informed. While the Regulation will replace the DPA rather than the Privacy Regulations, marketers looking to establish consent to comply with the Regulation will need to demonstrate unambiguous consent through a clear, affirmative action, and it is possible that the new definition of consent could be applied to the Privacy Regulations as well.

Given the importance of consent, organisations that engage in direct marketing by electronic means must keep clear records of which individuals have provided (or refused) consent, and have a method for ensuring that marketing is not sent to those who have refused it.

Direct marketing by e-mail and text message

'Electronic mail' marketing includes all forms of direct electronic messages, including SMS, MMS, instant messages and direct messages via social media (eg Facebook Messenger), as well as e-mail. It may also apply to other forms of marketing via social media, such as 'custom audience' marketing via Facebook and Twitter, which operates by displaying adverts to social media users whose e-mail addresses are stored in the advertiser's database.

Electronic mail marketing must not be sent to individual subscribers (see the section on 'Target audience' above) unless: (i) they have expressly consented to electronic mail marketing; or (ii) the conditions of the soft opt-in are satisfied (see below).

Marketing e-mails to corporate subscribers will be permitted provided: (i) the recipient is informed when his and/or her personal data are collected that his and/or her professional e-mail address may be used to contact him and/or her with marketing e-mails; and (ii) the marketer identifies itself and provides contact details. The requirement at (i) will not apply to communications sent to generic e-mail addresses of corporate subscribers (eg info@companyname.com).

Soft opt-in conditions

Within the context of an existing customer relationship, it is possible to directly market by electronic means similar products or services to customers without prior express consent (soft opt-in), provided:

- the company obtained the individual's details in the course of a sale or negotiations for a sale of a product or service;
- the company's marketing relates to its own similar products or services only;
- when the individual's details were obtained, the individual was clearly informed about the company's intention to use them for direct marketing and given a simple opportunity to opt out; and
- a simple way to opt out continues to be offered with each subsequent marketing message.

Negotiations for a sale

The customer must have actively expressed an interest in buying an organisation's products or services. Expressing an interest goes beyond, for example, sending a query. Rather, it refers to a customer actively expressing an interest in buying an organisation's product(s) or service(s). Registering with a retailer's website is not 'negotiating for a sale'.

Similar products and services

Organisations can only send electronic mail about similar products and services. The key question to consider here is whether the customer would reasonably expect messages about the product or service in question.

Opt-out requirements

Under the soft opt-in as described above, the marketer must give the customer the chance to opt out, both when the details are first collected and in every subsequent marketing e-mail.

Where the soft opt-in is not relied upon, and marketing is being sent on the basis of prior consent, there is no express requirement to include an opt-out method in marketing e-mails, although it is good practice to do so (and, as mentioned above, such individuals still have the DPA right to opt out).

Opt-out methods should be simple. It is considered good practice to allow individuals to reply directly to the message and opt out that way, or to provide a clear and operational 'unsubscribe' link in electronic mail. The ICO suggest that organisations undertaking SMS direct marketing should offer an opt-out via a stop message to a short code number, for example: 'text STOP to 12345'.

Viral e-mail campaigns

An organisation might use viral marketing messages or 'tell a friend' campaigns to tap into social networks of subscribers (current and potential). Viral campaigns are typically where a marketing e-mail is sent to an individual and they are asked to: (i) send the original marketing message to family or friends; or (ii) provide their family's or friends' contact details.

As these types of viral e-mail campaigns have the same consent considerations as the sending of unsolicited direct marketing e-mails, the ICO encourages organisations to take care in their design and implementation. For instance, organisations should advise individuals to forward e-mails or provide contact details only if they are reasonably certain that their family and/or friends would consent to receiving the marketing material in question.

Where an organisation wants to send a message to e-mail addresses obtained indirectly from a friend or relative, the ICO encourages the organisation to: (i) ask the information provider to confirm that they have the consent of the recipient for the marketing in question; (ii) check that the recipient hasn't previously opted out from receiving marketing from the organisation; and (iii) tell the information provider that it will tell the recipient how the organisation received the recipient's contact details.

ICO enforcement action – SMS marketing

Enforcement action by the ICO in relation to non-compliant e-mail marketing is rare; we are not aware at the time of writing of the ICO having issued any fines for non-compliant e-mail marketing.

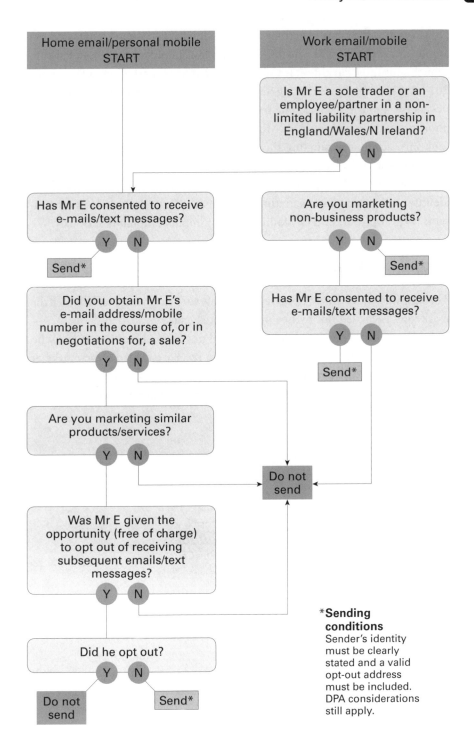

Home email/personal mobile
START

Work email/mobile
START

Is Mr E a sole trader or an employee/partner in a non-limited liability partnership in England/Wales/N Ireland?
Y N

Has Mr E consented to receive e-mails/text messages?
Y N

Send*

Are you marketing non-business products?
Y N

Send*

Did you obtain Mr E's e-mail address/mobile number in the course of, or in negotiations for, a sale?
Y N

Has Mr E consented to receive e-mails/text messages?
Y N

Send*

Are you marketing similar products/services?
Y N

Do not send

Was Mr E given the opportunity (free of charge) to opt out of receiving subsequent emails/text messages?
Y N

*Sending conditions
Sender's identity must be clearly stated and a valid opt-out address must be included. DPA considerations still apply.

Did he opt out?
Y N

Do not send

Send*

However, the ICO has sanctioned non-compliant SMS marketing. For example: a fine of £70,000 was imposed on a music festival organiser, Parklife Manchester Ltd ('Parklife'), for non-compliant SMS marketing in December 2014. Parklife sent a marketing SMS to 70,000 individuals who had booked tickets for a music festival. The message appeared on the recipients' mobile phones as having been sent by 'Mum'. It seems the main factors that the ICO took into account in singling this case out for sanctions were: (i) evidence of significant real distress (eg individuals whose mothers were dead or ill receiving the text); (ii) the organisation had deliberately concealed its identity; (iii) the large-scale nature of the marketing; (iv) lack of prior consent; (v) no opt-out; and (vi) failure to treat initial complaints seriously.

Telephone marketing

The considerations for telephone marketing vary according to whether the marketing is carried out by live or automated calls.

In summary, unsolicited live calls should not be made to: (i) anyone who has communicated that they do not want to receive calls from the marketer in question; and (ii) anyone who is listed on the Telephone Preference Service (TPS) or Corporate TPS (CTPS),[2] unless an individual has specifically consented to the calls.

Automated calls should not be made unless an individual has specifically consented to this method of calling. General consent for marketing or even consent for live calls is not enough.

For both live and automated calls, the name of the caller and a contact address or freephone number should be provided to the individual called.

ICO enforcement action – telephone marketing

In October 2015, a fine of £200,000 was imposed on Home Energy & Lifestyle Management Ltd (HELM) for non-compliant telephone marketing.

HELM had made or instigated over six million calls as part of an automated call marketing campaign offering 'free' solar panels. The factors that the ICO took into account were: (i) the automated calls were made without the recipients' prior consent; (ii) the calls were repeated; (iii) the caller did not identify themselves nor provide an address or freephone contact number; and (iv) HELM had not informed itself of the rules for marketing campaigns.

Direct marketing: summary

E-mail/SMS/MMS/instant message/voicemail

- Consent always needed?
  - Individual subscribers – Yes (unless soft opt-in applies)
  - Corporate subscribers – No
- Preference Service check needed?
  - Individual subscribers – No
  - Corporate subscribers – No

Telephone (live calls)

- Consent always needed?
  - Residential number/personal phone number – No
  - Business number/business mobile – No
- Preference Service check needed?
  - Residential number/personal phone number – legal requirement to check all telephone numbers against TPS
  - Business number/business mobile – legal requirement to check all telephone numbers against CTPS

Automated calling systems

- Consent always needed?
  - Residential number/personal phone number – Yes
  - Business number/business mobile – Yes

▶

- Preference Service check needed?
  - Residential number/personal phone number – General consent for marketing or live calls is not sufficient
  - Business number/business mobile – General consent for marketing or live calls is not sufficient

Post

- Consent always needed?
  - Residential address – No
  - Business address – No
- Preference Service check needed?
  - Residential address – Good practice to check all addresses against MPS
  - Business address – No: businesses not entitled to register on the MPS

Use of databases for marketing purposes

When marketers collect data for use in future marketing campaigns, eg at the point at which a website user subscribes to an online service, they must ensure that the individual knows the identity of the marketer and the purpose for which it intends to use the individual's data. This information can be communicated to the individual by means of a simple statement of use. Such a statement needs to be prominently positioned and marketers should ensure that there is some way of asking individuals to read it before providing any of their details (eg a box that must be ticked to show that the individual has read and accepts the statement).

Marketers cannot collect names and addresses for one purpose (such as fulfilling an order) and then use those names and addresses for an incompatible purpose (such as providing them to a third party for the third party's marketing purposes). Thought therefore needs to be given to the precise wording to be used at the point of collection of data from individuals.

Advertisers and marketers are increasingly looking to harness the power of so-called 'Big Data', by processing and/or analysing large amounts of data from multiple sources so as, for example, to better understand their audience and/or target their advertising.

The ICO has issued guidance on Big Data and Data Protection[3] which deals with the challenge that confronts all users of Big Data that includes personal data, of repurposing data, that is to say seeking to use personal data that were obtained for one purpose, for other purposes.

The ICO encourages organisations looking to exploit Big Data to first carry out a detailed privacy impact assessment in order to fully understand the impact of the planned project, what the applicable privacy obligations are, and how compliance will be attained. One of the most fundamental issues will be whether personal data are being processed for purposes that do not match individuals' expectations. The ICO encourages organisations carrying out Big Data analytics to inform individuals about what they are doing with their data.

The DPA requirements and ICO guidance are also complemented by Section 10 of the CAP Code, which imposes rules relating to the use of databases for direct marketing purposes.

Sharing customer databases

Whether an organisation can share its database of customer information (such as e-mail addresses) depends on what information was provided, and the scope of the marketing consents that were obtained, at the time the customer details were collected. To be able to share data, organisations must have made it clear that customer details would be passed on to third parties for marketing purposes and have obtained consent from the individuals to receive marketing e-mails from third parties. In its *Optical Express* decision,[4] the First-Tier Tribunal held that in order for third-party recipients to demonstrate consent for the purposes of the Privacy Regulations, it is necessary to: (i) specifically identify the particular third party who will undertake the planned unsolicited direct marketing; and (ii) explain the products to be marketed if they are different from those of the company that obtains the consent. It may be noted that *Optical Express* construes third-party consent more restrictively than the ICO's current guidance. The following example is an illustration of wording that should comply with the *Optical Express* ruling:

We would like to share your data with [J Bloggs & Co Limited], so that they may send you marketing communications relating to their [insert short broad description of products].

(Please) tick here if you do not wish [name of company obtaining consent] to make your details available to [J Bloggs & Co Limited]   □.

The use of cookies for advertising or marketing purposes

A cookie is a small text file that is downloaded onto terminal equipment (eg a computer or smartphone) when a user accesses a website. The cookie allows the website to recognise the user's device and collect information about him or her. This information can be used for various purposes. 'Targeted' cookies are used to build up user profiles which can be used for advertising or marketing.

Where cookies are used for advertising or marketing purposes, individuals must have a clear understanding of what the cookies do and why. Consent must be provided and, although it can be implied, it must be knowingly given.

Such cookies are likely to contain data linked to a name, e-mail address etc, which trigger requirements under both the DPA and the Privacy Regulations.

In its May 2012 'Guidance on the rules on use of cookies and similar technologies',[5] the ICO confirmed the basic rule that an organisation must tell users that cookies are there, for instance by using a banner on the website such as:

> This website uses cookies. Cookies allow us to find out a little bit about you
> and how you use our website, which helps us to improve the site and to tailor

our marketing to suit your interests. You can change your cookie settings at any time [add link to settings]. To find out more about the cookies we use please read our [privacy policy].

Users should understand what the cookies are doing and why, and then consent to the usage.

The ICO does not prescribe exactly what information should be provided or how, but there is a requirement under the Privacy Regulations that there must be 'clear and comprehensive' information about the organisation's purpose for using cookies.

Online behavioural advertising

The CAP Code, the DPA and the Privacy Regulations have potential application to online targeted or behavioural advertising (OBA), that is to say online advertising generated for a specific user based on his or her web browsing history.

OBA is normally generated through the use of cookies, so there is an obligation to obtain consent (see above). Data that can be linked to a specific user are likely to be personal data, so the principles of the DPA apply to those who control such data. Depending on how the OBA is generated, the data controller may be the organisation responsible for the website that publishes the ads ('publisher'), the advertising networks that match up the advertiser with the publisher, or a combination of the publisher and the advertising network.

The most relevant DPA requirement to OBA is the obligation to process data fairly (the ICO's Personal Information Online Code of Practice[6] makes various recommendations as to how best to achieve this, in particular through simply informing consumers that their personal data are being used to generate OBA and of opt-out options). The ICO also recommends the website www.youronlinechoices.com/uk, which provides further recommendations on best practice, and links to the OBA best practice recommendations of the European Advertising Standards Alliance (EASA) and the Internet Advertising Bureau (IAB) Europe.

The CAP Code sets out rules on OBA in Appendix 3 and CAP's website also contains a related Help Note.[7] The rules apply to advertising networks, not publishers or advertisers. The advertising networks are required to: give clear and comprehensive notices about use of OBA, both on the network's own website and 'in or around' the ad on the publisher's website (the notice can be an appropriate icon), plus a link to an opt-out; and not create interest segments specifically for targeting OBA at under-12s. Neither the ICO nor the ASA appears to have had to use its powers in relation to OBA.

OBA may be more restrictively regulated under the Regulation. For example, as noted above, the Regulation will provide a right for individuals not to be the subject of automated processing (including profiling) that has a legal or other similar significant effect on the individual, other than in certain limited circumstances (including where the individual provides explicit consent). Whether this restriction will apply to OBA remains to be seen.

Summary

The arrival of the Regulation will have a profound effect on many businesses in the UK, including advertising businesses, and across all Member States of the EU. Advertisers and agencies should start work now. Although the Regulation is not due to come into force until 25 May 2018, that may not seem long enough for some businesses to make the necessary changes. Even if the UK were to vote to leave the EU, it is highly likely that the UK would need to demonstrate comparable data protection law to the Regulation to enable UK businesses to trade with EU Member States.

Notes

1 In the direct marketing context the main guidance is the ICO's Direct Marketing guidance dated 24 October 2013.

2 The TPS is a central register of individuals who have opted out of receiving live marketing calls. The CTPS works in the same way as the TPS but for companies and other corporate bodies.

3 https://ico.org.uk/media/for-organisations/documents/1541/big-data-and-data-protection.pdf

4 *Optical Express* v. *Information Commissioner*, 31 August 2015, EA/2014/0014, paras 85–86

5 https://ico.org.uk/media/for-organisations/documents/1545/cookies_guidance.pdf

6 https://ico.org.uk/media/for-organisations/documents/1591/personal_information_online_cop.pdf

7 https://www.cap.org.uk/Advice-Training-on-the-rules/Advice-Online-Database/Online-behavioural-advertising-OBA.aspx

PART THREE
Do I comply? Key challenges and themes in advertising

Celebrities in advertising

08

INDIA FORSYTH AND RICHARD LINDSAY

Introduction

The use of famous people to market products and services has long been a favoured approach for advertisers, and a means for the famous to increase their income.

Traditional brand partnerships featuring celebrities in commercials can be seen in many award-winning campaigns. From Walkers' continued use of Gary Lineker to drive sales and market share for their crisps brand,[1] to Vinnie Jones' hands-only CPR saving lives campaign for the British Heart Foundation,[2] the power of celebrities to share their appeal with brands, and to draw attention to a message, is widely recognised.

In the past few years, society's concept of a 'celebrity' has expanded beyond people with traditionally high-profile careers, such as professional athletes and actors, to include influential individuals generating their own fame through the use of new media, typically vloggers and bloggers. At the same time, new media have expanded the ways in which brands can reach out to consumers. This has led to the adoption of new forms of marketing, often alongside more traditional campaigns.

This chapter looks at the various legal and regulatory matters that should be considered when making reference to a celebrity in advertising in a UK campaign. Where such rights are already discussed in general terms in other chapters, this chapter will focus upon how those rights are applied in context.

Vinnie Jones in the British Heart Foundation's Hands-only CPR campaign, courtesy of Grey London/BHF

What is a celebrity?

When referring to a celebrity, we mean an individual with a public profile. The elements of a celebrity's profile that might be exploited include their name, likeness, voice, mannerisms, catchphrases or other distinguishing features.

Certain types of celebrity are more likely than others to be willing and/or able to exploit their profiles for commercial gain. For example, footballers may enter into sponsorship arrangements with sportswear manufacturers keen to capitalise on their fame. Politicians, however, do not generally exploit their public profiles for money.

The distinction between those celebrities who exploit their profiles and those who do not becomes relevant when assessing the types of rights that those individuals can rely on to protect themselves, as well as their motivations for seeking protection.

Do you know who I am?

When the brand/celebrity combination works, the results should benefit both sides, of course, but when one side is unhappy the legal and regulatory issues can prove complex.

An obvious ground for dispute is the unauthorised use of a celebrity in an ad. Unlike many other legal jurisdictions:

> There is in English law no 'image right' or 'character right' which allows a celebrity to control the use of his or her name or image... A celebrity seeking to control the use of his or her image must therefore rely upon some other cause of action.[3]

As such, there is arguably scope for a brand to use a celebrity in a campaign without the need for consent, which can save money. Celebrities have to think of other ways to control the use of their profiles without their permission.

Even if use is authorised, disputes can still arise. Either side might act in such a way as to tarnish the reputation of the other, for example. Third-party rights in relation to the celebrity can also hinder the brand from fully exploiting what they have paid for. Innovative use of new media might cause confusion, with the risk that consumers could be misled.

When making use of a celebrity in advertising, the key legal and regulatory areas to consider are:

- intellectual property;
- self-regulatory codes;
- defamation; and
- privacy and data protection.

This chapter will consider each of these areas before listing, at the end, some specific points that should be covered in an agreement for the authorised use of a celebrity.

Intellectual property

Passing off

In the absence of a stand-alone image right, perhaps the most useful cause of action by celebrities seeking to stop unauthorised use of their profiles today is passing off. In essence, a claimant needs to show the existence of goodwill in their image or profile, that a misrepresentation has been made that is likely to confuse people into assuming an economic link with, or official endorsement by, the celebrity, and that this is likely to cause, or has caused, damage (see Chapter 4 for further details).

The successful use of passing off in false celebrity endorsement situations is a fairly new development which has arisen from the courts acknowledging that celebrities can have goodwill in their images and that celebrity endorsement is now a major revenue area. Indeed, entire businesses exist today to broker agreements between celebrities and brands. As such, celebrities and brands have a 'common field of activity', and unauthorised use of a celebrity's profile can, in certain situations, amount to a misrepresentation that can cause consumer confusion and damage to the celebrity.

This breakthrough came when Formula 1 racing driver Eddie Irvine successfully sued TalkSport Radio for doctoring an image of him speaking on a mobile phone to look as though he was listening to a radio branded with their station logo.[4] Previously, the courts had taken a more literal approach, considering celebrities to be operating in a different commercial area from brands and, as such, they could not see how confusion could arise as a result of a misrepresentation. For example, a radio personality who brought a passing-off action in the 1940s, against a cereal brand that had used his name and included wording that could have been understood as references to his physical characteristics, was unsuccessful in his claim because he did not operate within a common field of activity with the defendant.[5]

From a practical point of view, only celebrities who make money from exploiting their identity commercially are likely to bring successful passing-off claims. This is because of the need to show confusion on the part of consumers as a result of the misrepresentation by the brand. Individuals who do not exploit their profile commercially, such as politicians or religious figures, are unlikely to be able to show that consumers were confused into believing that they were somehow commercially involved with, or otherwise endorsing, the brand, even if they are featured in an advertisement for it.

Similarly, the need for confusion is also the reason why passing off may not help a celebrity against an advertiser's use of obvious lookalikes or soundalikes, particularly if used in a humorous way.

Bringing a legal action for passing off is expensive, can take several years to reach court and the evidential threshold for the claimant to meet is high. Even if damages are awarded, these tend to be relatively low compared to the legal fees involved, though advertisers should also remember that, if successfully sued, they may have to bear substantial claimant costs too.

SOURCE: Andy Buchanan/AFP/Getty Images

Trade marks

Chapter 2 looks at trade marks in detail, but it is worth just making a few points here with regard to trade marks and celebrities. Celebrities (and/or their estates) increasingly seek to protect aspects of their profiles by means of trade marks, including registrations of names, signatures, and even images of their own facial features, provided they are capable of functioning as a trade mark. For example, Audrey Hepburn's son has registered an image of his late mother for a wide range of goods.[6]

Trade marks are, however, of limited application in attempting to prevent unauthorised use of a celebrity's identity, because a trade mark used without permission in advertising will only infringe the owner's trade mark rights if it is used as a trade mark, rather than in a purely descriptive manner as a way of referring to that person. Moreover, celebrities may be wary of testing the strength of their trade marks in court because they are potentially vulnerable to a counterclaim which might invalidate their trade mark registrations.

Nevertheless, advertisers should still check relevant trade mark registers, even if intending to use a name or other insignia only descriptively and not in a trade mark sense. That a celebrity has registered a trade mark indicates that they are likely to seek to protect their rights, whether or not their case is strong.

Copyright, performance rights and moral rights

As discussed in detail in Chapter 1, copyright protects qualifying original creative executions by prohibiting third parties from copying them without permission from the copyright owner.

Copyright has limited scope for protecting a celebrity's profile. While it can exist in photographs and other representations of celebrities, in voice recordings and even their signatures, names do not normally qualify as copyright works. Likewise, a person's haircut, make-up[7] or personal style would not qualify for protection due to the lack of the permanence required of copyright works.

The difficulty with the application of copyright in this field is that the copyright owner is unlikely to be the celebrity featured. This is particularly relevant to photographs, as copyright first vests in the photographer. Copyright in a photograph of a celebrity might be licensed by an advertiser from a photographer or image bank, but the celebrity who does not own the copyright may still object successfully to the use of the image on other grounds (passing off, for example). It is notable that in two of the most prominent, recent passing-off actions brought to challenge false endorsement, *Eddie Irvine* v. *TalkSport* and *Rihanna* v. *TopShop*,[8] photographs of celebrities were involved and, in both cases, the images had been licensed legally from a copyright perspective.

It is, therefore, important that advertisers check the terms of any copyright licence carefully to establish whether the celebrity featured in the relevant image has given consent to its use for the purposes required by the advertiser. If not, or if the position is unclear, then although the celebrity may not have an action in copyright, they may have grounds to bring a passing-off claim.

Worth considering alongside copyright are performance rights and moral rights.

Distinct from copyright, performance rights give performers the right to prevent unauthorised exploitation of their performances. A performance can be a dramatic performance, including dance, a musical performance or a literary reading. While a celebrity might not own the copyright in the recording of their performance, they might still have grounds to challenge use of the recording in commercials if they have not given their consent to the use of their performance as recorded.

Aside from the moral rights given to creators of copyright works, there is also a privacy right to those who commission photographs or films for private domestic purposes.[9] This right would allow a celebrity who hires a photographer for a personal shoot, such as a wedding, to prevent that photographer from using the images for their own marketing or from licensing the images to third parties, even though the photographer might retain copyright in the work.

Self-regulatory codes

As discussed in Chapter 5, the UK self-regulatory system for marketing communications has two separate codes: the UK Code of Advertising, Sales Promotion and Direct Marketing (CAP Code) covering non-broadcast media, including online, and the UK Code of Broadcast Advertising (BCAP Code) covering broadcast media (the 'Codes').

One significant potential sanction for breach of the Codes is the withdrawal of the marketing communication. Obviously, this could have significant financial implications for the advertiser, but it is important to keep in mind that financial compensation is not awarded to a complainant as a result of an ASA adjudication. However, a complaint under the self-regulatory system may still be useful to celebrities if they are seeking a fast, easy and cheap way to protect their profile and/or privacy.

Both Codes cover misleading advertising, including testimonials and endorsements (Section 3), and privacy for living individuals (Section 6). However, the Codes are not always aligned, so it is important to check the particular rules in respect of the particular media to be used in a campaign.

Looking first at the issue of misleading advertising, both Codes require marketers to hold documentary evidence that a testimonial or endorsement used in a marketing communication is genuine unless it is 'obviously fictitious'. The marketer must also have permission to feature a testimonial unless an exception applies, such as quoting accurately from a published source or professional endorsement. In practice, this means that marketers need to be cautious before referring to celebrities who they believe use their products or services, as these references can amount to implied endorsements.

Unless they are merely referring to an unequivocal statement made by that celebrity published elsewhere, they ought to have permission to refer to the celebrity in this way.

In relation to privacy, the rules regarding television broadcast advertising are the strictest across all media. With limited exceptions, living persons must not be featured, caricatured or referred to in advertisements without their permission. The exceptions are, essentially, for incidental appearances or factual references referring to individuals featured in the product being advertised, such as a programme or film. Even then, the reference should be neither offensive nor defamatory.

The rules for radio broadcast are more lenient. There is scope to feature an individual without their express consent, provided it is neither offensive, adverse nor defamatory, and on the recommendation that legal advice is taken or permission sought. In particular, the BCAP Code states that:

> Impersonations, soundalikes, parodies or similar take-offs of celebrities are permissible only if those devices are instantly recognisable and if it could be reasonably expected that the person concerned has no reason to object.

In a similar approach to radio, the CAP Code rules for non-broadcast marketing generally allow for references to living individuals unless the reference unfairly portrays or refers to anyone in an adverse or offensive way, in which case written permission from the individual is required. Marketers are merely 'urged' to obtain written permission in other circumstances, though the CAP Code does state that 'marketers should recognise that those who do not want to be associated with the product could have a legal claim' (passing off being the obvious concern).

One notable limitation for non-broadcast media relates to references to members of the royal family. The CAP Code states that they should not normally be shown or mentioned in marketing communications without their prior permission unless the reference relates to the subject of the product being advertised. This is in line with the guidance issued by the Lord Chamberlain's Office.[10] There are no equivalent rules in the BCAP Code but, as noted above, the BCAP Code rules prohibit television advertisements to feature, caricature or refer to living persons without permission.

Neither the CAP nor BCAP Code prohibits references to deceased individuals. However, marketers need to be aware of the general rules on offensiveness in the Codes that could be relevant if a reference causes undue harm or distress to surviving individuals (Section 4).

Chapter 12 looks in detail at the rules around use of social media. The CAP Code's provisions on recognition of marketing communications (Section 2) are of particular importance to marketers when working in this area. It is increasingly important for advertisers to be familiar with these, and to ensure that any celebrities they work with are, too. This is because a brand can find itself responsible for the actions of a celebrity under their instruction, even if the celebrity does something they hadn't asked them to do. For example, the ASA upheld a complaint against Publishers Clearing House relating to a tweet by the celebrity Keith Chegwin, who was engaged in a commercial relationship with them and tweeted about a competition of theirs that he was involved in. Despite the fact that they had not asked him specifically to do this, they were deemed responsible for ensuring that promotional activity conducted on their behalf was CAP Code compliant.[11]

Defamation

Although discussed in more detail in Chapter 11, it is just worth mentioning defamation in relation to the use of celebrities in advertising.

Defamation, at a basic level, requires the publication of content that lowers the reputation of the claimant in the minds of right-thinking members of society, with the recent introduction of an additional requirement that the publication must have caused, or be likely to cause, 'serious harm'[12] to the reputation of the claimant.

An image or caricature of a famous person can amount to defamatory content for the purposes of bringing an action. Thus, as noted in Chapter 11, a famous amateur sportsman was able successfully to sue a chocolate manufacturer for use of a cartoon of his likeness on the basis that people would assume he had 'prostituted' his reputation for commercial purposes.[13]

This case shows how merely implying that an amateur sportsman might be involved in endorsing a product for money can be defamatory. More obviously, the content of an advert, rather than an implication of endorsement, can also defame someone famous. This is particularly important to keep in mind for advertisers who want to create controversial or humorous adverts referring to famous people and events without permission. Budget airline Ryanair reportedly settled a libel claim made by the founder of its rival, easyJet, after they ran an advert depicting him as Pinocchio and questioning whether he was 'hiding the truth' about the airline's punctuality record.[14]

Privacy and data protection

Since the introduction into English law of the Human Rights Act 1998 (HRA) and the Data Protection Act 1998 (DPA), a number of cases concerning privacy have centred around these two pieces of legislation.

These topics are complex and beyond detailed examination in this chapter. However, advertisers should be aware that, while there is no distinct privacy right in English law – as opposed to rights concerning personal data under the DPA – legislation should be interpreted so as to be compatible with the right to a private life under Article 8 of the European Convention on Human Rights, balanced against other rights, including Article 10 which grants the right to freedom of expression.

Advertisers should also be aware that a photograph or even a name can, in certain circumstances, amount to personal data,[15] and use without authorisation could breach the DPA (and the new EU General Data Protection Regulation when it comes into force).

Contractual obligations

When engaging a celebrity, it is important to document precisely what each party expects to get out of the arrangement.

In addition to the information in this section, agencies should keep in mind specific issues relevant to the production of a campaign, such as visa and insurance requirements.

Some points to consider in a celebrity contract include:

- the term of the agreement (and any licence(s) it may grant);
- the relevant territories in which the advertisement featuring the celebrity may be used;
- the required availability of the celebrity for shoots, PR, media and brand training;
- an obligation to comply with relevant laws and regulations;
- social media responsibilities;
- whether the agreement is exclusive;
- the extent of any licence to use intellectual property or other rights in the celebrity's profile;

- grounds for, and consequences of, termination;
- fees, including possible renewal rights or territory extensions; and
- warranties/indemnities relating to good conduct required of the celebrity, and a declaration about past behaviour/reputation.

Consider also any limitations from third-party agreements already in place. For example, athletes taking part in major sporting events, such as the Olympics, are often subject to team or event obligations that might prohibit them from being featured in marketing during the tournament period. It is essential that the celebrity is responsible for informing the agency about any such limitations.

Conclusion

The current legal and regulatory landscape relating to celebrities can be challenging for advertisers to navigate. Matters are becoming ever more complicated, particularly with online marketing blurring geographical boundaries. It is important to ensure that international advice is obtained when necessary, as laws around celebrity endorsement and image rights vary dramatically across different territories. However, the rewards of getting it right can be substantial enough to merit the time and effort involved.

Notes

1 Silver Award: Walkers Crisps: Staying loyal to Lineker – IPA Effectiveness Awards Case Study 2002. http://www.ipa.co.uk/effectiveness/case-studies/Walkers-Crisps-Staying-loyal-to-Lineker-IPA-Effectiveness-Awards-Case-Study-2002/5034

2 Gold Award: You've been Vinnied: How the BHF taught the UK to save lives – IPA Effectiveness Awards Case Study 2014. http://www.ipa.co.uk/effectiveness/case-studies/Youve-been-Vinnied-How-the-BHF-taught-the-UK-to-save-lives-IPA-Effectiveness-Awards-Case-Study-2014/10430

3 *Fenty & Ors v. Arcadia & Anr* [2015] EWCA Civ 3

4 *Irvine & Ors v. TalkSport Ltd* [2003] 2 All ER 881

5 *McCulloch v. Lewis A May* [1947] 5 RPC 58

6 https://www.ipo.gov.uk/tmcase/Results/4/EU010600799

7 *Merchandising Corporation of America Inc & Ors v. Harpbond Ltd & Ors* [1983] FSR 32

8 *Robyn Rihanna Fenty and others* v. *Arcadia Group Brands Ltd and another* [2013] EWCA Civ 3, 22 January 2015

9 Section 85 Copyright, Designs and Patents Act 1988

10 http://www.royal.gov.uk/MonarchUK/Symbols/UseroftheRoyalArms.aspx

11 https://www.asa.org.uk/Rulings/Adjudications/2013/1/Genting-Alderney-Ltd/ SHP_ADJ_209991.aspx#.VpWQdoT8uac

12 Defamation Act 2013

13 *Tolley* v. *J S Fry and Sons* [1930] 1 KB 467

14 http://www.bbc.co.uk/news/business-10645543

15 https://ico.org.uk/media/for-organisations/documents/1549/determining_what_ is_personal_data_quick_reference_guide.pdf

Advertising and children

09

NICK JOHNSON

Introduction

The impact of advertising on children has for many years been both a matter of public sensitivity and a reliable vote-winning cause for politicians of all stripes. It should be no surprise, then, that this is an area that is heavily regulated, in the form of both statutory protections and self-regulatory code provisions. This chapter looks at:

- what counts as a 'child' under UK law and regulation;
- rules to protect children;
- products that are prohibited or restricted in connection with children;
- scheduling restrictions and age-based targeting; and
- issues around the use of child performers in ads.

What counts as a 'child'?

There is no universal definition of a child under UK law and regulation. For the purposes of the UK Code of Advertising, Sales Promotion and Direct

Marketing (CAP Code) and UK Code of Broadcast Advertising (BCAP Code), a child is an individual under 16 years of age (16- and 17-year-olds are 'young persons' under the Codes). Yet for most legal purposes, anyone under the age of 18 is a minor. To add to the confusion:

- Guidance from the Information Commissioner's Office suggests 12 as an age when children can give consent to normal forms of collection and use of their personal data.

- Some specific product restrictions are based on other ages (see 'Restricted products' section below). For instance, some TV restrictions on advertising foods high in fat, sugar or salt apply only to ads targeted directly at pre-school or primary school children.

- The rules on child performers use a different test based on school-leaving age.

For these reasons, it is important to be clear exactly what age group is intended when discussing issues around children.

Rules to protect children

A number of different legal and regulatory rules are in place to protect children, bearing in mind their vulnerability and inexperience and the general interest in protecting them from inappropriate subject matter. Some of these rules relate only to ads directed at children. Others are of more general application. Others still – described in the 'Restricted products' section below – relate to product categories regarded as unsuitable for children.

The Consumer Protection from Unfair Trading Regulations 2008 (CPRs)

Misleadingness and children

The CPRs are one of the central pieces of consumer legislation under UK law and they cover a wide range of issues around misleading and aggressive trading practices (see Chapter 6 on consumer protection). So far as children are concerned, the CPRs include a requirement that commercial practices (including advertising) targeted at particularly vulnerable groups (such as children) must be judged by reference to the particular vulnerabilities and credulity of that group. So, whereas it may be quite apparent to an adult seeing a toy ad that particular sequences are imaginative illustrations and do not represent how the toy actually performs in real life, the ad could be misleading for a target audience of children. Further, on-screen disclaimers may not be effective in the context of a target audience that cannot read or can read only with difficulty. Note that the ASA upheld a complaint[1] about a mailing sent to a seven-year-old, inviting him to come to a theme park, as the mailing was seen as misleading for its target audience and could have been understood as an invitation to a birthday party.

'Pester power'

The CPRs also contain a specific 'pester power' prohibition. This prohibits 'including in an advertisement a direct exhortation to children to buy advertised products or persuade their parents or other adults to buy advertised products for them'.[2] This does not prevent ads from showing products, their prices and where they can be purchased. However, a call to action in the form of a command or encouragement to purchase or to get an adult to purchase would be a problem. For example, 'Join now for Exclusive Member Benefits' in the context of a paid-for feature of an online game was held by the ASA to be a direct exhortation to purchase.[3]

CAP Code and BCAP Code

The CAP Code and BCAP Code, the advertising codes enforced by the Advertising Standards Authority, contain detailed rules governing advertising to children.[4] As well as provisions closely reflecting the requirements of the CPRs, the Codes also include other rules covering a range of different areas.

Note that the CAP Code and the BCAP Code are not entirely aligned but, unless otherwise stated, it is likely – given the subject matter and the requirement under the Codes for the advertiser to act in a socially responsible way – that all of the different requirements listed below (some of which are from the CAP Code and some from the BCAP Code) would be seen as necessary regardless of the medium in which the ad appears.

Harm

Ads addressed to, targeted directly at or featuring children must contain nothing that is likely to result in their physical, mental or moral harm. In particular, children must not be encouraged to enter strange places or talk to strangers. They must not be shown in hazardous situations or behaving dangerously, except to promote safety. They must not be shown unattended in street scenes unless they are old enough to take responsibility for their own safety. Children must not be shown using, or in close proximity to, dangerous substances or equipment without direct adult supervision. Ads must not implicitly or explicitly discredit established safety guidelines. They must not condone, encourage or feature children going off alone or with strangers. Ads must not condone or encourage bullying. Distance-selling marketers must take care when using youth media not to promote products that are unsuitable for children.

Emulation

Ads must not condone, encourage or unreasonably feature behaviour that could be dangerous for children to emulate.

Possible emulation risks may not be front of mind when reviewing ads that are not specifically intended for children, but advertisers would be well advised to consider these risks in their clearance processes. Risks are likely to be particularly acute with ads that depict unusual/eye-catching activities that are easily replicated by children. For instance, the ASA upheld a complaint about a fashion ad appearing around Bonfire Night featuring models holding lit fireworks. Although the campaign was targeted more at adults and did not appear in any children-specific media, the regulator was concerned about the potential for easy emulation, especially at that time of year.[5]

Portraying children in a sexual way

Ads must not portray or represent children in a sexual way. Note that the fact a model is in fact 16 or older will not be a defence if the model looks younger and the ad appears to sexualise a child (*American Apparel* ASA case, March 2015).[6] School uniforms are likely to be unacceptable if used in a sexual context (*Ryanair* ASA case, January 2008).[7] Young girls wearing make-up may not of itself breach the CAP Code, but much depends on context (*no added sugar* ASA case, February 2007).[8]

Credulity and unfair pressure

Ads addressed to, targeted directly at or featuring children must not exploit their credulity, loyalty, vulnerability or lack of experience:

- Children must not be made to feel inferior or unpopular for not buying the advertised product.
- Children must not be made to feel that they are lacking in courage, duty or loyalty if they do not buy or do not encourage others to buy a product.

- It must be made easy for children to judge the size, characteristics and performance of advertised products and to distinguish between real-life situations and fantasy.
- Adult permission must be obtained before children are committed to buying complex or costly products.

Ads addressed to or targeted directly at children must not exaggerate what is attainable by an ordinary child using the product being marketed.

Charitable appeals

Ads must not exploit children's susceptibility to charitable appeals and must explain the extent to which their participation will help in any charity-linked promotions.

Price

If it includes a price, an ad for a children's product or service must not use qualifiers such as 'only' or 'just' to make the price seem less expensive.

For TV only, ads for a toy, game or comparable children's product must include a statement of its price or, if it is not possible to include a precise price, an approximate price, if that product costs £30 or more.

CAP Code/BCAP Code discrepancies

As noted above, it is important to be aware that some key differences still remain between the Children provisions of the broadcast and non-broadcast codes. An ad which is compliant for TV will not necessarily be acceptable for cinema, for example.

Product placement

Product placement is prohibited by law in children's programmes for viewing primarily by persons under the age of 16.[9] This applies both to television programmes and to on-demand programme services.

Restricted products

Particular categories of product are subject to advertising restrictions.

Alcohol

As discussed in Chapter 18, alcohol ads must not be likely to appeal particularly to people under 18, especially by reflecting or being associated with youth culture. They should not feature or portray real or fictitious characters who are likely to appeal particularly to people under 18 in a way that might encourage the young to drink. People shown drinking or playing a significant role should not be shown behaving in an adolescent or juvenile manner. Ads must not be directed at people under 18 through the selection of media or the context in which they appear. No medium should be used to advertise alcoholic drinks if more than 25 per cent of its audience is under 18 years of age.[10]

Electronic cigarettes

As discussed in Chapter 23, e-cigarette ads must not be directed at people under 18 through the selection of media or the context in which they appear. No medium should be used to advertise e-cigarettes if more than 25 per cent of its audience is under 18 years of age. Ads must not be likely to appeal particularly to people under 18, especially by reflecting or being associated with youth culture. They should not feature or portray real or fictitious characters who are likely to appeal particularly to people under 18. People shown using e-cigarettes or playing a significant role should not be shown behaving in an adolescent or juvenile manner. (Note that the Code rules may change to reflect the requirements of the EU's Tobacco Products Directive.)

Food

Various restrictions apply in relation to ads for food and drinks. The restrictions differ significantly as between the CAP Code and the BCAP Code, with the latter featuring specific controls on foods high in fat, salt or sugar. (See Chapter 20 on food advertising to children.)

Gambling

It is an offence under Section 46 of the Gambling Act 2005 to invite, cause or permit a child or young person to gamble (subject to certain exceptions). It is also an offence under Section 56 to invite, cause or permit a child (ie under 16) to participate in a lottery (again, subject to certain exceptions).

The CAP Code requires that ads must not be directed at under-18s (or under-16s in the case of lotteries, football pools, equal-chance gaming under a prize gaming permit or at a licensed family entertainment centre, prize gaming at a non-licensed family entertainment centre or at a travelling fair or Category D gaming machines) through the selection of media or the context in which they appear. The CAP Code also prohibits under-18s from appearing in gambling ads (and there are additional rules regarding people who are or seem to be under 25 being featured gambling or playing a significant role), but both the CAP Code and the BCAP Code provide that ads for family entertainment centres, travelling fairs, horse racecourses and dog racetracks, and for non-gambling leisure facilities that incidentally refer to separate gambling facilities as part of a list of facilities on, for example, a cruise ship, *may* include under-18s provided they are accompanied by an adult and are socialising responsibly in areas that the Gambling Act 2005 does not restrict by age. (See Chapter 21 on gambling and 13 on lotteries and prize promotions.)

Live premium-rate telephone services

Broadcast ads for live premium-rate services must not appeal particularly to people under 18, unless those services have received prior permission from PhonepayPlus to target people under 18.

Medicines

Ads for medicines and treatments must not be directed at under-16s (BCAP Code rule 11.24 and CAP Code rule 12.16).

Rolling papers and filters

Ads for tobacco rolling papers or filters must not be targeted at, or be likely to appeal to, people under 18. Anyone depicted in a marketing communication for rolling papers or filters must be, and be seen to be, over 25. No medium may be used to advertise rolling papers or filters if more than 25 per cent of its audience is or is likely to be males under 18 years of age or females under 24 years of age. No direct marketing communication for rolling papers or filters may be distributed to males under 18 years of age or females under 24 years of age. (See Chapter 23 on smoking and vaping.)

Weight loss and slimming

Ads for any weight-reduction regime or establishment must neither be directed at nor contain anything that is likely to appeal particularly to people who are under 18.

Scheduling restrictions and age-based targeting

Scheduling restrictions

Section 32 of the BCAP Code sets out various scheduling restrictions for broadcast advertising. It includes a general requirement for ads that might frighten, distress or otherwise be unsuitable for children: these must be subject to timing restrictions to minimise the number of children in the relevant age group being exposed to them. Well-considered daytime scheduling can be appropriate, but factors such as school holidays need to be taken into account.

Specific restrictions for different product categories also apply by reference to different ages.

Under-18s

Advertising in or adjacent to programmes commissioned for, principally directed at or likely to appeal particularly to under-18s is prohibited in relation to various categories of product, including among others: alcoholic drinks (with 1.2 per cent alcohol or more); various forms of gambling; betting tipsters; slimming products (but reduced-calorie foods and drinks are acceptable in the absence of slimming or weight-control themes); and electronic cigarettes.

Under-16s

A similar rule, but for under-16s, applies to lotteries, football pools, certain forms of gaming; medicines, vitamins and other dietary supplements; low-alcohol/no-alcohol versions of alcoholic drinks; computer games with an actual or expected rating of 15+, 16+ or 18+; foods assessed as high in fat, salt or sugar; matches; and trailers for 18-certificate or 15-certificate films.

Under-10s

Ads for sanitary protection products and condoms may not be scheduled in or adjacent to programmes commissioned for, principally directed at or likely to appeal particularly to under-10s.

Other scheduling restrictions

Before the 9 pm watershed it is prohibited to broadcast ads which show children having a medicine, vitamin or other food supplement administered to them. Ads featuring individuals or puppets who appear regularly in children's TV programmes must also not be broadcast before 9 pm if those individuals/puppets present or endorse products of special interest to children.

Other rules apply to help maintain a distinction between programmes and ads. Ads featuring any individual, cartoon character or puppet with a leading role in a children's programme must not be scheduled in or adjacent to that programme (although this does not apply to public service ads or characters specially created for ads). Ads featuring persons in extracts from children's programmes, or promoting merchandise based on children's programmes, must not be broadcast in the two hours before or after the programme is aired.

Age-based targeting

The way ads are targeted can impact directly on their acceptability under the CAP and BCAP Codes. With some product categories, unsuitable target-ing can be an automatic breach of the Code. Under the CAP Code, alcohol ads, for instance, cannot be run in a medium where more than 25 per cent of the audience is under 18.

In other cases, the analysis under taste and decency rules will depend on the age profile of the audience. For instance, the ASA held that a Diesel ad depicting a naked man, seen from the rear and with three pairs of women's legs straddling his body, was acceptable in *Elle* magazine but not in *The Sunday Times Style Magazine*, which was considered more likely to be seen by children.[11]

Particular difficulties have arisen in recent years with attempts to age-gate ads served online. The ASA has held in a number of adjudications that it is not sufficient to rely solely on the fact that a user has logged into YouTube and is known to be over 18, given that many parents may log in to allow a child to watch age-appropriate content. Advertisers should therefore additionally deploy measures to ensure that inappropriate ads are not served on sites or against online content/programmes that are regularly used by children.[12]

Child performers and licensing

The use of children as performers or models in ad shoots is governed by legislation designed to protect their education and well-being. In some cases, a licence must be obtained in advance from the relevant local authority or – for overseas shoots – from the magistrates' court. In all cases there are restrictions as to the hours during which the child can perform and specific requirements for breaks.

Licensing: shoots in Great Britain

Under Section 37 of the Children and Young Persons Act 1963 (the '1963 Act'), a licence must be obtained before a child can take part in certain kinds of performances and activities in Great Britain. These include modelling for which payment is made (to the child or to someone else for the child's participation) other than expenses. They also include any audio or video performance recorded (by whatever means) with a view to its use in a broadcast or such service or in a film intended for public exhibition – which may include online usage – unless an exemption applies (see below).

Note that a child for these purposes has a technical definition, namely anyone under the upper limit of compulsory school age, as defined by Section 8(3) of the Education Act 1996. As a general rule this means up to the last Friday in June in the school year in which they have their 16th birthday.

Exemptions

User-generated content

User-generated content falls outside these rules.

The 'four-day rule'

There is also an exemption for performances where there is no payment for the child's participation and the 'four-day rule' is observed. If a child has performed on this basis on no more than three days in the last six months, they will not need a licence on a fourth day. However, once they have performed on four days in a six-month period (whether on a licensed basis or otherwise), a licence is required unless some other exemption applies. Note that the four-day rule cannot be relied on if the child is to be absent from school. Note also that failure to get any necessary licence is a criminal offence and is punishable with a fine or imprisonment or both. Anyone seeking to rely on the four-day rule should have reasonable grounds for believing the child has not performed on more than three days in the previous six months – a written note documenting the investigations made with the child, their parents and others would be advisable.

Other exemptions

Other statutory exemptions – for school-arranged performances and 'Body of Persons' approval – are unlikely to be applicable to ad shoots.

Licence applications

For children resident in Great Britain, application should be made in writing to the child's home local authority. If the child lives outside Great Britain (for instance in Northern Ireland) but the performance will be in England, Scotland or Wales, the application should be made to the local authority in whose area the applicant has their place of business.

The applicant should be the person/organisation responsible for organising, producing or running the activity/performance. They must be able to take operational decisions during the course of the performance/ activity for the purpose of protecting the child and ensuring their well-being. For ad shoots, the applicant will typically be the advertising agency.

The information and documentation to include with an application are listed in Schedule 2 of the Children (Performances and Activities) (England) Regulations 2014 (the '2014 Regulations') (and corresponding legislation in other parts of Great Britain). Where any information required under the 2014 Regulations is not available, the local authority has a discretion nevertheless to process the application if there are good reasons for its absence. The authority must only grant a licence, however, if it is assured that the child's education, health and well-being will not suffer and that the licence conditions will be observed.

Timing

A local authority may refuse to consider an application if it is made less than 21 days before the child's participation is due to start (including any rehearsals). Careful advance planning is therefore required in order to ensure that all necessary information and paperwork are ready in good time.

Application form

There is no universal standard application form. A working group involving the National Network for Children in Employment and Entertainment has produced a recommended standard form (available on www.nncee.org.uk), but some local authorities insist on using their own form.

Child Protection Policy

A Child Protection Policy will generally need to be submitted with any application. The IPA has a standard template policy that its members can use.

Licence conditions

The local authority can impose conditions, for instance relating to travel to and from the location of the performance, accommodation, location restrictions and earnings-related conditions. If the dates for the shoot cannot be specified at the time of application, the authority must impose a maximum number of days of activity in a six-month period.

If a licence is refused, the authority must give reasons. Refusal can be appealed to the magistrates' court, as can any non-statutory conditions imposed.

Statutory restrictions: licensed performances

The 1963 Act and the 2014 Regulations impose various restrictions on all licensed performances.

Education

Any arrangements for the child's education during the term of the licence must be approved by the local authority. The Regulations stipulate minimum-hours requirements for education.

Absence from school

If a licence states the dates that a child will be absent from school for a performance then no further permission is needed from the school. If no dates are specified then absence is at the head teacher's discretion, so approval must be obtained.

Chaperones

During performance and rehearsal and while staying in accommodation for the activity, a child performer must be supervised at all times by a local-authority-approved chaperone, unless under the direct supervision of their parent or a teacher from their school (or home tutor).

Accommodation, location, travel

Where accommodation is provided, this must be approved by the local authority. The locations of performances and rehearsals must also be approved, and the authority must be satisfied that suitable arrangements are in place for meals, changing and washing. The responsible person must ensure that suitable travel arrangements are made.

Statutory restrictions: all performances

Various restrictions apply under the 2014 Regulations to all performances, whether or not a licence is required.

Other employment

A child must not take part in any other employment on the day of, or the day after, a performance. This does not prevent activities related to the performance – such as press conferences or rehearsals – as long as these are within the overall hours limits.

Working hours

Children cannot work earlier than 7 am or later than 11 pm (10 pm in the case of under-5s) without specific permission from a licensing authority. With licensed performances there is also a discretion for the child's chaperone to allow up to a further hour in the evening if the child's welfare will not be prejudiced and the need to extend hours arose from circumstances outside the licence-holder's control. The chaperone must notify the licensing and host authorities of the decision and the reason for it no later than the next day.

Table 9.1 Maximum permitted statutory hours by age group

Age of child	Maximum number of hours in one day at place of performance or rehearsal	Maximum total number of hours of performance or rehearsal in one day	Maximum continuous number of hours of performance or rehearsal in one day
Birth until child reaches 5	5	2	0.5
5 until child reaches 9	8	3	2.5
9 to school leaving age	9.5	5	2.5

Table 9.1 sets out the maximum permitted statutory hours (by age group) that a child performer may be at the place of performance or rehearsal and restrictions on the period(s) they may be engaged in performance/rehearsal. Required periods of education must be taken into account when assessing against these restrictions.

Breaks

The Regulations set out various minimum break-period requirements, including that children must have an overnight break of at least 12 hours.

Summary

'Never work with children or animals,' said WC Fields. With all of the rules in place to protect children, it may be tempting to take this a stage further and never advertise to children either. However, with common sense and good awareness of the relevant laws and Codes, it is usually possible to navigate a route through the compliance maze.

Notes

1 *The M&D Group* ASA case, March 2003 – https://www.asa.org.uk/Rulings/Adjudications/2003/3/The-MD-Group/CS_35617.aspx

2 Schedule 1, #28

3 *Mind Candy Limited t/a Moshi Monsters* ASA case, August 2015 – https://www.asa.org.uk/Rulings/Adjudications/2015/8/Mind-Candy-Ltd/ SHP_ADJ_305018.aspx

4 CAP Code section 5 and BCAP Code section 5

5 *Levi Strauss & Co t/a Levi's* ASA case, February 2012 – https://www.asa.org.uk/ Rulings/Adjudications/2012/2/Levi-Strauss-and-Co/SHP_ADJ_176549.aspx

6 https://www.asa.org.uk/Rulings/Adjudications/2015/3/American-Apparel-(UK)-Ltd/SHP_ADJ_285723.aspx

7 https://www.asa.org.uk/Rulings/Adjudications/2008/1/Ryanair-Ltd/TF_ADJ_43901.aspx

8 https://www.cap.org.uk/Advice-Training-on-the-rules/Advice-Online-Database/ Children-Sexual-imagery.aspx

9 Paragraph 3 of Schedule 11A of the Communications Act 2000

10 CAP Code, rules 18.14 and 18.15 – see also BCAP Code rules 19.15 and 19.16.

11 *Diesel (London) Limited* ASA case, March 2006 – https://www.asa.org.uk/ Rulings/Adjudications/2006/3/Diesel-(London)-Ltd/CS_40992.aspx

12 ASA adjudication on Isuzu (UK) Ltd – 25 March 2015 [https://www.asa.org.uk/ Rulings/Adjudications/2015/3/Isuzu-(UK)-Ltd/SHP_ADJ_285537.aspx (UK)-Ltd/SHP_ADJ_285537.aspx] and ASA adjudication on giffgaff Ltd – 4 February 2015 [https://www.asa.org.uk/Rulings/Adjudications/2015/2/ giffgaff-Ltd/SHP_ADJ_283958.aspx]

Comparative advertising

10

pillsbury

Introduction

Comparative advertising is one of the most complex areas of advertising law, and full of potential pitfalls. It is also one of the most important forms of marketing to get right. All companies look to grow market share through their advertising, which either directly or indirectly compares their goods/services with those of their competitors.

It is essential that the issues and risks associated with comparative advertising, and described further in this chapter, are carefully considered when compiling a claims and campaign strategy and before launching any new products or services off the back of strong claims and/or a comparative campaign.

A technical definition of comparative advertising is 'any advertising that explicitly or by implication identifies a competitor, or goods or services offered by a competitor'. Common examples are comparisons in terms of quality, price or performance. It is fairly obvious that direct comparisons with competitors are comparative advertising, but a claim to be the 'best', 'cheapest' or 'fastest' (or whatever the claim might be) is an indirect statement that your competitor is not, and is also therefore a comparison. Comparisons can be specific or generic, for example where advertising is used to criticise a competitor's service or brand generally, as opposed to the specific qualities of a particular product. It also includes the use of advertising to conduct a smear campaign against a competitor.

Fairy 'Fairyconomy' advert, courtesy of Grey London/Fairy

Examples of comparative advertising rules: past and present

Before 1994, the UK comparative advertising regime was strict, particularly in relation to the use of trade marks, and competitors *could not* refer to one another by names that were protected by trade mark registration. The 1938 Trade Marks Act meant that competitors in the UK wanting to run a comparative advertising campaign instead had to refer to the relative merits of their goods over 'Brand X'. The famous 'Take the Pepsi challenge' directly compared the Pepsi brand with the Coke brand, and while this was permissible in the United States (and very successful with consumers there), such advertising was not permissible in the UK.

The Trade Marks Act 1994 (the '1994 Act') replaced the 1938 Act. In the interests of promoting competition, the new Act *allowed* competitors to refer to their rivals and their goods or services by using the registered trade mark, but only so long as they complied with the new trade mark rules (very basically, being able to show objectively that the advertisement and trade mark use was 'honest'). The boundaries were far from clear as the rules were complex, so some ads looked to push them as far as possible (and in some eyes went much too far), such as the Ryanair campaign which compared their prices with British Airways under the slogan 'expensive ba****ds'.

Courtesy of Ryanair

There have been a number of cases on the use of trade marks in comparative advertising, and these will be looked at in further detail below.

What regulates comparative advertising?

There are a complex variety of advertising controls for comparative advertising, ranging from statutory legislation to self-regulation, and from common law to industry best practice. In particular, the 2006 European Comparative Advertising Directive (CAD), which consolidated a number of comparative advertising rules, is the primary legislation for the regulation of comparative advertising across Europe.

In 2008, there was a major shake-up of the existing UK regime, brought about by two new sets of rules which came into force on 26 May 2008.

The Consumer Protection from Unfair Trading Regulations 2008 (CPRs) implement the Unfair Commercial Practices Directive 2005[1] (UCPD) and repeal and replace many sections of the Trade Descriptions Act 1968, Consumer Protection Act 1987, Consumer Credit Act 1974 and the Control of Misleading Advertising Regulations 1988; and also the Business Protection from Misleading Marketing Regulations 2008 (BPRs), which implement the CAD into UK law. The CPRs are primarily aimed at business-to-consumer advertising and the BPRs at business-to-business advertising, hence the BPRs contain an all-important checklist with which comparative advertisers must comply (as discussed below).

These UK Regulations are enforced by a number of regulatory bodies, including the Advertising Standards Authority (ASA), the Trading Standards Institute (TSI) and the Competition and Markets Authority (CMA).

Applicable law and regulation

Agencies must, then, bear in mind a number of different laws and regulations when making comparative claims in advertisements, and all forms of comparative advertising need careful consideration. The rest of this chapter will consider each element in more detail in order to ensure that agencies avoid common pitfalls.

Trade mark infringement

Most comparative advertising will want to refer to a competitor's brand or specific product. Often this will involve the use of the competitor's registered trade mark which, therefore, could give the owner the option of suing for trade mark infringement if his or her trade mark is used incorrectly.

Generally speaking, it is not possible to use another entity's registered trade mark without permission. However, Section 10(6) of the 1994 Act provides a defence to trade mark infringement by stating that nothing in the Act prevents:

> the use of a registered trade mark by any person for the purpose of identifying goods or services as those of the proprietor or a licensee [but] any such use otherwise than in accordance with honest practices in industrial or commercial matters shall be treated as infringing the registered trade mark if the use without due cause takes unfair advantage of, or is detrimental to, the distinctive character or repute of the trade mark.

The majority of trade mark case law since 1994 addressed the meaning of 'honest use', 'taking unfair advantage of', 'use detrimental to repute' and how far an advertisement could go in its comparisons between competitors' goods/services. A number of key cases looked at these very issues.

In *Barclays Bank* v. *RBS Advanta*,[2] Barclays, as the proprietor of the trade marks 'BARCLAYCARD' and 'BARCLAYS', sued RBS when they used those marks in promotional comparative material for a proposed new credit card. Mr Justice Laddie held that Barclays had a weak case in view of Section 10(6) of the 1994 Act and that the balance of convenience lay in favour of allowing RBS to continue to refer to the trade marks in their literature. The onus was on Barclays to show that the mark was not being used in accordance with honest practices and 'it was most unlikely that any reasonable reader [of the advertisements] would take that view'.

In *British Airways* v. *Ryanair*,[3] British Airways brought an action under the 1994 Act for infringement of their trade mark, 'BA', and for malicious falsehood, when Ryanair used two advertisements under the headlines 'EXPENSIVE BA....DS!' and 'EXPENSIVE BA'. Mr Justice Jacob (Jacob J) held that sections 10(6) and 11(2)(b) of the 1994 Act saved Ryanair, as these sections permit comparative advertising when it is being used to describe goods in accordance with honest practices. Despite the fact the advertisements were actually incorrect in the fares quoted, showing the British Airways fares higher than they were, the court said that the average consumer would not find the price comparison misleading and would expect there to be some conditions to the comparison made. The judge said that in substance the advertisements were true (British Airways was still more expensive) and the comparisons were not significantly unfair. A number of commentators have differed in their views on this, particularly given the disparaging strapline and swear words used.

In *Cable & Wireless* v. *British Telecommunications*,[4] BT made some price comparisons with Cable & Wireless, using their trade mark in a brochure. Cable & Wireless were granted an interlocutory injunction. Jacob J held that the objective test to be applied was whether a reasonable trader could honestly have made the statements he made based upon the information that he had. On the facts, it was not established that no honest man would be prepared to put out these calculations as part of his advertising. Further, there was no reasonable likelihood of people being misled by the details in these tables to any significant degree. The judge lifted the interim injunction accordingly.

In summary, therefore, the guidance from the UK courts in relation to the use of a third party's trade marks was to consider whether the use is honest. Would a consumer be likely to take the view, upon being given the full facts available upon reasonable enquiry, that the advertisement is not honest? This honesty is tested against what the members of the public to whom the advertisement was addressed would reasonably expect of an advertisement for that product. Therefore, the test takes account of the fact that members of the public do expect a certain degree of 'puff'. However, how much puff is allowed will depend on the product in question.

The O_2 'Bubbles' case

The European Court of Justice (ECJ) judgment in June 2008, in the UK trade mark infringement suit O_2 v. *H3G* (O_2 case), helped clarify the law on trade mark infringement actions in relation to comparative advertisements.

In 2004, Hutchison 3G (H3G) launched a comparative advertising campaign in which it compared its mobile phone services to O_2's. H3G, in particular, ran a TV commercial which used bubble imagery very similar to O_2's famous bubbles (O_2 had registered various bubble device marks which it used in the marketing of its services). In the advertisement, the bubbles changed from blue (the O_2 colour) to black as the soundalike voiceover became quite ominous. O_2 sued for trade mark infringement under the 1994 Act.

Although on one level the case seemed to some to be fairly pedantic, for O_2 a huge element of the business's value was tied up in its very distinctive brand. The business had been transformed, with the help of IPA member agency VCCP, from the old BT Cellnet business into the UK market leader, by creating a hugely successful and award-winning brand identity. Anything that was seen to allow competitors to interfere with, and possibly damage or erode, that distinctive identity was a major threat, hence O_2's decision to sue.

Mr Justice Lewison ('Lewison J') initially found that there was *prima facie* infringement under Section 10(2) of the 1994 Act on the basis that the bubble use was confusingly similar, but that Section 10(6) provided a defence for H3G. He therefore ruled in their favour. He also rejected the claim of infringement under Section 10(3) as the advertisement did not take unfair advantage of, nor denigrate, the O_2 marks.

O_2 appealed (as did H3G against the finding of Section 10(2) infringement), but the Court of Appeal agreed with the High Court that H3G had a defence. The Court of Appeal's view was also that the CAD was the 'exhaustive' legislation to deal with comparative advertising and not trade mark law.

Therefore, given the uncertainties over the relationship of the 1994 Act to the CAD and whether the CAD should be viewed as the exhaustive set of rules, the court referred the question of priority between these two governing laws to the ECJ.

The ECJ decision largely agreed with this interpretation, but did leave the door slightly open for trade mark owners to sue in future. The ECJ ruled that:

1 Use of a trade mark identical or similar to a competitor's registered trade mark in a comparative advertisement *can* still be regarded as 'trade mark use'.

2 *However*, the provisions of the 1994 Act and those of the CAD are to be interpreted to the effect that a trade mark owner *cannot use trade mark rights to stop a competitor using his/her mark (or a similar sign) in a comparative advertisement, <u>provided</u> the advertisement <u>satisfies the CAD checklist</u>*. In effect, therefore, the CAD overrides the 1994 Act.

3 However, <u>if there is likelihood of confusion</u>, then one of the key CAD conditions will not have been satisfied, and therefore a claim under the 1994 Act is still possible.

H3G therefore won the case. Although they had used O_2's registered trade mark bubbles, there was no confusion and their use complied with the provisions of the CAD (which are dealt with in more detail below). H3G's use therefore fell within the honest use defence under Section 10(6) of the 1994 Act.

L'Oréal v. Bellure[5]

This later case, which was also referred to the ECJ by the English Court of Appeal, gave a ruling that was more favourable to brand-owners, but also demonstrates the fine line that advertisers tread when comparing brands.

The case concerned 'smell-a-like' perfumes ie perfumes which were designed to smell like those produced by L'Oréal and which were sold in bottles and packaging similar to various registrations for shape trade marks owned by L'Oréal. Comparison lists were also provided to distributors by Bellure, listing various L'Oréal perfumes and the cheaper imitations side-by-side.

L'Oréal brought proceedings in the English High Court against Bellure, alleging trade mark infringement due to Bellure's sale of imitation perfumes, its use of the comparison lists and its use of imitation bottles and packaging. Following an appeal by Bellure against the High Court's decision, the Court of Appeal referred various questions to the ECJ concerning the scope of 'unfair advantage' and its relationship with comparative advertising.

In summary, the ECJ ruled that it was not necessary to demonstrate harm to a trade mark in order for there to be unfair advantage; rather, the advantage would be unfair where the third party seeks 'to ride on the coat-tails of the mark with reputation'. Further, that the use of L'Oréal's registered trade marks in price and smell comparison lists could constitute infringement under the 2008 EC Trade Marks Directive, even though the essential function of a trade mark was not harmed (ie as an indication of origin). Provided that such use could affect one of the other functions of the marks, for example, guaranteeing quality, infringement could be found. The ECJ also went on to say that the CAD prevented an advertiser from stating explicitly or implicitly in comparative advertising that his product or service was an imitation or replica of a product bearing a well-known trade mark.

Applying the ECJ's ruling, therefore, the Court of Appeal reluctantly held in favour of L'Oréal, ruling that the comparison lists were not afforded the protection of the CAD because the perfumes were imitations and took unfair advantage of L'Oréal's marks. This amounted to trade mark infringement, despite there being no harm to the mark or product sales.

By providing a wide interpretation of the functions of a trade mark in this way, the ECJ arguably shifted the dial back towards brand-owners, making it easier for them to challenge comparative advertising via trade mark law, even where the advertiser's use of a trade mark does not jeopardise its essential functions.

Conclusion

These ECJ rulings marked a watershed for the use of trade mark rights in comparative advertising. The views of some lawyers that trade mark rights could always be relied on as a tool to prohibit comparative advertising activity and would take precedence over misleading and comparative advertising rules were shown to be completely wrong. The position is quite the opposite: strict compliance with the CAD by an advertiser will always provide a defence to any claim by a trade mark owner in respect of the former's use of the latter's registered trade mark in comparative advertising.

However, as *L'Oréal* v. *Bellure* shows, agencies should exercise caution. The CAD/BPRs checklist must be strictly followed if you wish to engage in comparative advertising (see later in this chapter). There is still a risk you/your client could be sued for trade mark infringement if there is a likelihood of consumer confusion or if one of the other elements in the CAD/BPRs checklist has not been met, for example denigration or discrediting or taking unfair advantage of the reputation of the competitor's trade mark.

Passing off

A claim in passing off has also been used by companies to attack competitors who they feel have overstepped the mark through a comparative campaign. For a passing-off action to succeed, the claimant must show a number of elements (see also Chapter 4):

- goodwill or reputation attached to the goods and services;

- a misrepresentation (express or implied) on the part of the defendant which leads to confusion or deception in the minds of the customers; and

- damage.

A good example of this is *McDonald's Hamburgers* v. *Burger King*.[6] Burger King advertised its Whopper hamburger on cards saying 'It's Not Just Big, Mac', continuing, 'Unlike some burgers, it's 100 per cent pure beef, flame grilled, never fried, with a unique choice of toppings.' McDonald's brought an action in passing off, trade libel and malicious falsehood. They argued that customers seeing the advertisement would think that they could get a Big Mac from a Burger King establishment, therefore McDonald's goodwill would be diluted. On passing off, McDonald's was able to convince the court that, despite clear Burger King branding, the advertising would confuse customers. As far-fetched as this argument may now seem, the court accepted that customers would be likely to purchase a Whopper instead of a Big Mac. The court held that there would be a direct loss of revenue to McDonald's by virtue of lost sales resulting from the advertising, and granted an injunction to restrain this.

Defamation and malicious falsehood

Defamation and, in particular, the tort of malicious falsehood have also been the basis of claims to prevent comparative advertising campaigns. Details of the components of these are set out in Chapter 11. The following cases illustrate how these claims have been used to attack inaccuracies in advertisements.

In *Compaq v. Dell*,[7] Compaq claimed that Dell's advertising amounted to a malicious falsehood because the claim that Dell equipment was cheaper but just as fast and powerful as the equivalent Compaq machines was false. Compaq argued that Dell had not made it sufficiently clear that the comparison was not strictly like-for-like. The price quoted for the Dell equipment was a special promotional price as opposed to its usual price and was being compared with the full recommended retail price for the Compaq equipment. The judge in this case held that the balance of convenience lay in favour of Compaq and granted an injunction to restrain Dell's advertising.

In *Vodafone Group & Vodafone v. Orange*,[8] Vodafone brought an action in response to an Orange advertising campaign, the basic slogan of which was: 'On average, Orange users save £20 compared to Vodafone... equivalent tariffs.' In this case, Jacob J held that Vodafone could not prove the elements of the tort of malicious falsehood, ie that the statement complained of was false; that it was made maliciously; that it was made either recklessly as to whether it is true or false or knowing it to be false; and that the making of the statement was calculated to cause Vodafone pecuniary damage. In fact, the judge found the statement to be true, describing Vodafone's claim in malicious falsehood as 'hopeless'. (See also Chapter 11.)

In *Jupiter Unit Trust v. Johnson Fry*,[9] Jupiter took issue over Johnson's ISA advertisements, claiming defamation and malicious falsehood. In the defamation claim, Jupiter complained that the advertisements suggested that Jupiter were unable or unwilling to work as hard as, or as effectively, in the management of its funds as Johnson and therefore achieved a substantially lower return on them than Johnson, leading investors to the conclusion that it would be foolish to entrust their money with Jupiter. The judge in this case, however, held that no reasonable reader of the advertisement could come to the conclusion that it contained any meaning defamatory of Jupiter in relation to its trading reputation, and the defamation claim therefore failed.

In its malicious falsehood claim, Jupiter complained that Johnson had maliciously made false statements. The judge, following a number of leading cases, including *Vodafone* v. *Orange*, said that Johnson had not, in 'puffing' its own products, overstepped the permissible limit of denigration or disparagement of Jupiter's products, so that a reasonable man would take the claim seriously. The judge said the advertisements were 'a clear example of comparative advertising with a degree of knocking', and the malicious falsehood claim also failed.

In *DSG Retail (t/a Currys)* v. *Comet*,[10] Currys sought an injunction against Comet when Comet used posters claiming their price was lower than a Currys '10% off' and '£10 off' weekend promotion. The judge in this case held that the posters were directed at Currys, that their meaning was clear and that the claims were, on the evidence, false. Further, the judge considered that Comet must have known that the statements were false when they were made, and that the statements were intended and likely to be taken seriously and amounted to a denigration or disparagement of Currys' goods. As such, there was a malicious falsehood and a likelihood of damage, and the injunction was therefore allowed.

In *British Airways* v. *Ryanair* (as mentioned earlier in this chapter), Jacob J held that there was no difference in the measure of damages recoverable between a claim for trade mark infringement and one for malicious falsehood. However, the tort of malicious falsehood requires a higher standard of liability than trade mark infringement. The judge commented that, although in some cases it might be worthwhile obtaining a judgment for malicious falsehood for publicity reasons, that was not the case here and, notwithstanding that Ryanair had incorrectly illustrated the higher cost of British Airways fares (although the judge agreed that the fares were higher), held the claim for malicious falsehood did not even 'get off the ground'.

Copyright infringement

Companies looking to take issue with a competitor's marketing have also used the claim of copyright infringement to prevent use of trade marks (see Chapter 1). When conducting a comparative advertising campaign, agencies should be extremely careful before reproducing any graphics, logos, photographs, music, straplines and other works used by a competitor and which may be protected by copyright. Logos are usually regarded as artistic works, and therefore protected by copyright. Agencies are therefore advised never to use a competitor's logo.

The CAD/BPRs checklist for comparative advertising

As mentioned above, the BPRs contain a checklist (taken from the CAD) with which advertisers must comply. They now permit comparative advertising provided it complies with *all* of the following key rules:

- It is not misleading (under either the BPRs or the CPRs – so this covers misleading both businesses and consumers).

- It compares products meeting the same needs or intended for the same purpose.

- It objectively compares one or more material, relevant, verifiable and representative features of those products, which may include price.

- It does not create confusion among traders, (i) between the advertiser and a competitor or (ii) between the trade marks, trade names, other distinguishing marks or products of the advertiser and those a competitor.

- It does not discredit or denigrate the trade marks, trade names, other distinguishing marks, products, activities, or circumstances of a competitor.

- For products with designation of origin, it relates in each case to products with the same designation.

- It does not take unfair advantage of the reputation of a trade mark, trade name or other distinguishing marks of a competitor or of the designation of origin of competing products.

- It does not present products as imitations or replicas of products bearing a protected trade mark or trade name.

'Product' in this context means 'any goods or services and includes immovable property, rights and obligations'.

The BPRs define 'advertising' as: 'any form of representation which is made in connection with a trade, business, craft or profession in order to promote the supply or transfer of a product and "advertiser" shall be construed accordingly'.

The BPRs further define 'comparative advertising' as: 'advertising which in any way, either explicitly or by implication, identifies a competitor or a product offered by a competitor'.

In short, therefore, the BPRs set out an all-inclusive checklist which applies widely and whether or not a competitor is expressly identified in the advertising. Agencies should ensure that any comparative advertising complies with this checklist.

Statutory and self-regulatory codes and bodies

In addition to specific statutes, agencies seeking to make direct (or indirect) comparisons need to be aware of, and comply with, the regulatory advertising standards codes.

The Committee of Advertising Practice is the industry body responsible for the UK's advertising codes for broadcast (BCAP Code) and non-broadcast (CAP Code) advertisements (together, the 'Codes'). These are enforced by the Advertising Standards Authority (ASA).

The latest editions of the Codes permit comparative advertising, but apply a number of rules and principles in the interests of ensuring compliance with the law. For example, they require: advertisements to compare products or services meeting the same need or intended for the same purpose; and advertisements to objectively compare one or more material, relevant, verifiable and representative features of products or services, which may include price.

In practice, under both Codes, agencies must seek to ensure that their comparisons with competitors are fairly selected and explained. It will not be enough, for example, to state that one car is 'better than' another simply because it has a higher top speed, particularly if the other car has, say, better fuel consumption or other superior qualities. On the other hand, in the same situation it may be acceptable to claim that the car is 'faster', provided that it is clear that the comparison is limited to speed. (Chapter 5 includes some examples of ASA rulings on comparative advertising.)

Penalties/sanctions

A breach of the applicable statutory provisions can be serious, given that in many cases a breach involves a criminal sanction by way of a fine (which can be unlimited) and a risk of liability for consenting and conniving, or even just negligent, directors, managers, company secretaries or other similar officers (eg marketing/sales directors etc) who may be prosecuted on a personal level and risk imprisonment.

Separately, if sued by a competitor by way of a civil action, a company might face a potential injunction, immediately preventing further use of the material (with the knock-on effect of the loss of any media that has already been paid for), a claim for damages, an order for delivery up or destruction of said material and, of course, costs.

Aside from fines and the civil remedies mentioned above, an infringing company may also face censure from one of the industry regulators, usually the ASA, in relation to breach of one (or both, if applicable) of the Codes.

Both the BPRs and CPRs provide the CMA and the TSI with significantly enhanced powers to investigate complaints, request information, enter premises (without warrant), seize products and documents, break open containers to get access to goods and documents and issue directions. It is also an offence to obstruct an officer of the CMA or the TSI.

The CMA also has the power to seek an injunction to prevent specific misleading advertising, and the activities of advertisers with a track record of producing misleading material. Generally, the CMA requires complaints to come via one of the regulatory bodies such as the ASA and will, more often than not, act on a referral from them, as in the Ryanair case. Since the implementation of the Consumer Protection (Amendment) Regulations 2014, individuals have a direct right of redress against traders for certain misleading practices, including advertising (see Chapter 6).

Advertisers should note that under the BPRs and the CPRs a misleading advertisement could result in a two-year prison sentence or an unlimited fine, or both. However, this sanction is not applicable to an advertisement that infringes the comparative advertising rules (so long as it does not break the rules by being a misleading advertisement). Advertisers who break the comparative advertising rules ultimately face a court injunction (and costs) not to repeat the advertisement and, of course, they may face a private suit with potential damages.

Options for the aggrieved

If a brand that is the subject of a comparative advertising campaign feels aggrieved, there are a number of options available for remedy. When deciding which avenue to pursue, one of the principal questions should be: 'What solution would we like?' For example, if damages are sought, a civil remedy is the only option. Alternatively, if it is desired to prevent publication, depending on the media involved, several options are open. Another consideration is the speed and cost balance.

If some urgency is desired, it is as well to bear in mind that finding grounds to sue directly (eg for copyright infringement or passing off or trade libel) allows the advertiser to move at its own pace and control the process. However, it can be expensive going the court route and there is the risk of further costs awards (from the competitor's side) if the advertiser loses.

Regulatory action (whether CMA, the TSI or ASA) is not guaranteed (although there is a duty to act) and the timing of investigations and adjudications can vary a great deal.

One major benefit of the regulatory process is its low cost and the fact that the administrative and cost burden is largely on the shoulders of the regulator; once the papers have been put together and filed with them, the advertiser can sit back to a large degree while the regulator goes to work and the competitor has to substantiate, answer queries, adduce evidence and so on. It can be a very cost-effective way to secure an injunction and prevent the comparison from being made.

The aggrieved must also think carefully about pursuing dual remedies. Although in some cases, where available, more than one remedy can certainly be sought and would be the right thing to do, this is not always the case. For example, it is important to note that the ASA will not investigate a complaint while another remedy is being pursued elsewhere. Furthermore, in *Cable & Wireless* v. *BT* the judge criticised the claimant's claim for both trade mark infringement and malicious falsehood. He made similar comments in *British Airways* v. *Ryanair*. Such criticisms often have costs implications.

Summary

Comparative advertising is, then, a highly complex area, made all the more so by the high degree of change brought about by the CPRs and BPRs implementing EU Directives into UK law.

With the O$_2$ and the L'Oréal cases, we have some very important ECJ guidance and clarification of the role of trade mark law in advertising and its relationship with the comparative advertising rules set out in the CAD.

These cases give greater clarity to those seeking to engage in comparisons using the registered trade marks of a competitor; such comparisons using others' trade marks are permitted provided the CAD rules are followed.

Certainly, some of the changes have made it easier for the comparative advertiser, but the reality of the increased sanctions and number of hurdles to navigate means advice should certainly be sought to help use comparative advertising in the least risky way.

In conclusion:

- Comparisons, whether explicit or implied, are notoriously fraught.

- Comparisons can expose advertisers to litigation from competitors and prosecutions from regulators.

- Comparative claims need detailed, independently reviewed, substantiation data to be robust.
- Comply with the 2006 CAD rules/checklist.
- Ensure your comparison or claim is 'honest' and not 'unfair' (is it like for like?).
- Note increased regulator powers to investigate and fine/prison risk for officers/managers.
- Seek specialist advice at any early stage – prevention is almost always better than cure.

Notes

1 Unfair Commercial Practices Directive 2005/29/EC

2 *Barclays Bank plc* v. *RBS Advanta* ChD [1996] RPC 307

3 *British Airways plc* v. *Ryanair Ltd* ChD [2000] FSR 541

4 *Cable & Wireless plc & Anor* v. *British Telecommunications plc* CHD [1998] FSR 383

5 *L'Oréal SA and others* v. *Bellure NV and others* [Case C-487/07]

6 *McDonald's Hamburgers Ltd* v. *Burger King* CA [1986] FSR 45

7 *Compaq Computer Corp* v. *Dell Computer Corp Ltd* ChD [1992] FSR 93

8 *Vodafone Group plc & Vodafone Ltd* v. *Orange Personal Communications Services Ltd* Chd [1997] FSR 34

9 *Jupiter Unit Trust Managers Limited* v. *Johnson Fry Asset Managers plc* [2000] EWHC QB 110

10 *DSG Retail Ltd (t/a Currys)* v. *Comet Group plc* QPD [2002] EWHC 116

Defamation and malicious falsehood

11

NICK WALKER AND JONATHAN COAD

 **LEWIS SILKIN**

Introduction

When any advertising or marketing communication refers to a living individual or a company, you should always consider whether there is a defamation risk. The law of defamation protects reputation, and since most advertisements (apart from comparative advertisements, which are dealt with in Chapter 10) do not threaten the reputation of others, this is not an area of law that arises frequently in an advertising and marketing context. It can, however, arise if any living individual or company is referred to – either expressly or implicitly – in a derogatory manner.

Clearing copy: assessing the risk

Unlike editorial material, there is generally less to be gained commercially from advertisements that are either defamatory or borderline, as they might generate the threat of legal action, which would undermine the commercial value of the work. But perhaps more importantly, the relationship between the agency and the client might be the most serious casualty if a campaign generates litigation.

Practically, advertising copy checks involve a two-stage process. The first is to determine whether the image(s) and/or text are defamatory of an identifiable, prospective claimant (or 'class' of prospective claimant). If the answer to that is 'no', then there is no need to worry. If the answer is 'yes', then the second check is to consider: will the prospective claimant sue? The answer to the second question might be 'no' because there is a viable defence which would deter the prospective claimant(s), or there may be other non-legal reasons why a claim would be unlikely.

Sometimes, an advertisement that is intended to be controversial, and for which the answer to the first question may be 'yes' and the second question is 'no', will be the basis of a successful campaign. For example, Major Charles Ingram, who was found guilty of deception on *Who Wants to Be a Millionaire?*, was featured in an easyJet advertisement with the headline 'Need a cheap getaway?' As he had been found guilty in the Crown Court of deception, Ingram would have been ill-advised to bring a claim for defamation against easyJet.

Courtesy of easyJet

Obviously, the second question is not always solely a legal one, but it should be asked. A specialist in this field should have sufficiently comprehensive knowledge of the media and entertainment industry to be able at least to make an intelligent judgment as to the likelihood of any prospective claimant investing legal fees in mounting a claim.

Generally, however, the lower the risk that can be achieved when creating advertising copy, the better. We will look first at the law of defamation, where most problems are likely to occur. Defamation is a *strict liability* tort, so it does not matter that you do not intend to libel anyone in the advertisement. Malicious falsehood is different, and the requirement of proof of malice (ie bad faith) creates a substantial hurdle to bringing such a claim.

What is defamation?

A defamatory statement about a person or company is most commonly defined as one that lowers the reputation of that person or company in the minds of 'right-thinking people'. Alternative definitions have included: words that expose the claimant to 'hatred, ridicule or contempt', or that cause others to 'shun or avoid' the claimant. Statements that an actor is hideously ugly or that an actress has a large bottom, or the portrayal of an actress without teeth in an advertisement for a dentist, have all been judged to have been defamatory.

The threshold under the Defamation Act 2013 (the 'Act')

Section 1(1) of the Act states that: 'A statement is not defamatory unless its publication has caused or is likely to cause serious harm to the reputation of the claimant.' For businesses, 'serious harm' will not be suffered unless the defamatory statement has caused or is likely to cause 'serious financial loss'. What amounts to serious harm will be considered in the circumstances of the particular case, but recent indications from the court suggest a higher hurdle than was previously required before the Act. In particular, simply because the words may be defamatory, there is no longer a presumption that damage has been, or will be, suffered. It will be a question of fact for the claimant to prove at the time the court determines the matter (ie at trial or other earlier hearing). The court will be entitled to take into account what has actually happened following publication of the defamatory words, for example, a retraction or apology. For corporate claimants, meeting the threshold of serious harm and serious financial loss may be difficult.

What is libel?

A defamatory statement, in writing or other permanent form, including statements on broadcast radio, television, film and new media, is called libel. The law looks at the words and/or images and, if they are defamatory, will assess the gravity of the allegation and synthesise, out of the totality of the material published, a defamatory meaning or 'sting'. A defamatory statement is only an actionable libel if:

- it is untrue or if one of the libel defences does not apply – if a defamatory statement about a person, even in an advertisement, is true or substantially true, that person cannot successfully sue for libel no matter how extreme or unflattering the statement; and

- it is published to a third party in a 'permanent' form, as is the case in virtually all advertising and marketing communications, and it refers to the claimant.

What is slander?

Slander is the oral or non-permanent form of defamation. It is, therefore, unlikely to arise in an advertising context, and the rules relating to slander are not covered in this chapter.

Can you libel somebody by implication?

Intention is irrelevant in libel (except, to some extent, in assessing the measure of damages), which means it is possible to libel someone inadvertently. It is also possible to include sufficient information in an advertisement to identify a prospective claimant without actually including a name. Words which are not inherently defamatory, or do not name any individual or company, may also still be actionable when they are read by people who know information supplemental to that conveyed by the words/images, which information, when combined with those words/images, creates a defamatory implication or 'innuendo'.

This is a particular danger where advertising or marketing material is targeted at a specific industry or profession. Visual representations of a person may convey an imputation defamatory of him/her either by their content or by their context. The same applies to a representation of a product or of a person in a cartoon or a caricature.

Picture libels are particular traps for the unwary. If a general allegation is made in a soundtrack or in subtitles accompanying images of individuals or specific premises, the net result can be defamatory. For example, if the voiceover in a television advertisement makes a general statement that some banks treat their customers badly, but the accompanying pictures show the premises of a specific bank, the general statement could be treated as referring to that specific bank.

By contrast, sometimes words that are associated with a picture may remove the otherwise defamatory sting which might arise from the publication of the picture alone. A court will always look at an advertisement as a whole, and decide on that basis whether or not it carries a defamatory sting.

Can endorsements and testimonials cause problems?

If endorsements or testimonials used in an advertisement are critical of a rival product, service or its provider, or if they falsely suggest that an advertised product or service has been endorsed by another company or person, particularly a celebrity (see Chapter 8), there is potential for a claim of defamation.

Many of the defamation cases in an advertising context are old but remain good examples of what can constitute libel in an advertisement. For example, describing a house erected by a builder as 'Jerry built'[1] and a claim that the kitchen of a famous chef was dirty were both found to be defamatory.

It is not, of itself, defamatory merely to use a person's name without their authority or publish their picture without consent, but in an age when celebrities increasingly seek to protect their 'image', any (alleged) endorsement of a product or service without a celebrity's consent could be subject to an action for passing off (see Chapters 4 and 8).

However, there may be a risk of a claim for defamation where the unauthorised endorsement carries some negative implication about the complainant. For example, in a New Zealand case, it was held that an advertisement featuring a reputable trader without his consent was defamatory as it implied that the trader was exploiting his regular customers by selling the same product as that advertised for a higher price.[2]

It may well also be defamatory to imply endorsement of a product or service by a celebrity in cases where the endorsement adversely affects the alleged endorser's reputation. Thus, an inferior but recognisable voiceover was held to be defamatory as it implied the actor's career had deteriorated to such an extent that he was reduced to making anonymous commercials.[3]

In another case, a caricature of an amateur golfer showing a packet of advertised chocolate in his top pocket was held to undermine his status as an amateur sportsman.[4]

It may also be defamatory to link a politician or other high-profile individual in an advertisement to a product that might, as a consequence of that association, reduce his or her professional standing. This might be either because the product itself carries some stigma or because a commercial endorsement of any kind would be inappropriate or even unlawful for that individual. Likewise, a high-profile performer, photographer or artist who has said publicly that his or her work would never be used for advertisements might be accused of hypocrisy by implication if their work is used in an advertisement.

Quoting, in advertising and marketing communications, defamatory remarks made by someone else can also be a trap for the unwary. The well-established 'repetition rule' in the English law of defamation requires the repeater of the remarks to defend them as if he had made them himself. That means he will either have to prove the truth of the allegations or show that some other defence applies, eg it is a legitimately expressed opinion (see the defence of 'honest opinion' below). Even if the remarks are not defamatory, it might be possible for the subject of them to sue for malicious falsehood instead (see 'Malicious falsehood' below).

Can lookalikes be used?

It is not, of itself, defamatory to use in an advertisement a photograph of an individual who closely resembles a celebrity or high-profile individual. However, if the 'lookalike' is depicted undertaking an activity or in a setting that would cast that celebrity/individual in a bad light, and the public was unaware that a 'look-alike' had been used, then the impersonated individual may be able to sue for libel. If this were done deliberately, so that the impersonated individual could be recognised, especially a celebrity, they may have a claim for malicious falsehood or passing off (see 'Malicious falsehood' later in this chapter and Chapter 4 on the law of passing off). An example of this was the use of a George Michael lookalike standing outside a public convenience in an advertisement for a radio channel, although no action was taken.

You can libel someone without meaning to, so the ignorance of a possible claimant is no defence (although it may mitigate the damages). With all advertising and marketing communications, it is therefore important to follow clearance procedures to check that any fictional characters or companies referred to do not have real-life namesakes who might become claimants.

However, it is not actionable to deploy in an advertisement a photograph of an individual who has consented to its use when, coincidentally, that photograph closely resembles someone else. In one case, a newspaper published an advertisement for an adult internet service provider that featured a well-known glamour model. The advertisement invited readers to join the service to see pictures of her, although she was not named. The model in the photograph happened to look identical to the claimant, with the result that she was associated with the pornography industry. She sued for libel because she had no such connection. Although the court accepted that anyone seeing the advertisement who knew the claimant would reasonably assume she was the woman featured, it said it would impose an impossible burden on publishers if they had to check whether a true picture of a person resembled someone else who might be defamed, and it would be an unjustifiable interference with the freedom of expression of commercial advertisers.

What is the time limit for bringing a libel action?

A libel action must generally be started within one year after the date of publication or broadcast; otherwise the claimant will be barred from bringing a claim in the courts unless exceptional circumstances can be shown.

Before the Defamation Act 2013 came into force, each time a defamatory article was published it was treated as a new publication, giving rise to a new action against a defendant. This was of particular concern in the context of online publications. By the same token, if a defamatory advertisement was included in an online archive, it could give rise to a new claim each time the advertisement was viewed. The Act introduced a single publication rule. A claimant cannot now bring a claim for defamation in respect of the same advertisement by the same publisher after one year has passed from its first publication. A claimant would, however, still be allowed to bring a new claim if the original advertisement was republished by a new publisher, or if the manner of publication differed materially from the first publication.

Who can sue?

Any living individual – can sue. But, in England, a deceased claimant cannot claim, their estate cannot claim and neither can their family or relatives.

Companies – can sue in relation to their business reputation, subject to the 'serious harm' test (see above), but not for hurt feelings or for distress caused by the publication. A director of a company can sue if he or she is so closely associated with a company that a defamatory allegation against it amounts to an allegation against one or all of its directors. It is not enough, however, simply to criticise a company's products or services; an allegation has to go beyond that to suggest some kind of incompetence or lack of skill or judgment in order to be defamatory. A company can recover 'special' damages if it can show that it has suffered financial loss as a direct consequence of a defamatory publication. One way for a company to demonstrate that it has suffered damage to its business reputation would be to show that its profits have declined or that it has, for example, lost a particular contract, as a result of the publication.

Partnerships – can sue in the name of the firm as a whole. The individual members of the partnership can also sue for injury they suffer as individuals.

Non-profit-making organisations eg charities – can sue in respect of statements which adversely affect their reputation or ability to carry out their objectives.

Groups of individuals – can bring actions if the group is small enough for the individuals to be identifiable. For example, an allegation that a regional CID officer had committed an offence, without naming the officer, entitled all 12 CID officers in the region to sue and receive damages. Therefore, not naming someone in respect of a particular allegation will not always prevent a libel action being brought.

Unincorporated associations and governmental bodies such as the departments of central government of the UK and local authorities cannot sue, nor can political parties. However, if in an advertisement defamatory statements that reflect badly on individual officers of such bodies are made, they may sue in their personal capacities.

Who can be sued?

A claimant could sue any or all of the following:

- the author of a defamatory statement;
- the publisher of a defamatory statement; or
- anyone having editorial or equivalent responsibility for the content of a defamatory statement or the decision to publish it. This could include the advertiser, the publisher and/or the broadcaster and also the advertising agency, the distribution company and the media owner.

This means that anyone involved in the publication of a defamatory advertisement is potentially liable to be sued.

What must the claimant establish?

The claimant must prove, on the balance of probabilities, that:

- the words and/or pictures in the advertisement have been published to a third party and were defamatory;
- the words identified the claimant; and
- the statement has caused or is likely to cause serious harm to the reputation of the claimant.

It is then up to the defendant to prove, on the balance of probabilities, that the words were true or that another defence is available (see below).

Is advertising covered by the right to free speech?

It is now established by the European Court of Human Rights and our own courts that advertisements are covered by Article 10 of the European Convention on Human Rights, the right to freedom of expression. However, that right is restricted in certain circumstances, one being where the rights of others are impinged – principally the right to respect for private and family life under Article 8 of the Convention.

What defences are available if a claim is made?

Not many defences are of much assistance in an advertising and marketing context, where the issues are most likely to be whether the advertisement is defamatory and/or whether it refers to the claimant. Here is a summary of the defences that may be available in a claim about advertising copy – the burden being on the advertiser to prove one of them if the advertisement is found to be defamatory and to refer to the claimant:

Truth – it is an absolute defence to show that the defamatory statement is true or substantially true.

Consent – it is an absolute defence if the claimant has consented to the publication of the defamatory statement.

Honest opinion – it is a defence to show that the statement complained of was a statement of opinion (ie not presented as fact), that the statement included, in general or specific terms, the basis of the opinion and that an honest person could have held the opinion on the basis of any fact that existed at the time the statement complained of was published. This defence can be relied on even where the facts turn out to be false or inaccurate, provided it was an opinion that an honest person could have held assuming the facts were correct. Although it would be difficult to prove in practice, if it were possible to show that the defendant knew the basis for his or her opinion was false or unsustainable or was made with malice, then the defence would most likely be defeated. It should be borne in mind that simply inserting a phrase such as 'in my view' or 'it seems to me' will not, on its own, offer complete protection. This will be particularly relevant if testimonials are being given or comparisons between products or services being made.

Publication on matters of public interest – it is a defence to show that the statement complained of was, or formed part of, a statement on a matter of public interest and the defendant reasonably believed that publishing the statement complained of was in the public interest. The court will take into account all the circumstances of the case and will make allowance for editorial judgment as it considers appropriate. This defence applies whether or not the statement complained of is a statement of fact or of opinion. The private activities of people in the public eye are likely to attract attention, and publications about them may be covered by this defence. But it is important to remember that statements that may be of interest to the public generally are not necessarily statements on a matter of public interest.

Absolute and qualified privilege – certain defamatory publications attract absolute or qualified privilege. It is difficult, however, to conceive of any circumstances in which such defences would be available for advertisements, so they will not be dealt with here.

There are also other specialist defences in respect of peer-reviewed statements and also for operators of websites where they respond promptly to a notice from a claimant about a defamatory statement (the so-called 'intermediaries' defence'). These defences are also beyond the scope of this chapter.

What remedies can a claimant seek?

Injunction – this is an order that can be granted by a court to prevent any further publication of the same or similar defamatory words. Claimants sometimes try to obtain an 'interim' injunction to prevent publication before a trial takes place. But this is notoriously difficult to achieve, particularly if the defendant argues that the defamatory publication is true or can otherwise be defended. If, however, a libel claimant wins at trial, a permanent injunction will normally be granted.

Damages – the courts' current view is that up to around £300,000 is generally accepted as the maximum amount that could be awarded in a successful defamation claim.

Can a claimant sue a UK-based defendant over something published abroad?

Yes, if the statement is defamatory under English law and is also actionable under the law of the foreign country in which the advertisement or marketing communication is circulated. This is a real concern with regard to the internet, as anything posted on a website is often accessible globally and, in theory, legal action could be taken in any country.

In an Australian case, a claimant sued the US news organisation, Dow Jones, in Australia for libel in respect of material published on its website. Dow Jones argued that, as the material was uploaded onto its website in the United States, the claimant should sue for libel in the United States. The Australian courts disagreed and allowed the claimant to sue in Australia, where he had a much higher profile. It took the view that publication had taken place in Australia because the website was accessible in, and the material complained of was read in, Australia. This same approach has been taken in the UK and it is likely also to apply to e-mail.

Can foreign claimants sue for defamation in the UK?

Foreign claimants can bring claims in this jurisdiction against UK defendants if: the communication complained of was published in the UK; and (in the case of non-EU claimants) claimants can show that they have sufficient connection with, and reputation in, the UK.

Malicious falsehood

Advertising and marketing communications that make statements about another person or company's products or services in comparative advertising, which are untrue and which are published maliciously, can be the subject of a claim of malicious falsehood. (See also Chapter 10.) The statement must also either have been calculated to cause 'pecuniary' (ie financial) damage to the claimant or must have actually caused such damage. Some claimants use this as an alternative to libel claims or in cases where false statements are made which are not, necessarily, defamatory.

Malicious falsehood is a useful and more frequently used tool than defamation in the advertising sector.

How is it different from libel?

- The words complained of do not have to be defamatory.
- In malicious falsehood, the claimant must prove both that the words were false and that they were published with malice. In libel the burden is on the defendant once the words have been shown to be defamatory. To show malice, it is not enough to show that the defendant was pursuing his or her own business interests; it must be shown that the statement was made with the direct intention of injuring the claimant's business.
- The claimant has to prove actual monetary damage – probably general loss of trade or possibly loss of customers.
- An action for malicious falsehood survives the death of either party.

How is it similar to libel?

- The statement must be understood to refer to the claimant.
- There must be publication of the statement to a third party.
- The same remedies are available – an injunction and damages.

How is it relevant to advertising and marketing communications?

In advertising and marketing communications, care should be taken to avoid making inaccurate, disparaging claims about rivals' products or services. A distinction should, however, be drawn between 'advertising puffs' and false representations about rival products or services.

'Advertising puffs' that extol the virtues of a particular product or service over that of a rival will not be actionable. For example, simply saying that one trader's goods are better than another's (or, indeed, any other) would not be actionable. If, however, inaccurate, factual claims are made, which criticise or disparage a rival's products or services, those could be actionable if the test for malicious falsehood is satisfied.

In one case, the claimant manufactured and marketed a natural diamond abrasive and the defendant manufactured and marketed a synthetic diamond abrasive.[5] The defendant circulated, at an international trade market, a pamphlet purporting to show the results of laboratory experiments comparing the two products and which contained statements reflecting adversely on the claimant's product. The court held that, as this purported to be a proper scientific test carried out by proper laboratory experiments, a reasonable man would take it as a serious claim and would not dismiss it as mere 'idle puff'. In another case, Vodafone sued Orange for malicious falsehood over the slogan 'On average, Orange users save £20 every month', used in a big advertising campaign in late 1995.[6] The saving was expressly stated to be in comparison with Vodafone's or Cellnet's 'equivalent tariffs'. Here, the court said:

> This is a case about advertising. The public are used to the ways of advertisers and expect a certain amount of hyperbole. In particular, the public are used to advertisers claiming the good points of a product and ignoring others, advertisements claiming that you can 'save £££££...' are common, carrying with them the notion that 'savings' are related to amount of spend, and the public are reasonably used to comparisons – 'knocking copy' as it is called in the advertising world. This is important in considering what the ordinary meaning may be. The test is whether a reasonable man would take the claim being made as one made seriously... the more precise the claim the more likely it is to be so taken – the more general or fuzzy the less so.

In this case, the court found that the advertisement was not false and consequently that malice was not established, so the claim failed. (See also Chapter 10.)

Some litigation tips

If you receive a claim letter, it is important at a very early stage to make a comprehensive assessment of the prospect of the claim succeeding. If necessary, you should seek specialist legal advice. Trying to assess whether something is defamatory can be very difficult, and there can often be good arguments either way.

It is sometimes worth seeking either the consent of the claimant, or an order from a judge, as to whether an advertisement that carries a defamatory meaning can be dealt with as a preliminary issue. Doing so can be a relatively inexpensive way of resolving a dispute of this sort.

If a claim looks weak because of the clear lack of a defamatory meaning, you can apply to a specialist judge for a determination of whether the advertisement is capable of bearing either the defamatory meaning contended by the claimant or any defamatory meaning at all. This is also sometimes a quick and relatively inexpensive way of dealing with a defamation claim.

One of the reasons why there is little modern case law on defamation in advertisements is that most claims will settle when an expert opinion is sought and a pragmatic view taken on a prospective claim. Other options, if you are faced with a pragmatic opponent, include agreeing to expert mediation, or jointly instructing a leading libel barrister to give his or her opinion, and agree that you will both be bound by that.

More information about comparative advertising can be found in Chapter 10.

Notes

1 *Erasmus* v. *Scott* (1933)

2 *Mount Cook Group Ltd* v. *Johnstone Motors Ltd* [1990] 2 NZLR 488

3 300 F.2d 256

4 *Tolley* v. *J S Fry and Sons* [1930] 1 KB 467

5 *De Beers Abrasive Prodcust Ltd* v. *Int. General Electric Co of New York Ltd* [1975] 1 WLR 972

6 *Vodafone Group plc* v. *Orange Personal Communications Services Ltd* [1997] FSR 34

The internet and beyond

12

Advertising on the internet and in social media

BRINSLEY DRESDEN

 **LEWIS SILKIN**

Introduction

It goes without saying that advertising on the internet is now a central focus for both brands and agencies, particularly if within that remit one includes social media. In 2015 the proportion of UK advertising spend going on digital media was set to pass 50 per cent for the first time.

Some assume that the internet is a 'wild west' in which the old-fashioned laws and regulatory systems that apply to traditional print, broadcast and outdoor advertising can be ignored. But such assumptions are incorrect. While new methods of delivering advertising via digital media are constantly developing, the safest rule of thumb is to assume that the laws and regulations applicable to traditional media will be broadly applicable to advertising on the internet as well.

There are, however, some particular hot topics that it is useful to highlight, and that is the purpose of the rest of this chapter. The following sections will look at who is responsible for regulating internet advertising from a UK perspective; the law relating to search-based advertising (such as Google AdWords); special considerations to bear in mind when dealing with clearance of online content (eg user-generated content or UGC); so-called 'native advertising'; online reviews and endorsements; and the use of social media.

For discussion of the data protection and privacy issues that arise online, particularly in respect of targeting of advertising through the use of cookies and similar technology, see Chapter 7.

Who regulates advertising on the internet?

The global nature of the internet and its implications for ads

Perhaps the most important point for this chapter to make, and also the most basic, is to flag up the implications of the internet being a global medium. Unlike traditional advertising media that can be targeted exclusively at a particular country (or selection of countries), it is considerably more difficult to prevent material made available on the internet from becoming more generally accessible. Technical steps (known as geo-targeting) can be taken to try to minimise online ads reaching unintended audiences, but none can be assumed to be entirely effective. Therefore, the advertising laws and regulatory approaches of any number of countries, potentially, have to be considered, not to mention the foreign privacy, defamation and intellectual property laws that may also apply if the campaign features identifiable people, copyright content or protected brands.

Some pragmatism can be applied to limit the need for a completely global clearance programme, for example by focusing on the requirements of those countries being directly targeted, plus other high-risk jurisdictions that are important for the advertiser's business. But there will frequently be a need to seek clearance advice from lawyers in a range of jurisdictions in order to minimise risk and satisfy the requirements of insurers.

As this is a book about UK advertising law, the rest of this chapter will focus on some of the specific considerations that apply here. But it is important never to forget the potential international ramifications of anything that you put on the internet.

The ASA's digital remit

The Advertising Standards Authority (the ASA) is the most active UK player in terms of regulating advertising activity on the internet. For many years, the ASA's remit has included ads sent by e-mail, online sales promotions, paid-for search listings and paid-for space online such as banner-ads and pop-ups. And from 1 March 2011 this digital remit (as set out in the UK Code of Advertising, Sales Promotion and Direct Marketing – the CAP Code) has been extended to include ads and marketing communications on advertisers' own websites and in other non-paid-for space online, such as social media.

The ASA's online regulatory reach is therefore now almost all-embracing, although there are certain specific exclusions that apply online as well as offline (for example, purely editorial material, classified private ads, press releases and PR material, investor relations and historic 'heritage ads'). When announcing the extended remit, the ASA said that its approach would be to focus on communications by or from companies, organisations or sole traders 'that are directly connected with the supply or transfer of goods, services, opportunities and gifts, or which consist of direct solicitations of donations as part of their own fund-raising activities'.[1]

It can sometimes be tricky to draw a precise dividing line between editorial material and advertising in the non-paid-for online context (see the discussion of transparency and native advertising later in this chapter). The ASA applies different tests in different contexts. For example, user-generated content is only within the ASA's remit when it is 'adopted and incorporated' into marketing by the advertiser,[2] while blogs and vlogs will be outside the ASA's remit unless the material is both paid for and controlled by the advertiser.[3]

According to the CAP Code, the ASA's digital remit does not extend to 'marketing communications in foreign media',[4] and CAP has explained that the remit covers website content of companies registered in the UK, regardless as to the top-level domain of the website, and the content of '.uk' websites.[5] The CAP Code[6] also says that problems with advertising on websites that originate outside the UK will usually be treated by the ASA as 'cross-border complaints' and referred to the regulatory authority in the country of origin if that authority operates a suitable cross-border complaints system. Most countries in Europe (and some outside, including South Africa, Australia, New Zealand and Canada) have a regulatory authority that is part of the European Advertising Standards Alliance (EASA) which co-ordinates a recognised cross-border complaints system. If the relevant country does not have a regulatory authority that is part of a cross-border system, the ASA will take what action it can.

A particular feature of the online environment is the number of affiliate marketers (and related web pages) rewarded by commission for steering new business to a particular site or brand. The ASA has taken a firm line, set out in numerous adjudications, that the ultimate brand-owner/advertiser whose product or services the affiliate is promoting must take responsibility for the compliance of the affiliate's advertising or marketing material in terms both of content and of correct targeting (where the product has age-restrictions).

In addition to its usual array of sanctions, the ASA has a special web page for complaints upheld about online advertising[7] on which it names and shames advertisers who have failed to respond appropriately to an adverse adjudication. The ASA also has arrangements in place with major search engines to enable the removal of sponsored links that are in breach of the CAP Code. Finally, the ASA can place ads of its own through search engines and use its own Twitter account (@ASA_UK) to highlight the continued non-compliance of repeat offenders.

Other relevant UK regulators

The Competition and Markets Authority (CMA) and Trading Standards also have a role in respect of internet advertising, mainly through their responsibility for enforcing the Consumer Protection from Unfair Trading Regulations 2008 (CPRs) (see Chapter 6). The CPRs do not single out online advertising for special attention, but many of their provisions have obvious relevance (for example, when it comes to social media campaigns or review websites, it can be tempting for brands – or their employees – to breach the prohibition on falsely representing oneself as a consumer).

The CMA lets the ASA take the lead in dealing with one-off infringing ads or campaigns, but may look to get involved when there are more systemic problems in the online market as a whole (for example, in 2015 it conducted an enquiry into the use and abuse of online reviews and endorsements). Trading Standards can be called in by the ASA to deal with enforcement against repeat online offenders. Equally, both the CMA and Trading Standards do, on occasion, refer specific cases to the ASA (it is recognised as the established means for gaining compliance with the CPRs in respect of advertising).

Ofcom also has a regulatory role in the online advertising space in respect of advertising shown alongside regulated on-demand programme services (ie 'video on demand' or VOD). It has sub-contracted this role to the ASA, however, much as it has done in respect of terrestrial broadcast advertising. In addition to the advertiser potentially being subject to an adverse ASA adjudication, this means that the on-demand service provider (ie the website publisher) can also be brought to book by the ASA if an ad shown alongside VOD material breaches the CAP Code.

Search-based advertising issues

ASA adjudications on link/results content

While the content and ranking of the natural listings of results produced by using an online search engine, such as Google, are outside the remit of the ASA, the content of paid-for listings displayed on the same results page ('sponsored links') is very much within the ASA's remit.[8] The full range of CAP Code requirements applies to the wording of the sponsored link itself (as well as to any marketing material on the destination web page(s) to which the link leads).

The most commonly upheld complaints in respect of sponsored links tend to result from the constrained length of the link's text, leading to an ASA finding that the link is misleading due to the omission of significant conditions or terms. For example, in January 2015 the ASA ruled that a sponsored search result reading: 'Unibet £20 Risk Free Bet – Join Today and Bet on Football... Great Odds & Live Betting' was misleading as it failed to mention some significant conditions applying to the availability of the free bet. (See below under Space constraints and CAP Code compliance.)

While a sponsored link will usually have insufficient space to spell out such conditions in full, best practice is to provide some clear indication in the sponsored link itself that significant conditions apply and then to set the details out, fully and clearly, just one click away (ie on the landing page). In the above example, not even the landing page set out the conditions, which were a further two clicks away.

Law on use of third-party trade marks in search advertising and e-commerce search functionality

Much legal attention has been focused on the question of whether an advertiser can legitimately pay a search-provider to use a third party's trade mark (often that of a competitor) as a 'keyword', so that its use in a search request will trigger the appearance of sponsored links for the advertiser's own goods or services on the results page. For example, in one of the cases to hit the headlines, Marks & Spencer paid Google to use the word 'Interflora' (a trade mark belonging to a competitor) as one of its keywords – so that sponsored links for Marks & Spencer's own floristry services were displayed when users searched for 'Interflora'.[9] (See also Chapter 2 on trade marks.)

As a result of a number of European Court of Justice rulings, the principles relating to the use of third-party trade marks as keywords and in sponsored links to promote a rival's own goods and services are now fairly clear:

- The use of a third party's trade mark *as a keyword* does not infringe the trade mark owner's rights *unless* the resulting ads (sponsored links) do not easily enable internet users to ascertain whether the goods or services covered by the ads originate from the trade mark owner. So if an advertiser is bidding on a trade-mark-protected term as a keyword in its search-based campaign, the advertiser should ensure that the sponsored links generated make it quite clear that it is its own goods or services that are being promoted. The links must not imply that they might be the goods or services of the competitor trade mark owner.

- The use of a third party's trade mark *in the text of a sponsored link* itself should generally be avoided, as that use will be at a high risk of infringing the mark. (Exceptions are rare, but such use can be legitimate where the trade mark is used properly to describe genuine goods or services that are being legitimately resold, to sell replacement parts corresponding to the trade mark, or to provide an information service about the trade marked goods or services.[10])

- The *search-provider* (eg Google) will not usually be liable itself for the way that trade marks are used as keywords unless it can be shown to have been actively involved in the selection of the keyword or the drafting of the sponsored link (which would not usually be the case). However, search-providers can become liable (alongside the advertiser) if they fail to take down misleading sponsored links once put on notice by the trade mark owner.

- Providers of sophisticated *e-commerce websites* that use similar keyword technology to optimise search functionality also need to be careful. In a recent case in the UK High Court, Amazon was found to be infringing the LUSH trade mark when – in response to a customer inputting 'Lush' as a term in the Amazon search box – the list of results appeared to show LUSH-branded products as being found on the site, but actually linked through to competitor products stocked by Amazon (no LUSH products were in fact available on Amazon).

Content clearance, UGC and customer reviews

As stated above, there are many principles of law that apply equally on the internet as they do offline. One such principle is the need to clear copyright (and designs, trade marks, passing off etc) in any third-party material that you wish to use in an online ad (see Chapters 1 to 4 for the general rules). As also discussed above, because your online ad is likely to have an international audience, your IP clearance will almost certainly have to look beyond just UK law.

Reuse of content found on the internet

Just because material has been found by your creatives on a publicly accessible website (even one that specifically encourages sharing, such as Pinterest) does not mean that you can assume its creators/copyright owners have given you *carte blanche* to reuse it in a different context. Website terms and conditions frequently restrict reuse and it will be difficult to argue that previous publication of material online implies permission to reuse it in a commercial context such as an ad campaign. Moreover, much of the material to be found online has itself been posted there without the appropriate permission of the underlying rights-owners.

In some specific circumstances, the platform terms of service may mean that you have a limited licence to reuse copyright content *within* a particular social media environment for marketing purposes (eg by re-pinning on Pinterest). But, in general, caution is still necessary: an acknowledgement is likely to be required; no editing or alteration is likely to be permitted; and other IP rights and privacy/publicity/defamation issues may still need to be cleared. And bear in mind that a brand-owner is far more likely to be sued when making commercial use of such material than an individual doing so for purely personal reasons.

Use and abuse of user-generated content

IP, privacy and defamation risks

The same principles apply to user-generated content, which in the advertising context is usually taken to mean material submitted to a brand-owner online by members of the public (whether or not in response to a specific promotion). Of course, consumers are not generally expert or careful about the laws of intellectual property, data protection, defamation etc. So the UGC that they submit will frequently include – without permission – material the underlying rights in which are owned by third parties, such as third-party branding or copyright material, or it may include personal details of individuals that should not be republished etc. Brand-owners must, therefore, be vigilant in checking UGC on all such grounds before adopting or republishing it themselves.

If the UGC is merely to sit passively on the brand-owner's site (perhaps as reviews or feedback), more of a balance has to be struck as to the extent of moderation (reviewing, editing etc) to be employed. As a general rule of thumb, the more hands-on a website-owner is in moderating, editing and/or reusing the UGC it receives, the more likely it is to be legally liable for any infringing or defamatory content that slips through the net and continues to appear on its site. Even if a policy decision is taken to be entirely hands-off regarding submitted comments or reviews, there are circumstances in which the site-owner will (at the very least) have a responsibility to remove such material swiftly if notified that it is infringing or defamatory (see Chapter 11 for more details).

It is good practice, when soliciting UGC from consumers for use in marketing communications, to ensure that appropriate terms and conditions apply (requiring a warranty that all content is original and no third-party or defamatory content is used, for example). This will at least have the benefit of making those submitting the UGC consider such issues, even if relying on warranties against individuals is far from ideal. If infringing or defamatory content remains, in practice it will usually be the brand-owner who is on the receiving end of legal proceedings, rather than the individual who supplied the UGC.

Regulatory risks

There are also regulatory risks to be considered when using UGC. As soon as an advertiser 'adopts and incorporates' UGC (ie makes use of it for its own marketing purposes), the ASA will treat the content of the UGC as if it was created and published by the advertiser themselves. This means that all of the usual CAP Code requirements will apply to such UGC, including the need to hold substantiating evidence for any claims made about products or services, the need to avoid being misleading, harmful or offensive etc.

Customer reviews and interaction

Customer reviews (whether on a brand-owner's website, a third-party e-commerce site or a reviews-centred site such as TripAdvisor) are a type of

UGC, and if they are simply listed in the order that they are posted without editorial interference from the site-owner, then they are unlikely to be treated by the ASA as having been adopted and incorporated by the site-owner. However, should the site-owner intervene to highlight positive reviews, they are likely to fall within the ASA's remit. (The same would be the case if a brand-owner were to cherry-pick and quote particularly glowing customer reviews from third-party sites.) As positive customer reviews will often discuss the merits of products or services in sweeping terms, there is a high risk of unsubstantiated claims unwittingly being adopted by the brand-owner.

Equally, if the site-owner intervenes simply to suppress or edit negative reviews (but presents the list of reviews as if it is complete and unedited), this is likely to be regarded by the ASA as misleading. However, some moderation of customer reviews to edit out posts that are malicious or use bad language, or those that are simply rather dated, will not usually render the remaining reviews misleading. (See also the section of this chapter below dealing with blogs and review sites.)

Brand-owners must also be careful how they interact with customers on publicly accessible areas of their sites. If they ask leading questions that solicit favourable responses from customers about their products or services, those responses could arguably have been adopted and incorporated. Likewise, if the brand-owner includes overtly promotional material in response to customer queries or comments, the overall conversation may well be treated as a marketing communication.

Transparency and native advertising

The need for transparency

The legal and regulatory requirement that advertising should be transparent – ie disclosed by the advertiser in such a way as to be obviously identifiable as advertising – was not newly created for the online world. The CAP Code has always expected advertising to be 'obviously identifiable' and already required that non-digital advertorial material was flagged up by a heading, such as 'Advertising Feature'. But the digital environment has introduced many new formats and functionalities offering fresh scope for advertising to test the boundaries of transparency, not least in the guise of native advertising. This section will look at the underlying rules as they apply online, while the next section will look more closely at native advertising in particular.

CPRs

While any advertising that is misleading has the potential to fall foul of the CPRs, there are three aspects that are particularly pertinent when considering whether online advertising is unfair because it is not sufficiently transparent. First, one of the general types of unfair misleading omission under the CPRs is committed when a trader 'fails to identify its commercial intent, unless this is already apparent from the context'.[11] More specifically, two of the 'black-listed practices' in Schedule 1 of the CPRs deemed to be 'always unfair' are directly relevant: (1) 'using editorial content in the media to promote a product where a trader has paid for the promotion without making that clear in the content or by images or sounds clearly identifiable by the consumer (advertorial)'[12]; and (2) 'falsely claiming or creating the impression that the trader is not acting for purposes relating to his trade, business, craft or profession, or falsely representing oneself as a consumer'.[13] (See Chapter 6.)

So, if an advertiser posts promotional messages that do not make it clear that it is operating commercially as a business, those messages will breach the CPRs (and amount, potentially, to a criminal offence).

CAP Code

As noted above, Section 2 of the CAP Code reflects these transparency requirements in its own provisions, including:

2.1 Marketing communications must be obviously identifiable as such; and...

2.3 Marketing communications must not falsely claim or imply that the marketer is acting as a consumer or for purposes outside its trade, business, craft or profession; marketing communications must make clear their commercial intent, if that is not obvious from the context.

CMA report on online reviews and endorsements

The CMA is responsible for seeing that the CPRs are generally being observed in the online marketplace. In a report published in June 2015, the CMA highlighted a potential breach of the transparency requirements of the CPRs and/or the CAP Code as follows:

- businesses paying for advertising or sponsored content in blogs and other online articles without ensuring that this is obviously identifiable to consumers.

The CMA report included guidelines for businesses on how to minimise breaches of the CPRs and CAP Code. The points relating to transparency include advice that businesses should:

- ensure that advertising and paid promotions are clearly identifiable to readers/viewers as paid-for content (whether the payment is financial or otherwise);

- disclose any commercial relationships with businesses that appear on their site and explain how this might affect businesses' ratings and/or rankings; and

- clearly identify all advertising and paid promotions, including when reviews have been paid for.

The challenge of native advertising

Broadly speaking, 'native advertising' refers to types of advertising so well adapted to their digital environment – be it website, social media, e-mail, text message etc – that they only minimally disrupt (or, ideally, even enhance) the consumer's experience of that environment. As a result, in theory, it is advertising that the consumer will be more positively disposed towards and likely to engage with: there is none of the jarring disruption of (say) pop-ups or pre-roll ads. Common examples of native advertising include online advertorial material, ads in newsfeeds on social media and paid-for links to material provided by content aggregators.

The problem with native advertising from a regulatory point of view is that – almost by definition – it tests the boundaries of transparency. The whole point of native advertising is that it blends into its environment and does not disrupt the user experience; but this is hard to square with the CAP Code requirement that all marketing communications should be 'obviously identifiable as such'. CAP has emphasised in guidance that the native approach must not mean that advertising is camouflaged: transparency must be maintained to ensure that consumers are not misled.

An early example of the regulatory response to website-based native advertising was the ASA's June 2014 adjudication relating to Outbrain Inc. Here, Outbrain provided content recommendations which appeared as headline links and teaser text at the foot of articles on publishers' web pages. The recommendations were paid for by third parties (to whose material they linked) and were signposted with messages such as 'Recommended by' or 'You may also like these'. Although a small, clickable logo did lead to a pop-up box which disclosed that the links were paid for, the ASA found this to be insufficiently clear and prominent. The Outbrain material, which the ASA described as 'contextually-targeted branded content', was thus not obviously identifiable as marketing communications, and so was found to be misleading.

When it comes to native advertising in the form of celebrity tweets and vlogs, CAP has developed more detailed guidance (based upon a series of ASA adjudications) which is discussed in separate sections of this chapter below.

Blogs and review sites

There are obviously numerous blogs and websites on the internet that have absolutely no content of relevance to a book on advertising law. It is usually only when products or services are being evaluated, recommended or criticised that a potential marketing angle emerges, and even then, there will be no regulatory impact if the product evaluation is being made – unprompted – by an individual consumer on their private blog or web page.

CAP guidance on reviews by bloggers

In March 2014, CAP clarified that the criteria the ASA can be expected to apply when deciding whether blog/review content comes within its regulatory remit are the same criteria that are applicable to advertorial material more generally. This means that for blog or website reviews to fall within remit, there must *both* have been *payment* of some kind (not necessarily monetary) by the advertiser to the reviewer *and control* by the advertiser over the resulting copy.[14] When assessing who has control, the CAP guidance says a good benchmark is whether the marketer has final approval of text and any visuals. If, on the contrary, goods or services (eg sample products distributed in an outreach programme, or a free holiday given to a travel journalist) have been provided for evaluation but the brand-owner has retained no control over what the blogger/reviewer says about them (good or bad), then the resulting review will not be within the ASA's remit.

If a blog or review site does fall within the ASA's remit, the full range of considerations applicable under the CAP Code will apply to whatever the paid-for content might say. In particular, there must be sufficient signposting of the fact that the review has been paid for to ensure that it is obviously identifiable as marketing material (see the section of this chapter, above, about transparency and native advertising). In addition, the content of the review must not be misleading – for example, substantiating evidence must be held for all claims made.

Impact of the CPRs

If blog or review site material is paid for but is not within the ASA's remit because the 'control over copy' element of the two-stage test is not fulfilled, it is still necessary to proceed with caution because of the requirements of the CPRs. As discussed above in the context of transparency, any use of paid-for editorial-style content for promotional purposes will be in breach of the CPRs unless the paid-for commercial nature of the content is made clear. In 2011, the Office of Fair Trading took action against an agency called Handpicked Media who subsequently gave undertakings not to 'engage in promotional activity unless bloggers within its network prominently disclose that the promotion has been paid for'.

CMA report on online reviews and endorsements

In a report published in August 2015, the CMA conducted a detailed analysis of how reviews and endorsements were being used in the online marketplace. It highlighted a number of practices that potentially breached the CPRs and/or the CAP Code:

- businesses writing or commissioning fake positive reviews about themselves to boost their ratings on review sites relative to rivals;
- businesses writing or commissioning fake negative reviews to undermine rivals;
- review sites cherry-picking positive reviews, or suppressing negative reviews that they collect and/or display, without making it clear to readers that they are presenting a selection of reviews only;
- review sites' moderation processes potentially causing genuine negative reviews not to be published; and
- businesses paying for advertising or sponsored content in blogs and other online articles without ensuring that this is obviously identifiable to consumers.

The CMA report included guidelines for businesses so as to minimise future breaches of the CPRs and CAP Code. Businesses wishing to promote their goods or services online should:

- not pretend to be a consumer and write fake reviews about their own or other businesses' goods and services; and
- ensure that advertising and paid promotions are clearly identifiable to readers/viewers as paid-for content (whether the payment is financial or otherwise).

Review sites should:

- be clear about how reviews are collected and checked;

- publish all reviews, even negative ones, provided they are genuine and lawful, and explain the circumstances in which reviews might not be published or might be edited (eg swearing, abusive language or defamatory remarks);

- make sure that there is not an unreasonable delay before reviews are published;

- disclose any commercial relationships with businesses that appear on their site and explain how this might affect businesses' ratings and/or rankings;

- clearly identify all advertising and paid promotions, including when reviews have been paid for; and

- have in place appropriate procedures to detect and remove fake reviews and act promptly in response to reports of suspected fake reviews.

ASA adjudications on purported review sites

On a number of occasions, the ASA has upheld complaints about websites that have purported to be providing independent and objective reviews of products or services in a particular sector, but in fact have been hosted by a particular player in that sector (usually with that player's products receiving greater prominence and praise than its competitors). Recent examples have been the Review Steam site claiming to be an 'independent voice' on steam showers[15] and the www.accountingreviews.co.uk site claiming to be 'the most comprehensive review of accounting software online today'.[16] In both cases, complaints were upheld that the advertisers had not been transparent about the marketing nature and commercial intent of the sites and that the material on the sites was misleading in the way that it dealt with the products of identifiable competitors.

Vlogging

The term 'vlogging' is a portmanteau word derived from 'video blogging' and refers to people video-recording themselves and sharing their views with the world online, often on matters of fashion, beauty, music, film and lifestyle. Recently, there has been a boom in the number of vloggers who have attracted sufficient followers to be treated as minor celebrities in their own right, with the power to influence their audiences in the choice of products or services (see Chapter 8 for more information on celebrities). This in turn has led brands and agencies to begin paying such celebrity vloggers to have their products or services favourably mentioned in the vlogs.

As neither the brands nor the vloggers want such endorsements to seem too overtly commercial, there are inevitably issues regarding how transparent the resulting marketing communications are (on transparency requirements in general see the section above on transparency and native advertising). A high-profile, adverse ASA adjudication against Mondelez in respect of a series of vlog posts promoting its biscuit brand, Oreos, has now been followed up by some very detailed guidance from CAP as to how to approach different types of vlog-related marketing.

The vlogs that were subject to the ASA's Mondelez adjudication featured various celebrity vloggers participating in a 'lick race' (licking the cream filling off the Oreo biscuit) to promote a particular type of Oreo. A BBC journalist complained that the material was not obviously identifiable as marketing communications and the ASA agreed. Although most of the vlogs had hinted at a commercial relationship by saying in text descriptions or as part of the video 'thanks to Oreos for making this video possible' or referring to the product as being provided by Oreos, the ASA considered such references too oblique to establish the commercial intent of the videos. Moreover, the ASA said that it would have wanted to see the disclosure of the marketing nature of the videos take place *before* the consumer engaged with the material at all, ie before the consumer set the video running.

The CAP guidance ('Video blogs: Scenarios')[17] issued in August 2015 distinguishes between various types of vlog-promotion and explains the different wording and positioning of disclosures that may be required to signpost their marketing nature. In summary, CAP suggests that the following distinctions can be drawn (although this has yet to be fully confirmed in ASA rulings):

Online marketing by a brand

If the brand works with a vlogger to produce a promotional vlog that is *solely* hosted on the brand's own page or channels (not on the vlogger's), and promoted by the brand through its social media channels (not by the vlogger), that will be advertising subject to the CAP Code, but it is likely to be obviously marketing material and thus no special prior disclosure may be needed. However, as confirmed by the ASA's adjudication against Procter & Gamble in relation to its Beauty Recommended YouTube channel in May 2015, to rely on this approach it will be important for the relevant site or channel on which the vlog is featured to be transparent about its association with the brand.[18]

Advertorial vlogs

If the whole vlog is in the vlogger's usual editorial style but fully controlled and paid for by the brand (as per the ASA's Mondelez ruling), it will be treated as advertorial and requires sufficient disclosure signposting its marketing nature *before* the consumer engages with the video. CAP advises that the disclosure should be in the title of the video or in a related thumbnail. Signpost labels such as 'advertorial', 'ad', 'ad feature' etc are likely to do the trick, but wording such as 'sponsored by' or 'brought to you by' should be avoided as that might imply a different type of relationship (see the section on sponsorship below) – this point was also made by the ASA in its Procter & Gamble Beauty Recommended adjudication of May 2015.

Commercial breaks or product placement within vlogs

CAP here suggests that if a vlog is largely made up of independent editorial material controlled by the vlogger, but includes a specific promotional segment or the use of products/props supplied by a brand, then only that segment or product placement needs to be signposted as marketing communication. (Thus the signposting can happen within the vlog, rather than having to take place before the consumer engages with the video.) This guidance has yet to be confirmed in an ASA ruling.

Sponsorship, or provision of free products/services for review

It is possible that a brand could sponsor a vlog or provide free samples/services for the vlogger to try out but have no control over the editorial content. In such circumstances – because there is not control as well as payment by the brand – the vlog would not amount to advertising for CAP Code purposes and so would not be within the ASA's remit. The CPRs would still require disclosure of the commercial relationship, however. For sponsorship arrangements, CAP suggests that a traditional sponsorship credit would be sufficient. When free products/services are provided, CAP comments that 'the CMA would expect brands and vloggers to tell consumers if an item was given on the condition that it was talked about' and, if there was an incentive to do so (financial or otherwise), what the incentive was.

Social media

The content, targeting and presentation of advertising material posted in social media is subject to the full range of CAP Code and CPRs requirements as discussed in the previous sections of this chapter. The aim here is to highlight a number of considerations that are particularly relevant to social media marketing.

Platform terms and conditions

The operators of social media platforms have to balance the need to monetise their online investment (usually by engaging with brands and advertising) against the desire of many of their users not to have their online experience interrupted by (or their data used for) marketing content/purposes. This balancing act is partially played out through the platforms' terms and conditions, which – depending upon the size and sophistication of the platform – often set out very detailed, and regularly changing, rules on whether/how brands can run advertising and promotions. (The T&Cs can also contain significant rules about the ownership of intellectual property in content posted to the site – frequently including a licence for the platform owner to reuse any content posted.)

It is, therefore, vital for brands/agencies planning ad campaigns or promotions in social media to consider the latest T&Cs of the relevant platforms, alongside the legal and regulatory considerations discussed in the rest of this chapter. There is not space here even to scratch the surface of all the different platform rules that can be encountered, but the approaches of two particular platforms are briefly mentioned below by way of example.

Facebook has a number of detailed sets of terms and conditions, including 'Self-Serve Ad Terms', relating to the use of promoted/boosted/sponsored posts, which incorporate, by reference, a series of advertising policies covering issues such as prohibited/restricted content, targeting, positioning, text in images, use of Facebook brand assets and data use restrictions.[19] In addition, rules set out in the Facebook 'Pages Terms'[20] include the following section on promotions. Note, in particular, the requirement for Facebook to be released by each entrant and the ban on the use of sharing or tagging as a mode of entry:

E. **Promotions**

1 If you use Facebook to communicate or administer a promotion (ex: a contest or sweepstakes) you are responsible for the lawful operation of that promotion, including:

a The official rules;

b Offer terms and eligibility requirements (ex: age and residency restrictions); and

c Compliance with applicable rules and regulations governing the promotion and all prizes offered (ex: registration and obtaining necessary regulatory approvals).

2 Promotions on Facebook must include the following:

a A complete release of Facebook by each entrant or participant.

b Acknowledgement that the promotion is in no way sponsored, endorsed or administered by, or associated with, Facebook.

3 Promotions may be administered on Pages or within apps on Facebook. Personal Timelines and friend connections must not be used to administer promotions (ex: 'share on your Timeline to enter' or 'share on your friend's Timeline to get additional entries', and 'tag your friends in this post to enter' are not permitted).

In response to complaints from users about the increased amount of promotional content that they were having to wade through emanating from brand-owner pages, Facebook announced that from January 2015, its algorithms would begin to discriminate against unsubtle promotional material such as non-paid-for posts that solely push people to buy a product or install an app, push people to enter promotions and sweepstakes with no real context, or reuse the exact same content as ads. Facebook said: 'People told us they wanted to see more stories from friends and Pages they care about, and less promotional content... Pages that post promotional creative should expect their organic distribution to fall significantly over time.'

On Twitter, participation in their Ads Program ('promoted tweets') now requires agreement to a Master Services Agreement and Program T&Cs[21] which vary from country to country. There are separate guidelines for running promotions on Twitter[22] and a whole bank of other sets of rules and policies relating to intellectual property use, personal data etc.

Space constraints and CAP Code compliance

As with the sponsored links generated in search advertising, the space constraints imposed in social media (such as the maximum number of characters available in a tweet or Facebook post) can pose challenges in terms of regulatory compliance. The ASA has upheld numerous complaints about promoted tweets and sponsored posts that have been misleading because they fail to disclose all significant conditions of a promotion. For example (as noted above under 'Search-based advertising issues'), in its Unibet International Ltd ruling of 7 January 2015, it had to analyse the following sponsored post on Facebook: 'Will Man City beat Liverpool? Join Unibet for a £20 Risk Free Bet on today's game! MANCHESTER CITY V LIVERPOOL £20 RISK FREE BET... Open an account today and we will cover the risk of your first bet up to £20.'

Unibet argued that the significantly limited space available in the post justified their omission of various conditions upon which the 'free bet' was dependent, and also claimed that it was 'common industry practice to display the ads in this manner'. The ASA upheld a complaint that the ad was misleading, however:

> [G]iven the omission of a qualification in the ads to indicate that the offer was subject to terms and conditions, some of which were particularly significant, and the fact that the full terms were more than one click away from the ads, we considered material information about the offer had not been presented clearly enough to consumers in order to enable them to make an informed decision.

Celebrity and brand ambassador endorsements

Whereas 'promoted tweet' and 'sponsored post' tags serve to make clear that such paid-for social media advertising is in the nature of a marketing communication, there is much more of an issue when marketing material is communicated in non-paid-for tweets or postings, for example by a celebrity who is a paid brand ambassador (see Chapter 8 on celebrities for more information).

In such instances, there is clearly a potential concern over transparency, ie whether the tweet or post is obviously identifiable as a marketing communication as required by the CAP Code. The brand ambassador's promotional tweets or postings about the brand may instead be seen by followers as an independent, personal recommendation of the product or service. It should be noted that CAP has also issued guidance regarding the need for special care in any use of children as brand ambassadors,[23] and the Advertising Association has a scheme whereby brands pledge not to use under-16s as brand ambassadors.

There is also a preliminary issue as to whether celebrity/brand ambassador social media activity falls within the ASA's remit at all. CAP guidance on celebrities[24] indicates that: 'if a celebrity spontaneously tweets about a brand and a consumer complained, it would not be investigated by the ASA.

However, if a celebrity is being paid to endorse a product on social media, it needs to be clear that the communication is an ad.'

The CAP view seems to be that if celebrities are being paid to endorse a product, such a role inevitably involves editorial control as the celebrities are required to state positive opinions of the service or product – thus the requirements of both payment and control are fulfilled, and the activity falls within the ASA's remit.

When it comes to the requirement of transparency (see the section of this chapter above on transparency and native advertising for a reminder of the general principles), the ASA has issued a series of high-profile adjudications. The basic rule is that marketing tweets by brand ambassadors must be obviously identifiable as ads. So, in adjudications relating to Wayne Rooney and Jack Wilshere tweeting about Nike (June 2012), and Keith Chegwin tweeting regarding a sales promotion for Publishers Clearing House (January 2013), the ASA ruled that the tweets were in breach of the Code as they should have included an identifier such as #ad or #spon to make the advertising obviously identifiable (though note that #spon is unlikely now to be acceptable – see practical tips below). It was not sufficient to rely upon any (alleged) fact that consumers would have known about the brand ambassador role.

A subsequent adjudication, again regarding Wayne Rooney/Nike (September 2013), has indicated that, in appropriate circumstances, the ASA is willing to take a slightly more nuanced approach. In this case the tweet read: 'The pitches change. The killer instinct doesn't. Own the turf, anywhere. @NikeFootball #myground pic.twitter.com/22jrPwdgC1.'

Although there was no #ad or #spon type of disclosure, in this case the ASA felt that it was sufficiently obvious that this was a marketing communication because of the specific reference to Nike, and because the wording of this tweet and inclusion of a Nike-branded picture contrasted so starkly with the (less poetic) nature of Wayne Rooney's usual tweets.

Also showing some flexibility in its approach was the ASA adjudication (Mars Chocolate, 7 March 2012) in respect of tweets from Rio Ferdinand and Katie Price in which only the final tweet in a series of bizarre teaser tweets from each celebrity revealed that the whole series had been part of a marketing campaign for Snickers. The final reveal tweet included the #spon signpost (again, note that #spon is unlikely now to be acceptable – see practical tips below), the Snickers brand name and the campaign slogan: 'you're not you when you're hungry'. The ASA was happy that the previous un-signposted teaser tweets were covered by that single disclosure in the reveal tweet, as they had all been tweeted within a relatively short time period and had not contained any commercial message or call to action.

In terms of practical tips for dealing with brand ambassadors in social media, best practice would therefore include the following:

- Disclosure must be in the body of each and every marketing communication unless the commercial intent is already clear (or becomes clear) from the context such as in the second Rooney/Nike case or the Snickers case.

- It isn't good enough to make disclosure of a paid relationship in the profile section for the celebrity on Twitter, Facebook, Pinterest, Google+, etc.

- Contracts with brand ambassadors should require them to be transparent when they engage in social media posts.

- Brand ambassadors should be provided with guidelines to explain when and how they should use social media.

- In the light of subsequent ASA rulings and CAP guidance, '#spon' and '#sp' must now be avoided – sponsored content is seen as a distinct category of material from advertising content – and so '#ad' or wording to similar effect is to be preferred.

Notes

1 Section H of Part 1 of the Introduction to the Scope of the Code

2 https://www.cap.org.uk/News-reports/Media-Centre/2014/~/media/Files/ASA/News/ORE%20Update%20Dec%202014.ashx

3 See Section K of Part III of the Introduction to the Scope of the Code and also CAP AdviceOnline on Advertisement Features. https://www.cap.org.uk/Advice-Training-on-the-rules/Advice-Online-Database/Advertisement-Features.aspx

4 See Section C of Part II of the Introduction to the Scope of the Code

5 See CAP's Q&A of March 2011: https://www.cap.org.uk/News-reports/Media-Centre/2011/~/media/Files/CAP/CAP/DRE%20FAQ.ashx

6 See Section C of Part II of the Introduction to the Scope of the Code

7 https://www.asa.org.uk/Rulings/Non-compliant-online-advertisers.aspx

8 See Section D of Part I of the Introduction to the Scope of the Code

9 The UK's Court of Appeal has – unusually – sent the *Interflora* v. *Marks & Spencer* case back to the High Court for a retrial

10 See Trade Marks Directive Arts 6 and 7

11 See Regulation 6(1)

12 See Schedule 1, para 11

13 See Schedule 1, para 22

14 See Section K of Part III of the Introduction to the Scope of the Code and also CAP AdviceOnline on Advertisement Features: https://www.cap.org.uk/ Advice-Training-on-the-rules/Advice-Online-Database/Advertisement-Features. aspx. See also CAP media release 'New words on the blog': https://www.cap. org.uk/News-reports/Media-Centre/2014/New-words-on-the-blog.aspx

15 ASA ruling on AEB Solutions Ltd, 26 November 2014

16 ASA ruling on TheAccountancyPartnership.com Ltd, 1 July 2015

17 See CAP AdviceOnline on Video Blogs: Scenarios: https://www.cap.org.uk/ Advice-Training-on-the-rules/Advice-Online-Database/Video-blogs-Scenarios.aspx

18 https://www.asa.org.uk/Rulings/Adjudications/2015/5/Procter-and-Gamble- %28Health-and-Beauty-Care%29-Ltd/SHP_ADJ_288449.aspx

19 www.facebook.com/policies/ads

20 [January 16, 2015] www.facebook.com/page_guidelines.php

21 https://ads.twitter.com/terms/

22 https://support.twitter.com/articles/68877#

23 https://www.cap.org.uk/~/media/Files/CAP/Help%20notes%20new/Brand%20 Ambassadors%20and%20Peer-to-Peer%20Marketing%20Help%20Note.ashx

24 https://www.cap.org.uk/Advice-Training-on-the-rules/Advice-Online-Database/ Celebrities.aspx

Lotteries and prize promotions

13

CHARLES SWAN

swanturton

Introduction

There are various methods an advertiser can use to achieve increased sales. One of the most common is to provide an inducement to consumers to buy its goods. A very popular inducement is to offer consumers the chance to win a prize, by entering either a competition or a prize draw.

There are many types of prize promotion. Some have one large prize for only one winner; some have a number of smaller prizes for a larger number of entrants. Some promotions can be entered simply by handing in coupons or filling in questionnaires; some will require a degree of skill in order to win. The size and scale of both the promotion and the prizes are entirely at the discretion of the advertiser.

An advertiser and its agency must take care when running a promotion to ensure that it complies with all legal and regulatory requirements. This chapter will examine the legal pitfalls involved in running a prize promotion or competition.

In order to stay on the right side of the law, when running either a prize draw or a competition, an advertiser needs to avoid any activity which is classified legally as gambling.

The Gambling Act 2005 (the 'Act') defines gambling as:

a gaming,

b betting, or

c participating in a lottery.[1]

Gaming and betting are considered in more detail in Chapter 21. This chapter deals with lotteries and prize promotions.

Lotteries and prize draws

Lotteries are illegal unless they are organised within statutory provisions regarding, for example, the National Lottery and lotteries at local fetes.

Running an unlicensed lottery is a criminal offence, and great care should therefore be taken to ensure that any prize promotion which an advertiser wishes to run complies with the provisions of the Act.

It is also illegal under Section 2 of the Act to advertise a lottery, subject to certain exceptions. The main exception is the advertising of the National Lottery. The Office of the National Lottery has issued guidelines regulating the advertising and promotion of the National Lottery. Advertising agencies should always be fully aware of this important prohibition.

Euromillions advert, courtesy of Camelot Group

What is a lottery?

The Act provides a statutory definition involving two types of lottery, a *simple lottery* and a *complex lottery*. An arrangement is a lottery if it falls within these definitions, irrespective of how it is described.[2]

A simple lottery is one where:

- persons are required to pay in order to participate in the arrangement;
- in the course of the arrangement one or more prizes are allocated to one or more members of a class; and
- the prizes are allocated by a process which relies wholly on chance.[3]

A complex lottery is one where:

- persons are required to pay in order to participate in the arrangement;
- in the course of the arrangement one or more prizes are allocated to one or more members of a class;
- the prizes are allocated by a series of processes; and
- the first of those processes relies wholly on chance.[4]

An example of a simple lottery is a normal raffle. You pay for a number and the winning number is picked out of a hat. An example of a complex lottery is a quiz on a television show where participants dial a premium-rate telephone line and callers are randomly selected to answer the question.

An arrangement is *not* a lottery if the first stage involves skill and the second stage relies wholly on chance. It is therefore lawful to pick the winner of a paid-for crossword competition out of a hat. The first stage of the competition, completing the crossword, relies on skill, so the arrangement is not a lottery.

The prize in a lottery may include any money, articles or services, whether or not described as a prize. If the prize is provided by participants rather than the organiser, the arrangement will still be a lottery.[5]

Some competitions are so easy that, in reality, they are lotteries. Before the Act, competition organisers were setting questions that were so simple that few people could fail to get the right answer. For example: 'The capital of England is: (a) London (b) Paris (c) Timbuktu?' The Act has introduced a statutory test for the skill level in such competitions, which is considered later in this chapter.

Prize draws and payment to enter

One of the essential elements of a lottery is payment to enter. The most important change introduced by the Act was to allow product promotions where prize draws are linked to the purchase of goods or services. Previously, these were considered as involving payment to enter and promoters were therefore obliged to provide a free entry route in such circumstances. It is now legal in Great Britain to offer entry into a prize draw as an inducement to buy a product.

The term 'payment' includes both paying money and 'transferring money's worth'.[6] Prize draws are often used as an incentive to encourage people to provide data, for example in customer satisfaction surveys. The Gambling Commission has issued guidance on this subject. The Commission does not, as a general rule, think that the provision of data by individuals amounts to payment and will not seek to argue that 'proportionate requests for data' involve transferring money's worth. However, the Commission considers that the position might be different where large quantities of data are requested, particularly where data are obtained in circumstances where they are intended to be sold to third parties.

It makes no difference whether a payment is made to the promoter of the prize draw or to someone else, and who receives benefit from a payment.[7] Hence, if a prize draw organiser makes no charge for entry but a telephone company does, that will involve payment (but see below on the subject of stamps, telephone calls etc). It is also irrelevant whether participants know when they make a payment that they are thereby participating in a draw.[8]

As stated above, paying for goods or services at their normal price is not considered as payment to enter. However, there will be payment for the purposes of the Act if participants in a product promotion are required to pay for goods or services 'at a price or rate which reflects the opportunity to participate in an arrangement',[9] ie where the advertiser increases the price for the duration of the promotion.

In most cases this is unlikely to cause difficulty; however, the Gambling Commission has issued the following guidance:

> As a general rule... a [product] linked to a promotion charged at a price that bears little relation either to its cost of production or to comparable products may mean the promotion will be challenged as an illegal lottery. On the other hand, an increase in price just before or coincident with the introduction of a promotion need not necessarily give rise to difficulty if it can be shown that the price rise is unrelated to the promotion itself, for instance because of higher costs of such things as raw materials or transport... The Commission acknowledges that ultimately the costs of any product promotions must be recovered through the revenues obtained from sales. However, the test is whether an identifiable element within the price of the product during the promotion can be said to be a participation fee.

Most prize draws can only be entered by post, telephone, text or internet. Participants generally pay for these services, but do they amount to payment to enter? The Act now provides statutory rules in this area. The following do not amount to payment to enter:

- sending a letter by ordinary post;
- making a telephone call; or
- using any other method of communication,

provided any expense incurred is at the 'normal rate' for that method of communication.[10] Ordinary post means 'ordinary first-class or second-class post (without special arrangements for delivery)'.[11]

Text-to-win promotions are only acceptable if the text message is charged at the standard rate. Premium-rate text entry would be regarded as payment.

Internet entry is not regarded as payment to enter, despite there being a general charge to use broadband (or analogue) connections by the service provider.

The Gambling Commission has issued the following guidance on 'normal rates':

> The test for whether a charge is at the 'normal rate' is whether or not it reflects the opportunity to enter... This is a question of fact in each case. However, it is irrelevant to this test whether different methods of communication cost different amounts. For instance, different mobile phone operators have different tariffs. The fact that, as a result, some participants pay more than others for their call to enter... does not affect the question of whether or not that method involves 'payment to enter'. The test is rather whether the costs of the call includes an element which involves a payment to enter... if the call is charged at a tariff which includes an element of paying for a service... that involves, in the Commission's view, a payment, for the opportunity to enter, again regardless of who benefits from that element of the payment. Here there is some additional payment over that which relates to the provision of the telecommunications facilities.

The following are also treated as payments to enter: a payment in order to discover whether a prize has been won;[12] and a payment in order to take possession of a prize which has or may have been allocated.[13]

The Gambling Commission has stated that this second example does not cover instances where the prize is, for example, a digital camera, and the winner is required to pay normal delivery costs which might be charged if that same camera was bought from a retailer. Nor does it prevent the winner of a car being required to pay road tax. On the other hand, a requirement to phone a premium-rate number for entrants to find out if they have won would not be acceptable.

The Gambling Commission's guidance on payments required to take possession of a prize concerns the status of a competition or prize draw under the Act. There are separate issues under the Unfair Commercial Practices Directive (the Directive). Paragraph 31 of Annex I to the Directive states that the following is an unfair practice in all circumstances:

- Creating the impression that the consumer has already won, will win, or will on doing a particular act win, a prize or other equivalent benefit, when in fact:

- there is no prize or other equivalent benefit; or

- taking any action in relation to claiming the prize or other equivalent benefit is subject to the consumer paying money or incurring a cost.

The Court of Justice of the European Union has held[14] that it is irrelevant that the cost imposed on the consumer, such as the cost of a stamp, is *de minimis* compared with the value of the prize or that it does not procure the trader any benefit. It is also irrelevant that the trader offers the consumer a number of methods by which he may claim the prize, at least one of which is free of charge, if, according to one or more of the proposed methods, the consumer would incur a cost in order to obtain information on the prize or how to acquire it.

Free entry routes

Under the legislation prior to the Act, it was generally accepted that if you included a genuine method for entering a prize draw that did not involve either buying the product or making any other payment, then you would avoid the draw being an illegal lottery. This principle was never clearly defined and led to difficulties and abuse.

You no longer need a free entry route if entry into a prize draw involves buying a product at its normal price, as this is not treated as payment to enter. In other cases, where there is payment to enter, you will still need to provide a genuine free entry route, and the Act now defines what this means. There is no payment to enter if:

- each individual who is eligible to participate has a choice whether to participate by paying or by sending a communication;

- the communication… may be:

  - a letter sent by ordinary post;[15] or

  - another method of communication which is neither more expensive nor less convenient than entering the lottery by paying;

- the choice is publicised in such a way as to be likely to come to the attention of each individual who proposes to participate; and

- the system for allocating prizes does not differentiate between those who participate by paying and those who participate by sending a communication.[16]

If an alternative route involves payment, but that payment costs the same as ordinary first or second-class post, that alternative route will still not qualify as free.

The Gambling Commission has issued the following guidance on the issues involved in free entry routes:

... to qualify as a method which does not involve payment, it is not sufficient that the alternative route costs nothing for those who use it. It also has to be such that, for instance, individuals wishing to participate have a choice whether to use the alternative route and it is no less convenient than the paid route. As an example, many people do not have ready access to the internet at home. Although, for many of those that do, use of it costs nothing in the sense that they pay a single amount for access and nothing for subsequent use, others cannot access it, at least quickly. A competition which offers an alternative 'free' entry route via the web may not offer substantial proportions of those who wish to enter a genuine choice, or at the very least, that alternative may not be as convenient for them as the paid route. This is particularly the case where the need for immediate responses is emphasised to enable the participants to win the prizes on offer, or the competitions are run only for relatively short periods. Reflecting all this, the Commission has developed the following principles, which we intend to use as a guide when considering whether web entry is a sufficient alternative route for those who seek to use it:

- potential participants who do not have home web access need sufficient time to gain web access elsewhere. The Commission considers three working days around the date of the particular draw as a reasonable length of time to obtain such access;

- participation by web access should be available at all times while the scheme is being actively promoted and until the closing date/time for entries. Therefore, a quiz taking place during a television programme should permit web entries while the programme is being aired if entries by other means are permitted at that time as well;

- the availability of free entry via the web should be made widely known, for example as the general policy for schemes organised by the operator concerned; and

- where any doubts exist as to whether the web entry arrangements in any particular case fully satisfy the Act's requirements, other routes, for example by post that has been specifically sanctioned by Parliament, should be offered in addition.

Summary

The main change introduced by the Act was to allow product-purchase-linked prize draws without requiring a free entry route, provided that the price of the product is not increased for the promotion. Agencies should note, however, that when running pay-to-enter prize draws, the requirements for the free entry route are stricter than before.

Prize competitions

Prize competitions, like free draws, are not regulated under the Act and are therefore lawful. A free draw is essentially a lottery that doesn't involve payment to enter. Prize competitions are defined negatively in the Act. They are not gambling unless they are gaming, participating in a lottery or betting.[17]

Prize competitions and gaming

Gaming means 'playing a game of chance for a prize',[18] including games that involve pure chance, such as roulette, or an element of chance and an element of skill, such as backgammon.[19] A game that involves an element of

chance that can be eliminated by superlative skill is still gaming.[20] A game that is 'presented as involving an element of chance' is still gaming,[21] but a sport is not gaming.[22]

Computer games can amount to gaming, which may involve only one participant in a game, and may involve computer-generated images or data representing the actions of others in the game.[23] Care is therefore needed if agencies intend to run online tournaments.

It is irrelevant whether or not a player risks losing anything in a game. The essential element is acquiring a chance to win a prize by playing the game.[24] Prize means 'money or money's worth' and includes both a prize provided by the organiser of the game and winnings of money staked.[25]

Gaming is generally of little relevance in the context of prize competitions. Of more relevance are the other two types of gambling – lotteries and betting.

Prize competitions and lotteries

When running a prize competition, it is important to include a sufficient element of skill to avoid the promotion being considered a lottery. As explained above, a lottery is defined as involving the allocation of prizes by a process that relies 'wholly on chance'. However, the Act defines certain low levels of skill which are ignored for these purposes. The wording of the section is difficult:

> A process which requires persons to exercise skill or judgment or to display knowledge shall be treated for the purposes of this section as relying wholly on chance if:
>
> a the requirement cannot reasonably be expected to prevent a significant proportion of persons who participate in the arrangement of which the process forms part from receiving a prize; and
>
> b the requirement cannot reasonably be expected to prevent a significant proportion of persons who wish to participate in that arrangement from doing so.'[26]

In simpler terms, a game involving a low level of skill may nevertheless be treated as a lottery if the skill element does not: (1) prevent a significant number of players from receiving a prize; and (2) deter a significant number of players from entering in the first place. If either one of these barriers to success or entry is present, the competition will not be a lottery.

The Gambling Commission has issued detailed guidance on this issue, including:

First, the intention of the law is clear: competitions that genuinely rely on skill, judgment or knowledge are to be permitted to operate free of any regulatory control under the Act. In many cases, it will be obvious that such competitions meet the test. See the crossword puzzle example above, for example. The law makes it clear that these qualify as prize competitions even if those who successfully complete the puzzle are subsequently entered into a draw to pick the winner.

Secondly, at the other extreme, there are some competitions that ask just one, simple question, the answer to which is widely and commonly known or is blatantly obvious from the material accompanying the competition. The Commission considers that these do not meet the test in the Act. It is not easy to say where the dividing line between these two extremes lies. The more questions or clues that have to be solved, or the more obscure or specialist the subject, the more likely it is that application of the statutory test leads to the conclusion that the competition is not a lottery. But we do think that the requirement to exercise skill or knowledge in the test in the Act is not met where the answer can be found easily on the internet, is widely or commonly known by the general public, appears in the accompanying text or narrative, or is obvious within a programme.

In cases where it is not self-evident that the competition involves sufficient skill, judgment or knowledge, the test that must be applied is the one in section 14(5) of the Act. In other words, the test is whether there is a reasonable expectation that the skill, judgment or knowledge requirement would either deter a significant proportion from entering or prevent a significant proportion from receiving a prize. Did the skill, judgment or knowledge requirement in fact eliminate a significant proportion from participation or success and, if it did not, on what basis did the organisers conclude it was reasonable to expect that it would have done so?

In case of doubt, the Gambling Commission's guidance note should be consulted, although ultimately it is for the courts to decide whether any given promotion amounts to a lottery or other type of gambling. The guidance issued by the Commission is just that, guidance. However, most advertisers will be anxious to avoid having to defend their arrangements in court, even if they believe the Commission's interpretation of the law is incorrect. For this reason, it is important to be aware of the guidance, which as well as providing useful assistance on the interpretation of the Act, also gives an indication of when advertisers can expect to be challenged by the Commission.

Prize competitions and betting

It is important when organising a prize competition, not only to include a sufficient skill requirement to avoid a lottery, but also to avoid setting questions the answers to which require participants to guess certain matters which turn the arrangement into another form of gambling, ie betting.

A prize competition will amount to betting if:

1 participants are required to guess any of the following:

   a the outcome of a race, competition or other event for process;[27]

   b the likelihood of anything occurring or not occurring;[28] or

   c whether anything is or is not true;

2 participants are required to pay to participate; and

3 if the guess is accurate, or more accurate than other guesses, participants are to:

    a win a prize; or

    b enter a class among whom one or more prizes are to be allocated (whether or not wholly by chance).[29]

The term 'guessing' includes 'predicting using skill or judgement'.[30]

These provisions are designed to ensure that prediction competitions such as fantasy football games are regulated as betting products and can therefore only be offered under a relevant betting licence. Agencies must, therefore, ensure that their client has a betting licence if they wish to run prediction-based league table competitions.

The provisions on payments to enter, including free entry routes, correspond to those for lotteries (see 1(a) and (b) above).

Prize promotions and the CAP Code

The UK Code of Non-broadcast Advertising, Sales Promotion and Direct Marketing (CAP Code) governs sales and prize promotions.[31] The rules set out in the Code are designed, primarily, to protect the public and to ensure that consumers are not misled.

The Code states that: 'Promoters must conduct their promotions equitably, promptly and efficiently and be seen to deal fairly and honourably with participants and potential participants. Promoters must avoid causing unnecessary disappointment.'

The rules also apply to consumer and trade promotions, incentive schemes and the promotional elements of sponsorships.

In practice, it is the CAP Code that regulates most aspects of prize promotions, and anyone running a promotion should familiarise themselves with the detailed rules as well as the various guidance notes published by CAP on its website.

Northern Ireland

The sales promotion provisions of the CAP Code apply throughout the United Kingdom, including in Northern Ireland. The Gambling Act 2005, however, only applies in Great Britain. The law in Northern Ireland regarding lotteries and competitions is set out in the Betting, Gaming, Lotteries and

Amusements (Northern Ireland) Order 1985 and, so far as the areas covered by this chapter are concerned, is the same as the law which, until the Gambling Act, applied throughout the United Kingdom. The key differences between Northern Irish and British law are as follows:

1 There is no statutory definition of a lottery in Northern Ireland. Nor is there any statutory definition of what the Act now refers to as 'payment to enter', or of what amounts to a valid free entry route. The principles of lottery law are largely similar, the main difference being that you cannot in Northern Ireland link entry into a prize draw with the purchase of goods or services. This is why, where you have a prize draw advertised on the packaging of products sold throughout the United Kingdom, you may now find a free entry route applicable only to Northern Ireland purchasers of the product.

2 Article 168 of the Order repeats Section 14 of the now repealed Lotteries and Amusements Act 1976. As a result, the Gambling Act provisions referred to in Section 2(c), which define as betting certain types of prediction competitions, do not apply in Northern Ireland. Instead, the Order makes unlawful:

a any competition in which prizes are offered for forecasts of the result either:

i of a future event; or

ii of a past event the result of which is not yet ascertained, or not yet generally known;

b any other competition in which success does not depend to a substantial degree on the exercise of skill.

It should be noted, however, that Northern Irish gambling law is likely to be amended soon. The rule in Northern Irish law that you cannot link entry into a prize draw with the purchase of goods or services would in any event be unlikely to survive an EU legal challenge.[32]

Summary

The Gambling Act 2005 has opened up a more flexible regime for prize promotions by allowing entry into prize draws to be linked to the purchase of products, without the threat of it being an illegal lottery. However, the Gambling Commission can be expected to prosecute advertisers in cases where the provisions of the Act are breached, although they may not always prosecute the first time an advertiser commits what they regard as an offence. Care should therefore be taken to comply with the Act's provisions, and cautious advertisers anxious to avoid a test case would be well advised to steer clear of the grey areas where the wording of the Act is open to interpretation.

Notes

1 Gambling Act 2005, Section 3

2 Gambling Act 2005, Section 14(1)

3 Gambling Act 2005, Section 14(2)

4 Gambling Act 2005, Section 14(3)

5 Gambling Act 2005, Section 14(4)

6 Gambling Act 2005, Schedule 2 paragraph 2(b)

7 Gambling Act 2005, Schedule 2 paragraph 3

8 Gambling Act 2005, Schedule 2 paragraph 4

9 Gambling Act 2005, Schedule 2 paragraph 2(c)

10 Gambling Act 2005, Schedule 2 paragraph 5(1)

11 Gambling Act 2005, Schedule 2 paragraph 5(2)(b)

12 Gambling Act 2005, Schedule 2 paragraph 6

13 Gambling Act 2005, Schedule 2 paragraph 7

14 Case C-428/11: *Purely Creative Ltd and Others* v. *Office of Fair Trading*

15 'Ordinary post' means 'ordinary first-class or second-class post (without special arrangements for delivery)'.

16 Gambling Act 2005, Schedule 2 paragraph 8

17 Gambling Act 2005, Section 339

18 Gambling Act 2005, Section 6(1)

19 Gambling Act 2005, Section 6(2)(a)(i)

20 Gambling Act 2005, Section 6(2)(a)(ii)

21 Gambling Act 2005, Section 6(2)(a)(iii)

22 Gambling Act 2005, Section 6(2)(b)

23 Gambling Act 2005, Section 6(3)

24 Gambling Act 2005, Section 6(4)

25 Gambling Act 2005, Section 6(5)

26 Gambling Act 2005, Section 14(5)

27 It may still amount to betting even if the race, competition, event or process has already occurred or been completed, and even if one party to the transaction knows the outcome. Gambling Act 2005, Section 9(2)

28 It may still amount to betting even if the thing has already occurred or failed to occur, and one party to the transaction knows that the thing has already occurred or failed to occur. Gambling Act 2005, Section 9(3)

29 Gambling Act 2005, Sections 9(1) and 11(1)

30 Gambling Act 2005, Section 11(2)

31 The British UK Code of Non-broadcast Advertising, Sales Promotion and Direct Marketing (the CAP Code): paragraph 1.1 (g) Section 8: Sales Promotions

32 See Case C-304/08: Plus Warenhandelsgesellschaft

Music in advertising

14

SCOTT MCKINLAY

Harbottle & Lewis

Introduction

Music and advertising are inexorably linked, forming a partnership that grabs the audience's attention. It is not just advertisers and agencies who understand this, as artists and labels also appreciate the value of their music in this context and are increasingly receptive to the idea of their music being used in advertising and the exposure and rewards that this can bring. In this area, the ways in which music is exploited is continually changing. This chapter aims to address some of the key considerations for advertising agencies, advertisers and marketers when deciding upon, and negotiating the use of, music in commercials and the important legal issues to be aware of in this context.

After a brief summary of the basics of music copyright, the various methods by which music can be used in advertising will be considered, as well as the essential, relevant legal points. Finally, some of the common pitfalls to avoid when using music in advertising will be discussed.

Types of copyright

Although Chapter 1 touches on copyright pertaining to music, it is useful to discuss it in more detail here. With regards to music, under UK copyright law there are the following types of works which are granted copyright protection:

Cadbury Dairy Milk 'Gorilla' advert, courtesy of Fallon/Cadbury

Literary and musical works (ie songs)

A literary work is a work that is written, spoken or sung. This includes song lyrics, with the accompanying music being protected in its own right, separately, as a musical work. Together, the copyrights in the song lyrics and in the music are described in the music industry as 'music publishing' or 'publishing rights'. Copyright in music publishing lasts for 70 years from the end of the calendar year in which the writer dies (or if the song is written by more than one person, 70 years from the end of the calendar year in which the last writer dies). In the remainder of this chapter, references to the 'song' will mean the literary and musical copyright (ie lyrics and music) together. Note: a separate musical copyright may also exist in an arrangement (not a 'cover version') of a song, as distinct from the musical copyright in the original song from which the arrangement has been made.

Sound recordings

There is copyright in the sound recording of the music. Presuming that the sound recording is published, the copyright in the recording lasts 70 years from the end of the calendar year in which it was first published. (Note: this was recently extended from 50 years.) The copyright in the sound recording is often described in the music industry as the 'master rights', and in the remainder of this chapter will be referred to as the 'master'.

For the discussion that follows, we shall assume that the copyright works in question are within the duration of copyright protection and have not yet entered what is known as the 'public domain', as this is likely to be the case for the majority of music currently used in commercials. If a work has the benefit of copyright protection, then if a person uses the work without the consent or licence of the copyright-owner, he or she is potentially committing an act of copyright infringement.

In the most common situation in which an advertising agency is likely to use music in a commercial – the 'traditional approach' – the artist who has written the song and performed and recorded the master (and it may well be more than one individual) will have assigned their copyrights in the song and the master to a publisher and a record label, respectively. This means that in order not to be in breach of copyright for using the music in the commercial, the advertising agency must obtain a licence from both the relevant publisher(s) and the record label (as the ultimate rights-owners).

Traditional approach

If the commercial in question is for a television or other type of audiovisual campaign, these licences will need to include the right for the advertiser to 'synchronise' both the master recording and the song with the visuals of the commercial. As a result, these licences are known as 'synchronisation licences'. The key issues and terms of such licences are discussed below.

Parties/licensors

As songs are often co-written by a number of different writers, sometimes there are multiple owners of the publishing rights in any one song. Each of these co-writers may have deals with different publishers whereby they assign their interest in the song, which can result in multiple publishers being the rights-owners. It will be necessary, therefore, to enter into a synchronisation licence with each of these publishers for each share to ensure that 100 per cent of the copyright in the song is licensed. Note: if a writer has not assigned his or her copyright to a publisher, it will be necessary to obtain a licence direct from the writer (being the rights-holder).

Usually, only one record label will own the rights to the master, but it is possible that there may be more than one rights-owner for the world (see below). In addition, extra care should be taken to establish which artists have contributed to the master in question. It is not uncommon for multiple artists to collaborate and/or for 'samples' to be included on masters, and these contributions can be owned by third parties. Masters may also include contributions from backing and/or session singers/musicians. An advertising agency should, therefore, ask the relevant labels to confirm, for example by way of a warranty in the relevant licence, that no other licences or consents are required in respect of the master. Generally speaking, an agency would also want the parties with whom it contracts to warrant that they own the rights which they are purporting to grant (in whatever percentages that they may own) and that they are entitled to license such rights to the agency (or advertiser) on the terms of the licence (including for the relevant territories). In addition, an agency should try to protect itself further by obtaining an indemnity from the rights-holder(s) in respect of any breach of such warranties. This is, effectively, an undertaking by the rights-holder(s) that they will reimburse the agency in the event that the agency suffers loss due to the warranties being untrue.

Scope and extent of rights granted

One of the most important points when negotiating the licence is to ensure that the rights granted by the licensors correlate with what the agency needs. The licence should cover each of the types of media in which the music will be used, whether it is online, in social media, for television, cinemas, or for use in company promotional materials. It should also continue for a sufficient length of time to cover the period over which the campaign is designed to run. A detailed specification of what is needed should, therefore, be provided to ensure that the licence granted is wide enough. If there are certain details or aspects of the campaign which are yet to be decided or may change, then the most effective way to cater for this is to have options within the licence in relation to these areas, which can be taken by the agency as and when required in return for a specific fee. Advertising is increasingly distributed across a variety of media which can be accessed and promulgated worldwide, and so licences will need to cover a wide territorial use of the music. Agencies should be wary of the fact that in some instances the publishers and record labels may only control rights to the music in certain territories, and so care should be taken to ensure the music is cleared with all the relevant parties across all the territories of the campaign. While there is no guarantee of success, agencies may also want to request that the publishers and record labels in question do not license the same music to competitors and/or for a similar campaign, for a reasonable period of time. Agencies should also make the duration and territorial scope of the licence very clear to their advertiser clients so that the clients remember to take down the ad in the relevant territory(ies) on expiry of the licence.

Key: *Ensure that the licence covers all the potential uses of the music across all relevant media and territories.*

Which music?

Not only will it be necessary to specify to which song and which version of the master the licences with the publisher and record label relate, but it should also be made clear how much and which parts of the music will be required. Will it be just a short segment of the master, or the whole duration? It should also be made clear if the music will be adapted in any way, through editing and/or cutting sections together, as certain adaptations of the music will (depending on the terms of the agreements between the artist(s) and their publisher and record label) require further permissions from the artists. In addition, some artists, depending on how protective they are of their music and what level of success they have achieved, may have approval of use of their music in commercials generally, and so agencies should not presume that any particular music will be available (see below for further discussion of other options available in these circumstances). Nor, for obvious reasons, should agencies assume that they will acquire the rights that they want simply because they have reached agreement with the artist and/or their manager. As explained above, there are often numerous other entities included in the chain.

Fees

These points are all very important when it comes to licensing music in commercials via the traditional approach. However, it is the price for including the music in the commercial or campaign which is likely to determine whether the project is viable. This will depend on a wide variety of factors, such as the size and scope of the campaign, the popularity of the song and/ or artist in question, and the two sides' bargaining positions. Sometimes, in situations where there are multiple rights-holders in respect of any particular song, the agency will be asked by the publisher(s) to agree to a 'most favoured nations' clause. Under such clauses, the agency will agree, for example, that the fees it pays to publisher no. 1 will not be on any less favourable terms than those fees which it pays to any other publisher(s) in respect of the same song. If the fees payable to the other publisher(s) are higher, then the fees payable to publisher no. 1 will be increased accordingly. Also, often there are 'most favoured nations' clauses between the publisher(s) and the record companies.

The earlier an agency can begin planning and discussions regarding the licensing of any music, the easier it will be to avoid situations where the rights-holders are able to demand higher fees due to their awareness of the time constraints an agency may be under to get a deal finalised in time for the launch of a campaign.

Other legal considerations

Moral rights

Again as noted in Chapter 1, in addition to the copyrights which exist in literary and musical works, the authors of such copyright works have certain rights known as 'moral rights'. These include the right to be identified as the author of a copyright work (known as the 'right of paternity'), and the right to object to derogatory treatment of a copyright work. Any licensor should warrant to the advertising agency that any such rights will not be asserted by the authors, ie a waiver of moral rights, in order to protect the agency from any possible infringement of these rights in the commercial. Note: the laws regarding moral rights vary between different countries.

Performance income

Performance income will be payable by the relevant broadcaster, cinema or venue for the public performance of each of the master and song included in the commercial. Generally, this income will be split in relation to the master between the record label and the artist by the collecting society, Phonographic Performance Limited (PPL), and in relation to the song between the publisher and the writer by the collecting society, Performing Rights Society (PRS). Careful attention should be paid to the wording of any licences, to confirm that the rights for performance and broadcast of the music have been granted. Depending on the rights position with respect to the master and the performers on the master, certain additional fees or 'residuals' can become payable, and so it should be clarified whose responsibility these will be.

Even with a strong awareness of the key issues involved with the traditional approach of licensing above, there may be situations where the music which was originally planned to be included is simply too expensive to license and/ or that a different method is preferable, in which case an agency may want to consider some of the alternative routes for using music in advertising discussed below.

Alternative methods

Library music

One of the most inexpensive solutions is to license 'library music' (also known as 'stock music' or 'production music'). Library music is music specifically written for synchronisation or dubbing into audio and audiovisual commercials, websites and other types of campaign and there is no need to apply for permission of the composer of the music. In the UK, the copyrights (both in the song and master) in these works are administered on behalf of library members by the Mechanical-Copyright Protection Society (MCPS), which is able to grant licences according to each agency's requirements and across a wide variety of genres.

Ownership model

Another option for agencies is to commission the music themselves, with the intention of being ultimate rights-owner of the song and master. Subject to the musicians in question not already being signed (see below), the agency contracts directly with musician(s) to compose and record bespoke music for its advertising campaign. In return for a fee, the musicians assign all rights they may have in the song and master to the agency. The benefits of owning the music for the agency are that it will have complete creative control over the music and the ability to use and exploit it in the campaign however it wishes to do so, without the potential need for paying expensive reuse fees. The music will be exclusively reserved for the agency and will also generate a revenue stream for the agency (as rights-owner) when the music in the commercial is performed in public (see discussion above re performance income). The masters could even become popular and saleable in their own right as a result of the campaign. The drawbacks of this model are the level of costs of engaging the musicians and the recording costs, and creating the music will require a high level of engagement from the agency to produce a strong end product.

Agencies should also be aware that in a significant proportion of cases, the musicians and performers involved will already have signed agreements with publishers and record labels under which they will have assigned all their rights in the songs and masters that they write and record, respectively (as well as certain additional ancillary rights), including any new ones commissioned by the agency. This means that if agencies want these rights, they will still need to negotiate terms with the publishers and record labels, which are likely to request fees and other additional conditions regarding the use of the music.

Covers and 'soundalikes'

A slight variation on the above model, and one which has been particularly prevalent in recent times, is the re-recording of pre-existing songs, ie recording 'cover versions', to be included in commercials. While a synchronisation licence would still be required from the publisher to include the song in the commercial, because a new master is being made it would not be necessary to license a version of the master from the record label. There are, potentially, a number of reasons to do this, including: (i) the original master in question being too expensive to use; (ii) not being able to obtain permission from the label (or the label not being able to obtain consent from the artist); or (iii) wanting to give the music (and commercial) an original voice and relevance. If the artist recording the new master is not signed to a label, then the agency would also be able to own the master, providing some of the benefits of the ownership model (see above). Occasionally, agencies will also commission the writing and recording of new 'soundalike' songs and masters, but they should be wary of the dangers of this approach (as discussed below).

Pitfalls

Budgetary constraints, generally, or the level of licence fee requested by the rights-owner, will sometimes lead an agency to consider whether it can achieve what it seeks musically, but without as much expenditure. Using a cover version instead of an original version (as discussed above) can assist. Care needs to be taken, however, that the vocal is not so close that it appears to be the original performer, as that could amount in some circumstances to passing off (see Chapter 4 for a more detailed discussion of this). Similarly, the instrumentation and musical arrangement in the cover version could infringe the copyright in the original arrangement, so the new version has to be created from the underlying music (ie the melody) rather than any particular recording or arrangement of that music.

Another common approach is a variant on the ownership model discussed above, in which the agency commissions new music, but does so to a clear brief or specification; namely, to 'sound like' an established artist, writer or even a particular track. In other words, to produce something that is in the style of, or evocative of, another work. The risk here is that although the music is new, it could still amount to copyright infringement if it is a 'substantial reproduction' of an existing work. It could also amount to passing off. In theory, an artist or writer's 'style' can be adopted in the same way that an 'idea' is not a copyright work, although a particular expression of that idea in a permanent form is. This idea/expression dichotomy is a complex legal question, and beyond the scope of this chapter, but the following points should be noted in particular (and see Chapter 1):

- The test of what is a 'substantial reproduction' is a qualitative test, and not a quantitative test.

- There are various urban legal myths that are often relied on. They are just myths, however, and have no legal basis. For example: 'it's ok as long as you make five changes' etc. This same warning also applies to 'sampling' or taking very small snippets of a work, on the basis that this must be safe because using 'only' three seconds from a three-minute track is surely not 'substantial'. It probably is, especially if it is an important three-second extract.

- The facts are highly relevant, as the question is whether the original work was 'copied'. If proceedings are brought, all the internal creative work, briefs, notes to clients and correspondence will probably all be seen by the court and the claimant. So any descriptions and directions such as to create 'some 'Beatles-ey' music', or early versions of the commercial that actually use the original music 'for illustrative purposes', will tend to indicate to the court that there was, in fact, copying. Courts are not usually impressed by an argument that there was 'copying away', ie 'We started with the claimant's work, but we deliberately made changes so it can't be a substantial reproduction', on the basis that this means that the original work was used as an obvious reference point.

- If a claimant applies for an emergency ('interim' or 'interlocutory') injunction it will not have to prove its case completely at that stage. If the court is satisfied that the claimant has at least a realistic complaint of copyright infringement, it will then consider other factors in order to decide whether or not to grant that initial injunction.

The future

Music has been and will always be a critical element of successful advertising and, as explained above, will involve a collection of rights which can make its use highly complex and expensive. This chapter has considered some of the main, practical considerations relating to using music in advertising and the ways in which the two can be combined. The relationship between music and advertising, however, will continue to evolve, and it appears that the roles of artists, record labels and publishers in brand partnerships will become increasingly prominent.

A number of music rights-holders and content providers are establishing specific artist and brand partnership divisions within their businesses, recognising that it is not just new revenue that can be created. Added value can also be produced, through launching a new artist's career, or re-launching an already established one. Partnerships can also enable both the artist and the brand to reach a wider audience, and to maintain this over a longer period than the traditional 'album cycle', which lasts for only a matter of weeks.

All parties will want to find a campaign that is a good fit; that will depend (among other things) upon the nature of the brand, the genre of the music and the artist's public persona. An appropriate partnership will not only be based on subjective opinion and 'feel', but can also now be established through analysing the wealth of information which can be gleaned from social media, online statistics and the parties' databases of fans and users. It will be fascinating to see how agencies make use of these opportunities and the variety of new media available in order to exploit them effectively in the near future.

Price claims and indications

15

STEPHEN GROOM

Introduction

In the UK, price claims and indications are governed principally by the following:

a The Consumer Protection from Unfair Trading Regulations 2008 (CPRs), which impose penalties on traders who make price claims and indications (PCIs) in advertising and marketing that constitute 'unfair commercial practices'. The CPRs extend to all PCIs that are directly connected with the promotion, sale or supply of goods or services to consumers. Breach of the CPRs can give rise to serious criminal sanctions.

b The Business Protection from Misleading Marketing Regulations 2008 (BPRs), which, to a large extent, mirror the CPRs, including sanctions, but apply to PCIs addressed to traders as opposed to consumers.

c The Price Marking Order 2004, the Consumer Rights (Payment Surcharges) Regulations 2012, the Consumer Contracts (Information, Cancellation and Additional Charges) Regulations 2013 and the Consumer Rights Act 2015 all impact how PCIs should be made in particular circumstances.

d PCIs must also comply with the Committee of Advertising Practice's (CAP) UK Code of Non-broadcast Advertising, Sales Promotion and Direct Marketing (CAP Code) and its broadcasting equivalent, the UK Code of Broadcast Advertising (BCAP Code), which are enforced by the Advertising Standards Authority (ASA); and

e The Department for Business, Innovation and Skills' (BIS) Pricing Practices Guide (PPG) is a set of good practices which BIS recommends that traders follow when making PCIs. Additionally, the CAP and BCAP Codes (collectively the CAP Codes) require that 'price statements in marketing communications should take account' of the PPG. *At the time of writing, the PPG is due to be updated in 2016 following a review by the Chartered Trading Standards Institute (CTSI).*

This chapter will first of all summarise key parts of the legislation that governs how PCIs are given in particular scenarios. (A detailed review is beyond the scope of this book.) Then it will discuss the key principles governing PCIs before exploring various PCI types and the laws or regulations that apply.

Legislation governing PCIs in particular scenarios

Price Marking Order 2004 (PMO)

The PMO applies to traders, including online retailers, who sell products to consumers.

It provides that, with some exceptions, where a trader indicates that any product is or may be for sale to a consumer, he or she shall indicate the selling price of that product in accordance with the PMO. 'Selling price' is defined as 'the final price for a unit of a product, or a given quantity of a product, including VAT and all other taxes'.

The PMO does not apply in respect of an advertisement for a product, but will still apply to PCIs: (i) in advertisements intended to encourage consumers to enter into distance contracts; (ii) in a catalogue; (iii) in a price list; (iv) on a container; and (v) on a label, such as a price tag.

An indication of selling price and any charges for postage, packing or delivery must be 'unambiguous, easily identifiable and clearly legible'.

Consumer Protection from Unfair Trading Regulations 2008 (CPRs) and the Consumer Contracts (Information, Cancellation and Additional Charges) Regulations 2013 (CCRs)

Both the CPRs and the CCRs require disclosure of the total price of goods or services offered to consumers, including any taxes, or where the nature of the product is such that the price cannot reasonably be calculated in advance, the manner in which the price is calculated.

The CPRs require this to be disclosed in 'invitations to purchase' in a way which is not unclear, unintelligible, ambiguous or untimely.

An invitation to purchase is defined as: 'a commercial communication which indicates characteristics of the product (in this case defined as goods and services) and the price in a way appropriate to the means of that commercial communication and thereby enables the consumer to make a purchase.' So advertisements are covered.

The CCRs require the disclosure of the same information 'in a clear and comprehensible manner' before a consumer is bound by an on-premises, distance or off-premises contract.

Consumer Rights (Payment Surcharges) Regulations 2012 (CPSRs)

The CPSRs ban traders from charging consumers more than the direct cost borne by the trader as a result of the consumer using a given means of payment, such as a credit card. They apply to contracts however they are concluded.

Consumer Rights Act 2015 (the CRA)

The CRA has changed the previous rule in the now revoked Unfair Terms in Consumer Contacts Regulations 1999. The old rule was that any term in a business-to-consumer contract for the sale of goods or services that related to price was exempt from the rule that provisions in such contracts were generally unenforceable if they were unfair.

Now, a term as to price will only be exempt from this rule if it is transparent and prominent.

Main principle: price claims and indications must not materially mislead or be likely to do so

The main guiding principle for all traders making PCIs to consumers or other traders is that such claims must not mislead or be likely to do so.

The principle is enshrined in law through Regulation 5(4)(g) of the CPRs. This prohibits traders from misleading consumers about the price of a product (defined as 'any goods or service and includes immoveable property, rights and obligations') or the manner in which the price is calculated. The PPG advises that a commercial practice, such as an advertisement, using correct information can be misleading if it is likely to deceive the average consumer. Therefore, when assessing whether a PCI is misleading, rather than simply considering whether the PCI is true or not, the key consideration is whether the PCI will, or is likely to, cause the consumer to take a transactional decision he or she would not have taken otherwise.

The CAP and BCAP Codes also reflect this principle. CAP defines 'price statements' as 'statements about the manner in which the price will be calculated as well as definite prices.'[1] The first rule in both Codes relating to price statements provides that 'price statements must not mislead by omission, undue emphasis or distortion. They must relate to the product featured in the marketing communication.'[2]

The latter rule often gives rise to issues when car manufacturers advertise the headline price of their cheapest car alongside the image of a top-of-the-range model. Adding 'from' before the headline price will still be misleading due to the difference between the price indicated and that of the model shown.[3] The PPG recommends that PCIs using 'from' and 'up to' must not exaggerate the benefits that a consumer is likely to obtain. In this context a 10 per cent rule of thumb is often applied by the ASA. See more about this below.

The PPG also advises that when the price indicated only relates to certain sizes or colours of a product, this should be made obvious in an easily identifiable and legible way. In addition, if the PCI relates only to some parts of the image displayed, then this should be clear. For example, an advertisement for a tablet showing an attachable keyboard that only quotes the price of the tablet should make clear that the keyboard is not included.

The validity of a PCI while the marketing communication is in circulation is also paramount in ensuring that the PCI is not misleading. The PPG states that PCIs can still be misleading even if they were accurate when first given. For instance, particular care should be taken with print advertising, especially in publications with long copy deadlines, such as magazines. It is essential that when the magazine is published, the offer should still apply for a 'reasonable' period. What is reasonable depends on the circumstances but the PPG advises either seven days from the date of publication or until the next issue is published, whichever is longer.

Price claims

Recommended retail prices[4]

Any reference in a PCI to a recommended retail price (RRP) should be used carefully to ensure that it is genuine and not misleading. The PPG recommends that an RRP which is not genuine or 'differs significantly from the price at which the product is generally sold' should not be used. Traders should always ensure that RRPs are properly identified and substantiated.

In 2014, a consumer complained that a website product page showing an RRP of £49.99 for a car seat was misleading. The retailer produced screenshots of competitors selling the seat for various prices, including: £59.99, £49.99, £39.95 and £29.99. The ASA held that the range of prices did not establish the RRP and therefore the advertisement misled consumers concerning the saving that could be made.

Finally, there are other prices that cannot be advertised as an RRP. The PPG and CAP both advise traders not to use an RRP for exclusive products that are sold only by them. CAP also advises that a maximum legal price should not be used as an RRP, for example, by claiming that the RRP of an MOT is £50 if £50 is the maximum legal price for an MOT. In addition, CAP warns marketers to be careful with products that have not been sold yet, such as new DVD or game releases, even if the distributor has provided an RRP. This is because the RRP may not be the general full price at which the product is sold.

Introductory prices and availability

When a product finally reaches the market, the PPG discourages using an introductory offer if there is no intention to offer the same product for sale at a higher price after the introductory offer period is over. Furthermore, the PPG advises traders not to allow an offer to run for so long that it becomes misleading to describe the offer as an introductory offer (or any other special offer). The reasonable period for an introductory offer depends on the circumstances, but the PPG advises stating and committing to the date that the offer will end.

The PPG mirrors the provisions set out in the CPRs that prohibit misleading consumers about the existence of a price advantage, such as the limited availability of an offer. Schedule 1 of the CPRs lists a number of commercial practices that will, in all circumstances, be considered unfair and therefore contrary to law. Two apply to offers with limited availability:
Practice # 5 is:

> Making an invitation to purchase products at a specified price without disclosing the existence of any reasonable grounds the trader may have for believing that he will not be able to offer for supply,... those products or equivalent products at that price for a period that is, and in quantities that are, reasonable having regard to the product, the scale of the advertising and the price offered (bait advertising).

Practice #7 is:

> Falsely stating that a product will only be available for a very limited time, or that it will only be available on particular terms for a very limited time, in order to elicit an immediate decision and deprive consumers of sufficient opportunity or time to make an informed choice.

'Particular terms' could, of course, include a particular price. (See also Chapter 6.)

Savings and sales[5]

CAP divides savings claims into two categories: savings that all consumers *will* benefit from (such as a clothes sale) and savings that consumers *may* benefit from (such as car insurance, which will depend on the driver and car). CAP also differentiates between the wording '*can* save' (which it considers 'implies a stronger probability that savings will be attained') and '*could* save' (which is conditional). Traders should be careful when making a conditional offer to ensure that consumers are not disappointed or misled into believing that they can save.

Both CAP and the PPG advise applying a rule of thumb that a savings claim should only be made when 10 per cent or more of customers can expect to receive the maximum benefit from a saving. This 10 per cent threshold applies to the different types of savings that are offered too. For example, a PCI such as 'save up to 50% on all books' would mean that all books will be discounted, with at least 10 per cent of the books being half price. If only certain books are discounted, then the PCI should relate to designated lines only by using wording such as 'save up to 50% on selected books'. The savings claim must not be misleading and small print should be avoided.

If a savings claim is made as a result of savings from which other customers have benefited, then the basis of the saving and method of calculation should be clear to consumers. Every customer is different, so advertisers must appreciate that the savings made by each customer may not be the same. Therefore, PCIs such as 'Our insurance will save you an average of £x' will not be acceptable, but PCIs such as 'last year, our new insurance customers saved an average of £x' may be acceptable. Further to this, the PPG advises that, if the discount is in relation to a previous price not offered by the trader (for example, if the trader operates an outlet or specialist discount store), then this should be made clear to the consumer. In addition, the PPG states that traders should make it clear if any items were brought in especially for a sale.

The PPG advises that a genuine reference price has a number of facets, which may include: (i) being the price at which the trader might reasonably expect to sell a significant number of the products; (ii) a significant quantity of the products were placed on sale at that price; and (iii) the products were offered for sale at that price for a period at least sufficient to be a genuine offer of sale to the section of the public likely to be interested.

The PPG goes on to indicate that if the circumstances in which the previous price was charged are not described, it should be the price at which the product was available for at least 28 consecutive days within the previous six months. However, it is now considered that this is over-prescriptive. For instance, if taken literally it can be abused by traders artificially increasing their price for exactly 28 days before a reduction.

Therefore, it is now more likely that the court or the ASA would take a more flexible approach and apply the basic test of whether the higher price was genuine rather than focusing on any minimum number of days' availability at that price. *Indeed, the draft updated PPG produced by the CTSI at the time of writing (referred to in the Introduction above) removes references to 28 days.*

For instance, a furniture retailer claimed in respect of a nest of tables: 'Now only £169. Was £378.' On investigation, the ASA found that over the previous six months the tables had been on sale initially at the higher price for 28 days at all 50 of the retailer's stores, then subsequently sold at the higher price at only two stores for another 28 days.[6]

Furthermore, apart from in the two identified stores, the tables had already been on sale at £169 at all the trader's stores for five of the six months before the price reduction to £169 was claimed. The ASA concluded that the normal selling price was not £378 but £169 and that the claim was therefore misleading and breached the CAP Code.

In addition, the PPG requires that a sale price should not last longer than the previous, higher price. The ASA also applies this principle.

If advertising further price reductions during the same sale or special offer period, the PPG advises that the highest price in the series should have applied for a reasonable time and that the entire series of prices, from the highest to the intervening, should be quoted alongside the current selling price. Alternatively, the PPG recommends providing a suitable explanation so that consumers understand the saving that they can make.

'Lowest' price claims and price guarantees[7]

CAP advises that 'lowest' or 'best' PCIs must be properly substantiated to show that the price 'will always beat, and not merely match, competitors' prices'. If the price is based on a specific time period, then this should be made clear in the advertisement and the specified time period should be as recent as possible.

In terms of price promises and guarantees, CAP clarifies the difference as follows: 'lowest price guaranteed' is a claim that a product cannot be purchased for a lower price elsewhere; whereas 'lowest price guarantee' is a price promise, which may mean a low price is provided and a refund is offered if the price is found to not be the lowest. CAP recommends clarifying whether the PCI is offering to match or beat a competitor's price.

'Lowest' PCIs must also compare like with like. The most recent prominent complaint at the time of writing involved Sainsbury's challenging a Tesco advertising campaign that claimed its own-brand products were the cheapest. Sainsbury's claimed that Tesco's Price Promise campaign misled consumers as Sainsbury's own-brand products were of superior ethical or provenance standards to Tesco's, and therefore the products could not be fairly compared or matched. The ASA held that the comparison was permitted as the products were sufficiently interchangeable for the average consumer. Sainsbury's challenged this decision by way of judicial review, but was unsuccessful.[8]

CAP also advises that promises or guarantees to match or beat a competitor's price upon notification from a consumer will not justify a 'lowest' price claim and that any significant conditions attached to a price promise should be made clear.

Hidden costs and charges

Regulations 6(4)(d) and (e) of the CPRs prohibit the omission from any PCI of associated charges such as tax, delivery and postal charges, unless these costs are obvious from the context. The PPG advises that 'the object is to ensure that the consumer should always be fully aware of the total cost'. When a trader is unable to give full details of the additional costs and charges, the PPG requires them to give the consumer full details of what is included within an offer and how the remaining costs may be calculated. These points are reflected in the CAP and BCAP Code rules.[9]

The PPG's advice is particularly pertinent as online shopping increases in popularity. Postage, packing, import duty and delivery charges should be clear. This is to ensure that consumers are fully informed of the full cost of their purchase. If the costs are unknown, then an indication of how such costs will be calculated must be provided; for example, by warning customers that 'courier charges apply'.

The PPG also advises displaying price indications in one currency with value added tax included (unless advertising only to other businesses). In the context of ticket PCIs, CAP advises that if each transaction is subject to an extra charge, irrespective of the number of tickets purchased, that fee (and not just its existence) should be stated clearly at key points during the purchasing process.[10] The Competition and Markets Authority has made it clear that so-called 'drip feed' advertising of prices in an online context, with an initial quoted price added to later in the purchase process, will very likely be regarded as an unfair commercial practice and hence contrary to the CPRs.

'Free'[11]

The CPRs state that a product should not be described as 'free' if a consumer has to pay anything other than the cost of taking up the offer or paying for delivery. Therefore, the CAP Code allows traders to make delivery-related charges such as postage, packaging, administration, handling and insurance, when making an offer.[12] However, the costs of these delivery-related charges must not be inflated. The PPG advises traders to make it clear to consumers at the time of making the offer, exactly what is required to obtain the offer. If there are any other significant conditions, then these should be summarised. CAP has allowed an exception to the use of 'free' when there are other costs, such as one-off or upfront costs to set up a free service. CAP provides the example of free television channels: a channel can advertise itself as free even though this is conditional on consumers being able to take advantage of the channel, such as by owning a television and holding a television licence.

The PPG states that a product must not be described as free when the trader has included additional charges that it would not usually make (such as postage or a premium-rate telephone number), a related purchase has increased in price (such as increasing the price of a shirt when offering a free tie with every shirt purchase) and when the price will be reduced to consumers who do not take the free product.

Similarly, CAP permits a free offer as part of a conditional purchase promotion, provided that the other items are available to purchase separately, any associated costs are made clear, the quality of the purchase has not been reduced and/or the price of the purchase has not been increased to recover the cost of the free item. If the free item does not comply with these rules, then marketers should describe the item as 'inclusive' rather than free.

In comparison, an individual element of a package must not be described as free if the cost of that individual element is included within the price of the package. CAP and PPG recommend that any product that is part of a package deal should not be described as free if the remainder of the package is not, in practice, available for the same price. For example, a mobile phone contract will include minutes, text messages and a data allowance, and it is not possible to claim that any of these elements are free as they are all an essential part of the package. In addition, customers cannot exercise choice over the elements in the package as they all fall under one price. Therefore, none of the elements are free.

If a free item is added to an existing package without increasing the price of the package or reducing the quality of the package, then the addition can be described as free for a limited period. CAP advises that once the item has been part of the package for a certain amount of time, consumers will treat it as an inclusive part of the package. Therefore, additions should not normally be described as free for more than six months.

Summary

As is evident from this chapter, the legislative requirement for clarity and fairness set out in the CPRs underpins the approach to PCIs from CAP/ BCAP and the PPG. It is essential that PCIs do not materially mislead consumers or be likely to do so, and this principle applies to all types of PCI. The particular rules in place surrounding certain types of PCI, such as the requirement for advertisers to provide full details of any hidden costs, all aim to ensure that consumers receive straightforward pricing information so that they have all the information needed to make an informed transactional decision. As online shopping rises in popularity, it is crucial that advertisers present their prices are clearly as possible to provide fair competition and safeguard consumers in an increasingly competitive environment.

Notes

1 Rule 3 CAP Code and BCAP Code

2 Rule 3.17 CAP Code and rule 3.18 BCAP Code

3 Fiat Group Automobiles UK Ltd, 20 August 2008

4 CAP AdviceOnline – Recommended Retail Prices: https://www.cap.org.uk/ Advice-Training-on-the-rules/Advice-Online-Database/Recommended-Retail-Prices.aspx

5 CAP AdviceOnline – Savings Claims: https://www.cap.org.uk/Advice-Training-on-the-rules/Advice-Online-Database/Savings-Claims.aspx

6 https://www.asa.org.uk/Rulings/Adjudications/2014/12/Wren-Living-Ltd/ SHP_ADJ_268611.aspx

7 CAP Advertising Guidance on Lowest Price Claims and Price Promises: https://www.cap.org.uk/~/media/Files/CAP/Help%20notes%20new/Lowest_ Price_PricePromises.ashx

8 *R (on the application of Sainsbury's Supermarkets Ltd) v. Independent Reviewer of Advertising Standards Authority Adjudications* [2014]

9 See CAP Code rules 3.17–3.22 and BCAP Code rules 3.18–3.24

10 https://www.cap.org.uk/Advice-Training-on-the-rules/Advice-Online-Database/ Ticket-Pricing.aspx

11 CAP and BCAP Advertising Guidance on Use of 'Free': https://www.cap.org. uk/~/media/Files/CAP/Help%20notes%20new/Guidance_use_of_free.ashx

12 See CAP and BCAP Codes section 3: 'Prices' – 'Free'

Sponsorship and major events

16

RAFI AZIM-KHAN

pillsbury

Introduction

Sponsorship is an increasingly popular form of 'below the line' advertising which enables sponsors to raise the profile of its corporate name or brand by association with another, like-minded party which has a package of rights (the 'rights-holder') to, for example, an event, venue, merchandise, television or radio programme, team or personality (the 'sponsorship target'). The Olympic Games, the FIFA World Cup, FA Premier League, programmes such as *The X Factor* are all examples of high-profile sponsorship targets. The London Olympic Games in 2012 attracted investment from major sponsors, which was a large contributor to ensuring the event itself was economically viable. The Olympic Games in Rio de Janeiro is equally attracting lucrative deals. Such major events, however, also raise the debate about 'ambush marketing' (see later in this chapter).

Sponsorship differs from traditional advertising; while the latter is often accused of being valuable only in itself, sponsorship targets can themselves, in some circumstances, even benefit third parties by making available to them funding, products or services that would not otherwise be obtainable had the sponsorship target not received sponsorship. Sponsorship also embraces consumers by bestowing benefits on the sponsorship target, say a football team or its stadium, with which those consumers already have an existing emotional relationship. Further, endorsement by a sponsorship target in the form of a famous personality can be as powerful as a recommendation from a loyal friend. It is this association aspect of sponsorship that makes it an attractive proposition to companies wishing to acquire kudos with an identifiable group of consumers through celebrity affiliations (for example, Rory McIlroy and Nike, David Beckham and Gillette, Emma Watson and Burberry).

The way in which a sponsor associates itself with the sponsorship target will depend upon its nature. Similarly, the way in which the rights-holder is remunerated may vary depending upon what rights to the sponsorship target it grants to the sponsor.

Olympics laws and sponsorship trends

Every four years, the Olympic Games attract a lot of media attention, not just about the athletes or the political arguments, but also concerning the sponsorship deals which are vital to the economic viability of the Games. For example, prior to the London Olympic Games in 2012, the *Daily Telegraph* reported[1] Sir Keith Mills, the vice-chairman of LOCOG (the London Organising Committee of the Olympic Games), saying that deals would cost a sponsor a minimum of £50m. That is not surprising when you consider that LOCOG committed itself to raising £2bn to help finance the event, 35 per cent of which had to come from sponsorship deals. The high price did not, however, stop key market players from wanting to be officially associated with the Olympic 2012 brand: Adidas, British Airways, BT, EDF Energy, Lloyds TSB and Deloitte all signed up, and at the time of writing, the clamour to be part of the Rio Olympic Games in 2016 is already well under way.

New bespoke legislation is sometimes needed or regarded as desirable to reassure sponsors. Protection already existed for the Olympic Games brand before the London Games through the Olympic Symbol (Protection) Act 1995, which prevents ambush marketers (ie those without a formal association with the Games wishing to create an association by other means) from using the word 'Olympic', using the Olympic rings and other Olympic symbols and through trade mark, passing off and copyright law. However, the UK government wanted to ensure the London Games had the toughest anti-ambush laws in the world so that any official sponsor was assured that its investment would not be diluted. So, in order to protect official sponsors, the London Olympic Games and Paralympic Games Act 2006 (LOA 2006) introduced tough new restrictions and protections that went far beyond the legislative restrictions other Olympic host countries had introduced previously.

As regards trends, a well-established US sponsorship trend that has become much more fashionable this side of the Atlantic in recent years is that of stadium/venue naming-rights deals. In the UK, Arsenal play at the Emirates Stadium, the Kia Oval plays host to the England cricket team, and Ed Sheeran fills the O$_2$ Arena with fans at his concerts. In the United States, it has been common for many years for significant revenues for a sports club to be generated by long-term stadia naming-rights deals. This now seems to be the way things are headed in Europe.

SOURCE: Nigel French / EMPICS Sport / Press Association

However, although sponsorship trends come and go, the key questions and the ones that any sponsor should consider before entering into a deal remain the same, namely: What am I getting for my money? What exactly are the rights being offered?

What's in it for the sponsor?

The main attraction for any sponsor is the opportunity to raise its corporate image or brand profile and enhance its reputation by association with the sponsorship target through a comparatively inexpensive form of media exposure, thereby transferring the ideals of the sponsorship target to the sponsor's corporate image or brand profile.

What's in it for the rights-holder?

From the perspective of the rights-holder, sponsorship is usually viewed as a means of raising finance to support the sponsorship target and, typically where a representative body or sports authority is concerned, may even present an opportunity for the rights-holder to bind its members to present the united front it may not otherwise have had.

The package of rights

The rights on offer will determine what the sponsor will actually get for its money. Accordingly, attention to detail is the key.

Understandably, the rights granted under the sponsorship agreement would preferably be as broad as possible from the perspective of the sponsor (so as to maximise exposure) and as narrow as possible from the perspective of the rights-holder, who will be aiming to maximise its remuneration by carving up the rights it has to offer to attract a number of different sponsors.

Accordingly, the package of rights can be a fairly complex matter; the larger the event and the greater the global dimension of its scope, the deeper the attendant complexities and potential for conflict and confusion. It is not uncommon to find different sponsors potentially stepping on each other's toes. For example, at each Olympic Games, a sponsor can find that although it has written a multi-million-pound cheque to the host city organiser to be an 'Official Partner' in return for exclusive marketing rights in respect of a specific sector, the International Olympic Committee (the IOC, responsible for organising each Olympic Games with the host city) has separately already concluded a multi-million-pound sponsorship deal on a worldwide scale with someone else operating in a similar market sector. This is because the IOC sells sponsorship packages on a global basis, whereas the rights being offered by the host country are for the host country only (something that is often missed by sponsors when signing up for national sponsorship packages).

In the case of the London 2012 Games, for example, EDF Energy had exclusive marketing rights for the utility services sector and was listed as an Official Partner; however, General Electric was an IOC sponsor and was accordingly listed by LOCOG as a Worldwide Partner for the 2012 Games.

Sole sponsorships

The level of sponsorship will vary depending on the nature of the sponsorship target. Sole sponsorships are typically offered on a small scale; for example, sponsorship of a school football team by a local newspaper would typically be offered on a sole basis, with no other sponsors involved. On the other hand, a prestigious international football tournament would undoubtedly be the subject of a multi-sponsor format, with varying levels on offer to potential sponsors. In any agreement, the class of sponsorship on offer should be clearly defined.

Multi-sponsor formats

Multi-sponsor formats require careful organisation to achieve optimum returns. Primary sponsors will have paid considerable amounts to acquire rights similar to those of a sole sponsor, and their intention will be to have their names associated with the event in question, while secondary sponsors associated with the same event will have fewer rights and pay less for the privilege. And official suppliers may be appointed merely to supply their own merchandise or services for the event. The needs, expectations and desires of each type of sponsor must be carefully managed in order to balance and safeguard the interests of all the parties involved.

By way of an example, sponsorship opportunities offered by a major sports tour event, such as the British & Irish Lions four-yearly rugby tours, may include rights to: the whole tour; individual tour dates; venue(s); teams; individuals; corporate hospitality; event programmes; security; travel arrangements; broadcast rights, etc (although broadcast rights may not fall within the control of the rights-holder). Even in relation to these opportunities, the rights-holder may decide to sub-divide the rights further. For example, the corporate hospitality aspect may be broken down into sponsorship of the cocktail reception, individual courses, after-dinner speakers and so on.

This is not to say that the sponsorship opportunities will be divided up equally, and where there are a number of sponsors, each will want details of where it falls in the hierarchy.

Exclusivity

In some cases, the sponsorship target may offer exclusive rights. These rights may apply to the whole sponsorship target or just to specific areas. (Sole sponsors always have exclusivity by definition.)

Even where the rights on offer are not exclusive, most sponsors will want some kind of assurance from the rights-holder that it will not grant any identical or similar rights to a third party in respect of the same products or services supplied by the sponsor, ie they will want exclusivity within their category.

It is important to ensure that by granting exclusive rights, the rights-holder does not breach competition laws by preventing, distorting or restricting competition in any way. Similarly, extra care must be taken to avoid accusations of abuse if either the sponsor or rights-holder enjoys a dominant position in its market.

Conditional arrangements

Where a significant level of investment by the sponsor is at stake, the sponsor may make certain elements of the sponsorship remuneration dependent upon the achievement of specified goals, or the substantiation of claims made by the rights-holder.

For example, the sponsor may want an indication of the minimum expected numbers of visitors to a website, attendees at an event or viewers of a television programme. Perhaps it wants a guarantee of publicity across certain targeted newspapers or specified radio channels. It may want a firm assurance that nominated celebrities will turn up at an event or that the venue itself is available. Similarly, where the sponsor's products are a key element of the arrangement, the sponsor will be looking for guarantees relating to the placement of its products or other indicators of its brand.

If any of these factors are crucial to the sponsor, as opposed to just being on its wishlist, they should be made clear in the sponsorship agreement, which should contain provisions that cater for the withholding of funds, repayment of all or part of the sponsorship fees or some other form of appropriate compensation for the sponsor.

The sponsorship agreement

Whether you are a sponsor or a rights-holder, it is important to enter into a written agreement that clearly sets out the nature of the relationship and the rights and obligations of each party, whatever type of sponsorship target is in question. A sponsorship agreement is equally important whether you are sponsoring the Olympics, a television programme or a local event. There is a checklist of important issues which should be considered in any agreement at the end of this chapter.

Common requirements

Parties to a sponsorship agreement are likely to have certain requirements in common. For example, each party will typically want the right to use the other party's logo and brand names, in conjunction with its own if appropriate, for promotional and publicity purposes.

Bearing in mind the close associations that are likely to be made between sponsor and rights-holder, it is not unusual to require guarantees and undertakings relating to each party's reputation and protection of its image.

Assurances likely to be sought by sponsor

As well as requiring the rights to use the logo and marks of the rights-holder, where appropriate, a sponsor will wish to ensure that it maintains control over the use of its own logo and marks, eg relating to size, colour, location and the surroundings in which they are to be delivered etc. If it is a primary sponsor, it will certainly want the right to use any event logo, and will want to ensure that no other rights are granted which may undermine its status. Almost all sponsors will wish to be able to use any promotional materials generated by the sponsorship opportunity, eg photographs and other publicity materials and perhaps even any data collected, such as the names and addresses of participants, in which case particular regard should be had to data protection law (see Chapter 7).

One of the bonuses of the appointment may entitle a sponsor to presentation rights, eg at sporting events, together with complimentary tickets or free products, entitlement to all of which should be set out in the sponsorship agreement for clarity.

Depending on the sponsorship target, the sponsor may wish to be granted an option to sponsor further rights relating to the subject of the agreement, eg for its own post-event marketing and advertising purposes, films, videos etc.

Assurances likely to be sought by the rights-holder

Clearly, the rights-owner will only grant rights to those it perceives to be reputable sponsors. Nonetheless, it should still reserve the right to vet and, if necessary, prevent further usage of any sponsorship materials supplied by the sponsor.

Similarly, where the rights-owner is subject to certain rules and regulations, eg industry standards, it must obtain assurances from the sponsor that it will comply with them.

Remuneration

While a prime objective of the rights-holder will be to raise finance, the manner in which it is remunerated will largely depend on the nature of the rights granted.

In relation to one-off events, fixed amounts are commonly payable (up front or in arrears), while tours or rolling events may be payable in instalments or on a periodic basis. Going one stage further, certain arrangements may make remuneration conditional on the rights-holder achieving certain specified targets, for example, in the event that it secures personal appearances by nominated celebrities or gains publicity for the sponsorship target in the national press or on television, etc.

The sponsor's products or services may also be offered as well as, or in lieu of, payment.

Finally, where the rights-holder's trade marks or other intellectual property rights are used, eg in relation to merchandising deals, it may also be entitled to royalty payments.

Intellectual property rights

As previously discussed, while each party will normally reserve to itself its own intellectual property rights, granting limited rights of use to the other party, ownership and rights of use of any intellectual property rights generated as a result of the sponsorship deal should be addressed in the sponsorship agreement. Accordingly, ownership and use of the following intellectual property should be dealt with either within the agreement or under a separate licence:

- background intellectual property;
- intellectual property created or commissioned by one party to the agreement during the period of the agreement; and
- intellectual property created jointly by the parties during the period of the agreement.

Of course, the final outcome will largely depend on the negotiating strengths of the parties. This aspect will be particularly important where the intellectual property is created outside the UK, where the parties cannot rely on certain implied terms of ownership and where it is likely that such intellectual property will still be used after the event itself has come to an end.

Another aspect to consider is whether or not any copyright work to be used is still subject to the moral rights of the author (see Chapter 1 on copyright).

If so – and this may be the case where an individual has been commissioned to create a work – a moral rights waiver should be obtained by the commissioning party and covered by the appropriate warranties and indemnities in the sponsorship agreement.

If the sponsorship target is to have its own logo or mark or if a composite logo, made up of both the sponsor's mark and the rights-holder's mark, is to be created, the parties should ensure they take steps to register such logo or mark to ensure they are protected, particularly where merchandising is involved. Similarly, they should ensure adequate and appropriate copyright and trade mark notices are applied where such logos and marks are used.

Reliance on third parties

One aspect of sponsorship which is often overlooked is the necessary co-operation of third parties. Accordingly, a sponsor needs to obtain an assurance from the rights-holder that it has the capacity to grant the rights and bind any relevant third parties to the terms of the sponsorship agreement, particularly when they are indispensable.

The ability to bind third parties is particularly important when the rights-holder represents a group or association, eg a sporting body. While it may be an easy task to clarify whether or not that sporting body's rules of association confirm its ability to bind its members, ie the teams, its ability to bind individuals within those teams is less likely and will require further investigation. If necessary, the sponsor should insist upon proof of any existing contractual arrangements or that secondary contracts with the third parties are entered into.

A prime example of where things can go wrong was demonstrated in the Aprilia[2] case. A sponsor who had relied on the Spice Girls staying together during a sponsorship arrangement to promote a range of scooters was understandably upset when Geri Halliwell announced her decision to leave the group. In this particular case, the sponsor was eventually entitled to recover all of its losses on the basis of misrepresentation. However, had Aprilia had the foresight to make its sponsorship conditional upon maintenance of the line-up of the group for the duration of the promotion, the costly litigation might have been avoided.

It would also be prudent to make checks with any association to which the rights-holder belongs to ensure it is not going to be subject to other sponsorship arrangements or to hidden restrictions.

Ambush marketing

As discussed briefly above, ambush marketing refers to a company's attempt to capitalise on the goodwill, reputation and popularity of a particular event by creating an association with it but without the authorisation or consent of the necessary parties. Some popular indirect ambush techniques include buying commercial time prior to, and during, event broadcasts, sponsoring the broadcasts of events rather than directly sponsoring the event, sponsoring individual teams and athletes and using sporting events tickets in consumer giveaways, sweepstakes or contests. Purely defined, ambush marketing does not involve counterfeiting or the illegal use of trade marks, trade names, or symbols. Companies simply develop a creative advertising campaign around the event, never use the event logo, trade mark or trade name, and capitalise by association with the event without paying for 'Official Sponsor' status. When effectively employed, ambush marketing is not illegal and is therefore difficult for legitimate sponsors and event-holders to combat.

Ambush marketing may take the form of: unauthorised merchandising; blanket advertising in the vicinity of the event; broadcast sponsorship (which will probably be entirely separate from the event sponsorship); independent sponsorship deals with teams and team members; or even inter-ference with a broadcast such that images in and around the sponsorship target are altered to impose alternative brands and logos.

A classic example of ambush marketing took place at the 1996 Atlanta Olympic Games, where Linford Christie appeared wearing blue contact lenses with a white Puma logo in the centre, upsetting the official sponsor, Reebok. The photo of Christie with his startling, branded eyes appeared on the front pages of newspapers and in lead television news items all over the world, gaining Puma huge publicity.

More recently, the London 2012 Games were a hotbed for ambush marketing despite the draconian LOA 2006. Virgin Media was viewed by some to have 'ambushed' official sponsor BT, by using Usain Bolt to advertise its broadband services. Electronics company Beats Electronics (now owned by Apple) also got in on the act by giving free, Union flag-branded headphones to members of Team GB who wore them poolside and trackside and happily tweeted their appreciation. This gave substantial publicity without official sponsorship involvement.

Some countries – including the UK and its LOA 2006 – have stepped in and tried to deal with the problem through legislation. South African law, in particular, has gone a long way to crack down on ambush marketing,

Paddy Power advert, courtesy of Lucky Generals/Paddy Power

making it a criminal offence if carried out at certain events. This came into play as far back as 2002 at the cricket World Cup in South Africa, where advertising for anybody other than sponsors was prohibited by legislation not just in the arenas (as is usually the case), but also anywhere within a specific radius around the arenas.

A few years ago, New Zealand introduced the Major Events Management Act 2007 (MEMA), which created strict association right restrictions to help protect any major event organiser holding an event in New Zealand.

However, the concern is that major event-holders now have too much power, resulting in a lack of fair competition for local business and increased sponsorship fees because of the total monopoly such event-holders now have. This was one of the criticisms levelled at LOCOG with regard to the LOA 2006.

The Rio Olympics 2016 has produced its own suite of rules (which have a specific section on ambush marketing), made specifically for the Games.

Care should certainly be taken and specialist advice sought before running campaigns in any way connected with the Olympics and/or the sports represented.

Conflicting sponsorship rights

If an advertiser sponsors an individual player, it should ensure that it is fully aware of what rights it has under the sponsorship agreement. While an advertiser may, for example, sponsor Wayne Rooney, this does not necessarily carry with it the right to refer to or to portray the entire England team in an advertisement nor, necessarily, to portray the England team logo. It will almost certainly not entitle use of the logo for a major international event such as the World Cup.

There is another potentially difficult issue for international sporting events: conflicting rights of the official sponsors with the sponsors of individual players. If the rights-holder enforces a ban on any advertising within the arenas, other than that by official sponsors, this will be an issue for individual players if they want to wear, say, baseball caps with the logos of their individual sponsors. Technically, to do so would breach the rights-holder's regulations. What a rights-holder would do in these circumstances is difficult to predict, but it may, for example, prevent the individual player from wearing any item with the conflicting individual sponsor's logo during pre- or post-match interviews or even result in the exclusion of the individual from the event.

Regulatory codes of practice

There are a number of regulatory codes of practice that may apply to parties to a sponsorship agreement.

Non-broadcast media (including the internet)

The British Code of Advertising, Sales Promotion and Direct Marketing (CAP Code) applies to non-broadcast advertising in the UK. The CAP Code is administered and adjudicated by the Advertising Standards Authority (ASA) and requires all advertisements to be 'legal, decent, honest and truthful'. Although the CAP Code does not apply to sponsorship itself, it does apply to marketing communications that refer to sponsorship. It also applies, of course, to ambush marketing communications, and ambush marketers should pay particular care to ensure that their ads do not mislead and suggest an association with an event where none exists.

Broadcast media

The UK Code of Broadcast Advertising (BCAP Code) applies to all ads and programme sponsorship credits on radio and television services licensed by Ofcom. Ofcom requires that the content of programme sponsorship credits complies with the BCAP Code, although the ASA refers complaints about those to Ofcom.

In addition, the Ofcom Broadcasting Code (Ofcom Code) contains the regulations for sponsorship of broadcast programmes and sets out a number of key principles, including that:

- news and current affairs programmes must not be sponsored;

- programming (including a channel) may not be sponsored by any sponsor that is prohibited from advertising on television; and

- a sponsor must not influence the content and/or scheduling of a channel or its programming in such a way as to impair the responsibility and editorial independence of the broadcaster.

Further, it specifically addresses issues such as the categories of products which are prohibited from being placed in a broadcast (eg cigarettes and tobacco products, prescription-only medicines, alcoholic drinks etc) and the prominence with which sponsors may place advertising both during and around their sponsored programmes.

While the non-commercial section of the BBC is prohibited from allowing advertising or sponsorship of its broadcast programmes, the commercial sections of the BBC will sometimes engage in marketing initiatives around their products and services with other commercial parties, for example the sponsorship of BBC events and joint promotions, in which case advertisers should refer to the BBC's Producers' Guidelines.

These Guidelines – a code of ethics for BBC programme makers covering editorial policy in relation to commercially funded BBC channels – include the requirement that sponsorship should only be allowed for holding the event; no sponsorship money may go into any production budget or be used for any broadcasting cost.

Sponsorship agreement checklist

Parties

Sponsor
Rights-holder

Conditional arrangements

Sponsorship to be conditional upon:

- attendance by designated celebrities;
- availability of venue;
- use of office facilities;
- number of attendees/website hits etc;
- appointment to management board; and
- television coverage, celebrity endorsement etc.

Sponsor's rights

Set out in schedule, eg:

- approval/control of staging of event;
- entitlement to use sponsor's name in sponsorship target etc;
- entitlement to use rights-holder's name and logo in connection with event;
- whether exclusive or non-exclusive;
- merchandising rights;
- any associated advertising rights or other rights of publicity (if necessary, deal with sponsor's right to lay cable for its own filming purposes etc);
- permitted designations, eg title sponsor or official supplier;
- allocation of free tickets, availability of hospitality areas etc;
- restrict appointment of other sponsors without consent or limit to non-competitors; and
- rights should comply with any applicable regulatory code.

▶

Broadcast agreements

- Live for-free terrestrial, or pay-per-view, satellite, cable etc;
- governing body should try to control copyright in broadcast by negotiating for a full assignment to it with an exclusive licence of copyright back to broadcaster; and
- broadcast sponsorship should be dealt with, as sponsor will not want a competitor involved.

Sponsor's obligations

Sponsor must:

- comply with confidentiality requirements;
- pay the sponsorship money;
- pay any prize monies etc;
- co-operate with rights-holder regarding media and publicity etc;
- supply any products or services;
- not bring rights-holder into disrepute;
- comply with regulatory codes etc; and
- all sponsorship materials to be approved by rights-holder.

Rights-holder's obligations

Rights-holder must:

- register event if necessary;
- keep to the agreed format;
- promote and publicise event;
- provide and circulate regular press releases with accreditation of sponsor;
- credit sponsor;
- ensure all persons concerned attend functions etc;
- provide press conferences;
- provide all necessary facilities etc (specify, eg insurance, referees, event venue etc);
- not bring sponsor into disrepute;
- use sponsor's products;

- indemnity for breach of warranty;
- limit advertising space around event to prevent ambush marketing;
- where appropriate, permit all advertising to be approved by sponsor;
- comply with regulatory codes etc; and
- achieve any specified target, eg celebrity endorsement.

Remuneration

Consider:

- fixed fee payable in advance/arrears;
- instalments;
- periodic payments;
- conditional payments;
- non-monetary payments;
- royalties;
- conditional fees; and
- compensation for the sponsor in the event of non-achievement of crucial targets, the subject of conditional fees.

Duration

- Specify, and allow 'run-on' time if linked to specific number of events which may overshoot;
- allow the rights-holder to appoint a new sponsor in the event of termination; and
- consider granting the sponsor an option to renew.

Intellectual property rights

Deal with:

- ownership of, and rights to use: (i) background IP; (ii) IP generated by either party under the sponsorship agreement; and (iii) IP developed by the parties jointly;
- sub-licensing;
- goodwill;
- moral rights;

- include an obligation to register any event logo;
- deal with rights to use event logo/other joint IP post-termination;
- provide indemnities and warranties; and
- if necessary, set any licences out in separate agreements, particularly if they are to survive termination of the sponsorship agreement.

Warranties

Rights-holder to warrant that:

- it can bind clubs, team members etc;
- material agreements with venues, individuals etc have been concluded;
- it owns, or has the right to use the rights;
- it has all necessary insurances;
- there are no conflicting arrangements with the sponsor's competitors; and
- it is not itself subject to any commercial arrangements likely to conflict with the spirit of the agreement.

Termination

- Upon notice;
- material breach (specify what constitutes material breach throughout agreement);
- insolvency;
- cancellation;
- if either party ceases to exist; or
- loss of a venue, endorsement or celebrity.

Consequences of termination

- Upon termination:
  - rights-holder reserves right to appoint another sponsor;
  - sponsor to cease associating itself with the event; and
  - sponsor to remove any facilities, hoardings etc from the venue within a reasonable time.

Additionally, upon early termination:

- repayment of sponsorship fees.

Notes

1 25 January 2006
2 *Spice Girls Limited* v. *Aprilia World Service BV* [2002] EWCA Civ 15

Usage FAQs 17

BRINSLEY DRESDEN

 **LEWIS SILKIN**

Introduction

This chapter will deal with issues relating to the use of common, everyday items in advertisements. Some of these require consent, while others do not; this chapter seeks to help agencies decide when to seek permission and from whom. It is important to note that this chapter covers law and regulation in England and Wales. The legal and regulatory position may be different in other jurisdictions and you may need to obtain foreign legal advice if you are using everyday items from other jurisdictions, especially if your advertising will be targeted and/or viewable in such jurisdictions.

Badges

If a badge is to appear reasonably prominently in an advertisement, for instance if it is to be worn by an actor so as to be clearly visible, then permissions may be required in respect of any image or design that appears on the badge. The High Court case of *The Flashing Badges Company Limited* v. *Brian Groves*[1] has confirmed that if the design on a badge can exist independently of the badge, then it will be deemed surface decoration and an artistic work. It may, therefore, be protected by copyright and any use may require the consent of the copyright owner.

However, if the badge design is integral to the configuration of the badge and cannot be used independently, then it will be a design work and any use through copying will fall within the defence in section 51 of the Copyright

Design and Patents Act 1988 and will not usually need to be cleared with the owner of the design right.

Even if the image on the badge does have copyright protection, it may be possible to argue that its inclusion in an advertisement is merely 'incidental', or insufficiently substantial to infringe. This may be of assistance where the inclusion of the badge is very fleeting or partial and clearly not central to the commercial purpose of the advertisement. However, the courts seem less inclined to treat the inclusion of copyright works in an advertisement as incidental or insubstantial (given that most advertisements are usually very carefully planned and staged) when compared with, for example, footage shot live for a documentary or news report. If in doubt, the safest option would be to avoid the inclusion, even quite fleetingly, of a badge with distinctive surface decoration, or alternatively, to obtain permission from the relevant copyright owner.

Care should also be taken to check that any image on a badge is not a registered trade mark. If it is, clearance from the trade mark owner is advisable to avoid any suggestion that the owner is endorsing or somehow connected with the advertised product or service.

Banknotes

Courtesy of the Bank of England

The Bank of England holds the copyright to British banknotes. Section 18(1) of the Forgery and Counterfeiting Act 1981 provides that permission must be obtained from the Bank of England before an image of a British banknote may be legally reproduced. Prior written consent is required whether the front or back of the banknote is reproduced, whether or not the note is the same scale and whether the note is still legal tender or not, and for all possible reproductions, including modified or distorted versions. Although it does not allow banknote reproductions on articles for sale, such as T-shirts, the Bank will clear the use of banknotes in advertisements subject to certain conditions which it has published.

The following pre-conditions must be met before permission will be granted. For physical reproductions or reproducing the images of banknotes in broadcast, video (including online) and cinema advertisements, conditions 1, 2, 3, 4 and at least one of the options in condition 5 must be satisfied. For all other reproductions, including print and static online ads, conditions 3, 4 and 6 must be satisfied:

1 Reproductions must be one-sided, ie nothing should appear on the reverse which might give the impression that it is a genuine banknote. (However, in TV, video and film ads, genuine banknotes can usually be used – contact the Bank of England to confirm that this is the case in your particular circumstances.)

2 Reproductions (partial and entire) must differ in size from actual banknotes. If smaller, they must be at most two-thirds as long *and* at most two-thirds as wide. If larger, they must be at least one-and-a-half times as long *and* at least one-and-a-half times as wide.

3 Reproductions may not appear in an offensive context (for example, in conjunction with violence or pornography).

4 The Queen's image should not be distorted (other than by enlargement, reduction or slant).

5 At least one of the following conditions must also be met:

    a The reproduction is shown on the slant, not flat to camera. In this case the distortion must be such that right angles are reduced to angles of 70° or less, or increased to angles of 110° or more; or

    b the reproduction is printed on a material clearly different and distinguishable from paper or paper-like material; or

    c the colours on the reproduction differ distinctly from the main colours on any of the current series of Bank of England banknotes; or

d in the case of a partial reproduction of a banknote, at most 50% of the total surface area of one side of the original banknote may be reproduced; or

e if the reproduction is flat to camera it must be overprinted with the word 'SPECIMEN' twice in accordance with Condition 6.

6 The banknotes must also include the word SPECIMEN twice in solid black capital letters, once from the bottom-left corner to the top-centre and again from the bottom-centre to the top-right corner of the banknote. The word SPECIMEN must be not less than one-third of the length of the reproduction in length, and not less than one-eighth of the height of the reproduction in height. This applies whether the entire banknote is reproduced or just part.

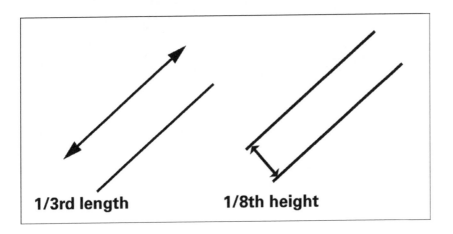

1/3rd length   **1/8th height**

In order to seek permission to reproduce banknotes, advertisers should contact the Notes Reproduction Officer of the Bank of England (e-mail: banknote.reproductions@bankofengland.co.uk), or visit the Bank of England's website and submit the online Banknote Reproductions Application form (see: http://www.bankofengland.co.uk/banknotes/Documents/banknote_repro_app_form.pdf). The site indicates that a response can usually be expected within five working days.

(See also the entries in this chapter on Coins; Postage stamps; and Royalty and the Crown.)

Buildings (exteriors and interiors) and sculptures

Although buildings are protected as copyright works (assuming that the copyright has not expired), UK copyright legislation provides a specific exemption allowing buildings to be reproduced in drawings, photographs, films and broadcasts without the permission of the copyright owner,[2] provided that they are permanently situated in a public place or in premises open to the public.

The same section also permits drawing, painting, photographing or filming sculptures and works of artistic craftsmanship, such as furniture and ironwork, in similar circumstances. Thus, merely using the outside of a building in the UK as the backdrop for an advertisement will not in itself usually raise any copyright issues. In the case of sculptures and works of artistic craftsmanship, however, there could still be a claim for passing off by the creator of the work, particularly if they have a reputation that is associated with a particular work or style of work. A similar risk applies in respect of buildings if they are sponsored or otherwise associated with a particular brand. As noted below in this section regarding rule 6.1 of the CAP Code, there is also a danger of complaint under the CAP Codes if you feature a private building prominently in an advertisement.

If agencies are shooting in the interior of a building, however, it is important to note that the exemption does not apply to any photographs, paintings or other graphic works situated within the building, so permission from the relevant copyright owner would usually be required to feature these. The same would be true if the exterior of the building had any such items displayed on it. Agencies should avoid showing any brand logos on buildings.

In some circumstances, it is possible to argue that the inclusion of copyright works in the background of advertisements is merely incidental, or insufficiently substantial to infringe, although this is rare in an advertising context (given that most advertisements are usually very carefully planned and staged). This defence may be of assistance where the inclusion of copyright works is very fleeting or partial and clearly not central to the commercial purpose of the advertisement. If in doubt, the safest option would be to avoid the inclusion of any such works, or to obtain permissions from the copyright owners of those works that are included.

It is also common for the owners of buildings to impose specific contractual conditions on filming, particularly of interior shots. If it is necessary to make arrangements with the owners for access, then it is likely that accepting such contractual terms will be unavoidable, and these will take precedence over any copyright exceptions. From the advertiser's point of view, it therefore makes sense to ensure that such an agreement includes a full release for the use of the location. Sports stadia frequently impose restrictions on commercial filming inside the stadia.

Rule 6.1 of the CAP Code contains a provision which urges advertisers to obtain written permission before 'referring to or portraying a member of the public or his or her identifiable possessions'; such possessions can include both buildings and land provided that the owner can be identified from them. However, there is an exception for the use of 'a crowd scene or a general public location', while for private locations it is usually possible to manipulate any images of buildings or land to render them sufficiently unidentifiable.

Cars (motor vehicles)

There are specific rules set out in the CAP and BCAP Codes for the advertising of motor vehicles and electric vehicles with which car retailers need to comply. This section, however, discusses the issues facing other advertisers who wish to feature cars or other motor vehicles in their advertisements. (Chapter 5 contains some information on car emissions and fuel consumption requirements.)

There are a number of potential issues that could arise when the images or brands of motor vehicles are used (either deliberately or incidentally) in advertisements.

Copyright

While mass-produced articles such as cars do not usually attract copyright in terms of their three-dimensional shape and configuration, hand-built or customised cars might be protected as 'works of artistic craftsmanship'. Some designer marques, such as Lamborghini, may also argue that their iconic and limited-production designs are 'artistic works' and therefore covered by copyright protection. There is no case law on such claims, but agencies should seek permission before using customised cars or designer marques.

There is also the potential for copyright to protect aspects of 'surface decoration' applied to mass-produced cars, including some logos. If a motor vehicle has particular graphics or logos incorporated into its paintwork which will be visible in the advertisement, then permission should usually be sought for its use or the shot should be taken so that the graphics or logos are obscured. The manufacturers' badges or logos usually appear at various places on a car, on the bonnet, steering wheel and hub of the car's wheels. (While in the UK it may be an acceptable option to remove or blur the logos or badges, this debranding of goods may constitute trade mark infringement in other countries where the ad may be viewed, so we recommend obtaining legal advice before doing this. See also Chapter 1 on copyright.)

Trade marks

The manufacturer's name and logo, and the name of the model of the vehicle used, are almost certain to be registered trade marks. In many cases, provided that undue prominence is not given to the vehicle's trade marks, it will be clear that the vehicle's brands and trade marks are not being used as trade marks for the advertised product – they are included simply because they are part of the vehicle – and thus the trade mark is not infringed. If the advertisement is comparing different makes of car, then the rules of comparative advertising will apply (see Chapter 10).

The owners of car brands may feel aggrieved if their brand is being associated with the product or service in the advertisement but their permission has not been sought. The owners of very well-known brands may object to the use of their trade marks if they can show that such use takes unfair advantage of, or is detrimental to, the distinctive character of their mark. (This would be most likely to be the case if the advert showed the car in a negative light, or implied that the brand-owner endorsed the advertised product.) While it is not always clear-cut whether the use of trade marks in such circumstances is infringing, the safest option would always be to avoid the marks/logos appearing in the advertisements. However, as noted in the copyright section above, in some countries outside the UK, removing or blurring the logos or badges on products may in itself constitute trade mark infringement, so local legal advice should be obtained before the ad is viewable in such countries. (See also Chapter 2 on trade marks.)

Design rights

There are a variety of design rights that attach to the external shape and appearance of motor vehicles. The law is not fully tested in this field, but it seems that the rights are only infringed when the design is incorporated in, or applied to, another traded product (so merely photographing, filming or broadcasting images of the vehicle is unlikely to infringe design rights). If a three-dimensional model of a car is made, then an infringement of the design rights in the original design will occur unless permission is obtained. (See also Chapter 3 on design rights.)

Passing off

Even if the registered trade mark is not visible in the advertisement, if the motor vehicle is clearly recognisable as being of a particular make then passing off may be an issue. To have the advert withdrawn or to claim damages, however, the car manufacturer would have to show that its goodwill or reputation was being damaged by the advertisement through customers becoming confused, for example, into thinking that there was some connection between the vehicle manufacturer and the advertised product. It is highly unlikely that this would be the case if the car was only briefly and incidentally part of the background of the advertisement, and passing off is rarely an issue for agencies in such circumstances. (See also Chapter 4 on passing off.)

Regulatory considerations

Rule 3.42 of both the CAP and BCAP Codes states that 'Advertisements must not discredit or denigrate another product, advertiser or advertisement or a trade mark, trade name or other distinguishing mark.' It is, therefore, essential that advertisements featuring identifiable cars or other motor vehicles do not show them in a denigratory light. This will include featuring, for example, crashed cars or broken-down cars. It is common practice, therefore, in such cases to ensure that the car used is not identifiable, and in many cases this may require the creation of a generic car, especially for television commercials.

Coats of arms

Coats of arms in England and Wales derive from the Crown, but control is delegated to the Kings of Arms, who are members of the Royal Household and regulate the devising of new arms by ensuring that each design is unique.

Coats of arms are the property of the person or family to whom the arms were granted by the Crown. They are governed by the Law of Arms which is not part of the common law, and so the normal courts do not generally regard coats of arms as either property or as being defensible by legal action. Instead, the Court of Chivalry has exclusive jurisdiction over the Law of Arms. It does not sit very often, the last time apparently being in 1954 to hear the case of *Manchester Corporation* v. *Manchester Palace of Varieties* in which a theatre was successfully sued for using the arms of the Corporation without permission. It does still have jurisdiction, although it is doubtful now whether the court is likely to sit again.

None of which is to suggest that coats of arms can be used with impunity. Where possible, they should be cleared with the rights owner, not least because other intellectual property rights could be infringed in unauthorised use, such as copyright (particularly if the coat of arms is relatively modern) or passing off. Defamation could be an issue too. It would also be wise to check whether any coats of arms that you intend to use have been registered as trade marks.

(See also the entry in this chapter on Royalty and the Crown.)

Coins

Courtesy of The Royal Mint

The UK coinage is technically protected by Crown copyright, but the Crown has delegated the administration of such permissions to the Royal Mint, and the Royal Mint has waived its right to charge a royalty fee for the use of coin images or designs in flat form, provided that the image or design does not form an integral part of a commercial product (for example, a coin reproduced on a T-shirt).

Agencies should follow the provisions below when using coins in advertisements:

- The reproduction of the coin should be reproduced in a faithful likeness and shown in good taste (in respect of which the Royal Mint relies upon the good sense of the advertisers and agencies).

- Parts of the designs used on the coinage should not be reutilised out of context. However, showing part of a coin will usually be acceptable, provided it is clearly recognisable as part of a coin and good taste is used.

- The 'Heads' (Queen's effigy) side of a coin, or the 'Tails' side if it shows the Royal Arms, must also be a faithful reproduction of actual currency in circulation, and must be shown unaltered.

- Technically, permission to use the Queen's effigy requires permission of the Lord Chamberlain (see Royalty and the Crown), so agencies are advised to use the Tails side when featuring coins. However, it is generally acceptable to feature both Heads and Tails when featuring a pile of coins.

It is, however, an offence under Section 19 of the Forgery and Counterfeiting Act 1981 to make a coin that resembles a UK coin in shape, size and substance, in connection with a scheme intended to promote the sale of any product or the supply of any service, unless the Treasury has previously consented in writing to such sale or supply.

(See also the sections in this chapter on Banknotes; Postage stamps; and Royalty and the Crown.)

Crowds/passers-by

(This section assumes that the passers-by or members of the crowd included are not people with a public reputation. Chapter 8 considers the use of celebrities in advertising.)

The BCAP Code (which applies to broadcast media) provides that 'with limited exceptions, living people must not be featured, caricatured or referred to in advertisements without their permission'. Thus the consent of all living individuals, not just celebrities, is normally required and best practice would be to obtain it by way of a signed release. One of the specific exceptions to this general rule under the BCAP Code, however, is for 'brief and incidental appearances, such as crowd scenes'. The inclusion of a passer-by who is caught on camera only briefly and incidentally would probably also benefit from this exception.

The CAP Code (which applies to all non-broadcast media, including the internet) has a slightly less stringent approach. It states that: 'Marketers are urged to obtain written permission before referring to or portraying a member of the public or his or her identifiable possessions... [or] implying any personal approval of the advertised product.' However, again an exception is made: 'the use of a crowd scene or a general public location may be acceptable without permission'. The CAP Code rules are, then, reasonably lenient in respect of crowd scenes or passers-by and the use of individuals without their consent.

There are also some more general legal rules to bear in mind. In particular, data protection and rights of privacy under the Human Rights Act may arise when individuals who are identifiable from a photo or footage are included without their consent, even if purely incidental to the message of the advertisement. The case law regarding data protection and privacy protection in such circumstances is still not fully developed, particularly in the advertising context, but the overall trend in recent years has been towards increasing court recognition for the rights of private individuals to have their private life respected. Although currently the damages awarded in such cases are minimal, generally speaking, and in accordance with the Information Commissioner's Office's Technical Guidance, the taking of a photograph of an individual in a public place in the UK is not an actionable breach under the Data Protection Act.

If an advertisement has to be shot in a place open to the public, it is therefore advisable to use signs to warn people away if they do not wish to be caught on camera. Anyone who does appear sufficiently prominently to be identifiable should be asked for their written consent, or agencies should edit the image(s) in order to remove the relevant individual or render them unidentifiable.

Designer clothes/jewellery

Mass-market clothing and jewellery do not usually raise copyright issues when used in photographs, films or broadcasts (although care should be taken if any trade mark is visible or a distinctive product 'get-up' is clearly recognisable).

Greater caution is needed with hand-made 'haute couture' clothes or designer jewellery, particularly if they are one-off items. These are likely to be treated as 'works of artistic craftsmanship' and so qualify for copyright protection.

It may be possible to argue that the inclusion of clothes and jewellery in photographs, films or broadcasts is merely incidental, or insufficiently substantial to infringe. This may be of assistance where the inclusion of copyright works is very fleeting or partial, and clearly not central to the commercial purpose of the advertisement. However, the case law is not clear-cut in this area, and the courts may be less inclined to treat the inclusion of copyright works in an advertisement as incidental or insubstantial (given that most advertisements are usually very carefully planned and staged). The safest option would be to obtain permissions from the copyright owners of any designer clothing or jewellery that is to be included.

If the clothes and/or jewellery are protected as works of artistic craftsmanship, then their creator will also have moral rights to be identified as such (if this right has been asserted) and to object to any derogatory treatment. Derogatory treatment includes distortion or mutilation of the work, or other treatment that is 'prejudicial to the honour or reputation of the author'. In theory, this could give the designer grounds to prevent an advertisement being shown if his or her design is being associated with products or services that might be detrimental to his or her reputation.

The more prominent the use of the clothes or jewellery, and the more recognisable their brand or origin, the more likely it is that the relevant designers would be aggrieved by any use in an advertisement without permission (particularly if they feel that being associated with the advertiser may be damaging to their brand's reputation, or implies an endorsement of the advertised product). To avoid any dispute arising, it would therefore be prudent to obtain a written release from the relevant designer in such circumstances.

Fictitious names and testimonials

It is common practice to make up a fictitious name for use in an advertisement (whether in respect of an individual or a business) in order to lend a greater air of reality to the content. Although this might seem to avoid the numerous pitfalls associated with using the names of real businesses or people (in particular celebrities: see Chapter 8), simply making up a name is not necessarily the panacea that one might think.

For example, if the name turns out to be that of a real person or business and it is used in a defamatory context (ie it unjustifiably damages the reputation of the person or business: see Chapter 11), then the advertiser may be liable for defamation even though it had no intention of referring to the real person or business in question. Equally, if the name chosen is that of a real individual or business and they have a registered trade mark or significant goodwill in the name, then the lack of intention on the part of the advertiser will not necessarily prevent legal action being taken for trade mark infringement (see Chapter 2) or passing off (see Chapter 4). In certain jurisdictions, there may be other rights which may be infringed by using a fictitious name. For example, in Germany, the use of a non-generic name without any further accompanying identifying information may infringe name rights which exist under the German Civil Code.

It is therefore prudent when using made-up names to conduct a trade mark search and potentially also to search Companies House or directories for relevant business names or individuals' names, and obtain local legal advice in the geographical territories at which the advertisement is aimed.

Advertisers may also be tempted to make up endorsements or testimonials for their products or services, and to associate these with fictitious names in order to make the endorsements seem more realistic. This practice is specifically addressed by the CAP Code, which makes it clear in rule 3.45 that if fictitious testimonials are used, they must be obviously fictitious, ie they should not be presented as if they are the genuine views of real people. Beware also of associating a fictitious testimonial with the image of a real person – in 2006, the ASA held a marketing brochure misleading when a woman complained about her photo being featured alongside a fictional testimonial. Likewise, in the BCAP Code, rule 3.45 provides that: 'Testimonials or endorsements used in advertising must be genuine, unless they are obviously fictitious [...] Claims that are likely to be interpreted as factual and appear in advertisements must not mislead or be likely to mislead.' Clearcast guidance indicates that 'where characters in a playlet are clearly expressing, in dramatised form, the claims of the advertiser, they are not regarded as testimonials'. But again it will be important that viewers are not left with the impression that the views expressed are those of real people.

If the advertiser does not make up a fictitious name, but uses the name of a fictitious character already made popular by others (for example, a character from a book, film or TV programme), then permission will almost certainly be necessary. There is usually no copyright in a mere name, but many popular characters are protected by trade marks in order to optimise income from merchandising opportunities. Even if not registered as a trade mark, an action in passing off may arise if the public perceive there to be an endorsement by the creators of a character where there is none and a licence has not been granted.

Flags

Flags of state and state emblems are generally free from copyright, not least because of their age. Care should be taken over any flag of modern design, however, in case copyright still subsists and is enforceable by the designer or commissioner of the flag's design.

In addition, flags cannot be registered as a trade mark by virtue of Article 6 of the Paris Convention for the Protection of Industrial Property of 1883, which states that any flag or emblem that has been communicated to the international bureau of the World Intellectual Property Organisation by any state party to the Paris Convention is prohibited from registration as a trade mark in any other state that is party to the Convention.

However, great care should be taken before using foreign national flags in advertisements and marketing materials if the materials are to be widely disseminated around the globe (for example on the internet). Many countries have rules and regulations specifying how their national flag should be used in order to protect its honour and reputation. In some countries these rules include a blanket ban upon the use of the national flag in advertisements or other commercial contexts (for example the United States of America and the Philippines).

The use of the UK's Union Flag and the national flags of England, Scotland and Wales is unregulated and they can be used freely, although obviously they should not be used in a manner that is likely to cause serious or widespread offence.

Care should also be taken not to use flags in a misleading way on marketing materials and packaging for food and other products which are subject to country-of-origin rules.

The emblem of the European Union flag of 12 yellow stars against a blue background (which it shares with the Council of Europe, an entirely separate institution) may be used without permission provided that the use does not suggest any form of association with or endorsement by either the EU or the Council and provided that the use is not made in connection with any objective or activity that is incompatible with the aims and principles of either institution or is otherwise unlawful.

Control of use of the flag is shared between the European Commission (on behalf of the EU) and the Council of Europe to ensure that use of the flag retains its dignity and reflects the values of the Union and Council. Requests for permission to use the flag/emblem should be addressed to the European Commission.

Commercial use of the United Nations flag and emblem is regulated by Section 2(a) of General Resolution 92(I), which places an obligation on Member States of the United Nations to take legislative steps to prevent usage of the emblem for any commercial purposes. It specifies that any commercial use of the seal must be authorised by the Secretary General of the UN.

(See also entries for Red Cross, Red Crescent; and Royalty and the Crown.)

Maps

Maps and mapping data are protected by copyright as a type of artistic and/ or literary work, except for those that are so old that the copyright has expired. The information contained in maps is also potentially protected by database rights. In the United Kingdom, most official maps and road atlases are based on the mapping conducted by the Ordnance Survey, until recently a Crown body, but from 1 April 2015 a government-owned limited company. Pre-April 2015 Ordnance Survey maps are subject to Crown copyright, while copyright in more recent maps is owned by Ordnance Survey Limited, but the administration of copyright licensing and permissions for use of both types of material is now entrusted to Ordnance Survey Limited. Ordnance Survey has not waived its copyright or database rights in its maps and permission should always be sought before reproducing them in advertisements unless the maps are old enough for the rights in them to have expired (see below). Given that other publishers (for example Philips) use Ordnance Survey maps as the basis for their own maps and road atlases, any reproductions of their material will require the permission both of that publisher and also of Ordnance Survey.

The range of licences available from Ordnance Survey can be seen on its website (www.ordnancesurvey.co.uk) and, depending upon the type of advertising or marketing use envisaged, the sections on publishing, partner or media use may be most relevant. It is recommended that advertisers contact the OS Pricing and Licensing Team to discuss the particular use/terms available (newbusinessenquiries@os.uk). Advertisers proposing to feature a substantial extract from an Ordnance Survey map in a print or billboard ad will usually need a publishing licence, the cost of which is based on the amount of mapping used, whether it is facsimile use or redrawn, and the size and number of copies of the publication printed. Some Ordnance Survey mapping data can be licensed for use free of charge (provided due acknowledgement of source is given) under the OS Open Data scheme. Again, see the website for details.

Advertisers may freely use and copy Ordnance Survey mapping data that are out of copyright, but should contact Ordnance Survey for confirmation that the mapping is of the requisite age. For maps created before April 2015 (when Ordnance Service was a Crown body), Crown copyright lasts for 50 years from the end of the calendar year in which the maps were first published. But for maps and mapping data (including updates to existing maps) created by Ordnance Survey Limited after 1 April 2015, copyright will last for 70 years following the death of all persons involved in creating it.

Agencies can create their own maps, but these must be their own work and not copied or traced from existing mapping.

Olympic symbols

Use of Olympic symbols, insignia and words are all heavily protected. Chapter 16 deals with this in more detail.

Postage stamps

The copyright in all designs for British Postage Stamps is owned by Royal Mail Group Ltd. Certain stamps are also registered as trade marks (for example the Penny Black). Written permission for the reproduction of stamps should be obtained from the Royal Mail by contacting stamp.team@royalmail.com.

The Royal Mail insists that stamps must be reproduced faithfully in every detail and in their entirety (for example showing the Monarch's head, the stamp value and the stamp's perforations) and that, if a licence is granted, final designs must be sent to its brand team for approval. When showing stamp images, they must not be obscured or partly covered with another object or illustration. However, if a number of stamps are to be shown, it is acceptable for some to be partly covered by others. Stamp, or stamp-related, imagery must not be altered in any way to suit the purposes of the advertisement, nor must their use impact negatively on Royal Mail or the stamp's designers. Stamp, or stamp-related, imagery must also be acknowledged as: '© Stamp Design Royal Mail Group Ltd (year)'.

In order to protect new designs, the Royal Mail insists that stamps must not appear in any media, including stamp-collecting publications, local or national press, electronically or on the internet more than 20 weeks before that stamp issue goes on sale.

If permission is to be granted, you will be sent a licence agreement and may be required to pay a fee.

If reproducing material for commercial use incorporating the profile or portrait of HM the Queen, or other members of the royal family, you must observe the rules laid down by the Lord Chamberlain's Office. (See the section on Royalty and the Crown in this chapter.)

Quotations

The use of substantial verbatim quotations without permission from works such as books, plays, journals and newspapers may constitute copyright infringement unless the amount quoted is very small, or covered by a fair dealing defence, or the copyright has expired. The moral rights of the author may also be infringed. (See Chapter 1 for further details.)

The same principles also apply to using spoken words that have been recorded in films, sound recordings or broadcasts. In the latter case, there may be two copyright owners, both the speaker and the maker of the recording, but again a single line from a film is unlikely to be an infringement.

The common example of using quotations in advertisements of excerpts from published reviews of new books, films, CDs, etc on promotional materials will be fine, provided that such quotes are kept very short, ie a line or two.

Another common example of the use of quotes is quoting a famous line from a film, such as 'I'll be back'. Very short excerpts from a film script such as this would usually be perfectly acceptable if used by themselves and without any other reference to the film. Agencies should always be aware, however, of the rules on fair dealing in the use of quotations and parodies (see Chapter 1 on copyright). There is no hard and fast rule as to the amount of material that can be quoted without infringing. This is because the courts will look at the quality rather than the quantity of material that has been reproduced before deciding whether the amount taken is substantial and thus infringes (again, see Chapter 1 on copyright). The case law on copyright has tightened in recent years, and while in the past it was thought safe to assume that one line is legitimate, this will now depend on the quality of what is taken. Copying even small extracts should now only be undertaken with caution. Brief quotations from poems and song lyrics may infringe, especially if the poem or song is itself very short.

Trade mark searches may also be necessary before using a quotation. For example, Muhammad Ali Enterprises LLC has registered trade marks for the former boxer's 'Float like a butterfly, sting like a bee' quotation. Any commercial use of this quotation will need permission.

Red Cross, Red Crescent

Agencies should avoid using the Red Cross and Red Crescent emblems, either in advertisements or when creating logos for clients. The 'Red Cross' and 'Red Crescent' terms and associated emblems are protected by the Geneva Convention Act 1957. Use of these marks is restricted, and making any unauthorised use of the words or emblems Red Cross or Red Crescent (or misleadingly similar symbols) is a criminal offence with a penalty of a fine up to £5,000. The guilty party will further be ordered to forfeit any goods in connection to which the infringing symbol was used.

If an advertiser's logo featuring a Red Cross or Red Crescent symbol was registered as a trade mark before the passing of the 1957 Act, it is a defence for the owner of the registered trade mark to show that his or her use of the design or wording was lawful.

(See also the section in this chapter on Flags.)

Road signs

Road signs are the subject of Crown copyright. However, any road signs determined by the Traffic Signs Regulations and General Directions 2002 (or by the TSRGDs 2016, which are due to replace them) are covered by a free Open Government Licence. In practice, this licence means that agencies and advertisers are free to reproduce and use the majority of official road signs in any advertising, provided that the signs are not used in a misleading or derogatory manner. Where practicable, an attribution statement should be included, stating the TSRGDs as the source of the signs and that they are licensed under the Open Government Licence v3.0. While there is no charge for use of material under the Open Government Licence, there may be a charge for supplying information, such as large quantities of data or high-resolution images.

The Department for Transport may object when signs are used on advertising material and sited on the roadside where they could be mistaken for a traffic sign. Agencies should ensure that their choice of media for advertisements featuring road signs is not likely to confuse motorists; particular care should therefore be given to roadside billboards and bus shelters.

The reproduction of a sign should also not imply that the advertiser has official status or that it, or its product, is endorsed by government.

In addition, the City of Westminster Council owns the copyright in the famous red and black rectangular designs of central London street signs. All products incorporating those street signs must therefore be licensed and failure to acquire a licence could leave unlicensed users liable to civil enforcement or criminal prosecution. It is debatable whether their featuring in an advertisement would infringe copyright, however, particularly if their inclusion is of an incidental nature, and no cases have yet been brought in this respect.

Royalty and the Crown

Generally, the use of royal images for advertising purposes in any medium is prohibited. The commercial use of all royal images is governed by rules issued by the Lord Chamberlain's Office. Royal images may only be used when advertising a book, newspaper, magazine article or television documentary that is itself about a member of the royal family, and only if express approval has been obtained from the Lord Chamberlain's Office. All necessary permissions must also have been obtained from copyright holders (ie in the photographs etc).

It is also not permitted to use photographs of any member of the royal family visiting a firm's premises or trade stands or being publicly involved with the firm, in order to advertise the firm's business activities.

Strict provisions also apply to the use of the Royal Arms, Royal Crown and emblems personal to members of the royal family. Enquiries should be made in writing on a case-by-case basis, with details of the intended advertising use and context, to the Deputy Comptroller, Lord Chamberlain's Office. More general advice can also be obtained from this office.

Royal warrants are awarded to 'tradesmen' (not professionals, media, government or places of refreshment or entertainment) based on a minimum of five years' supply to the relevant member of the royal family. A warrant gives the holder the right to display the Royal Arms on advertising, premises, packaging, stationery and vehicles, with the statement 'By appointment to...' HM the Queen, HRH the Duke of Edinburgh or HRH the Prince of Wales, as the case may be. Royal warrants are again administered by the Lord Chamberlain's Office, which issues very particular rules about how the Royal Arms should appear.

The above rules are reflected in sections 3.52 and 6.2 of the CAP Code, which state that: 'Marketing communications must not use the Royal Arms or Emblems without prior permission from the Lord Chamberlain's office. References to a Royal Warrant should be checked with the Royal Warrant Holders' Association' and 'Members of the royal family should not normally be shown or mentioned in a marketing communication without their prior permission but an incidental reference unconnected with the advertised product, or a reference to material such as a book, article or film about a member of the royal family, may be acceptable.'

There have been a number of cases in which complaints about (obvious) lookalikes, impersonators and cartoon images of members of the royal family were not upheld by the ASA, indicating that humorous references to royalty may be acceptable provided they are not likely to cause offence or mislead by implying an endorsement. On the other hand, complaints have been upheld regarding the use of photographs of members of the royal family without prior permission, particularly where it potentially implies an endorsement of the advertised product.

(See also the sections of this chapter on Bank notes; Coins; and Postage stamps.)

Uniforms

Under the Chartered Associations (Protection of Names and Uniforms) Act 1926, any association incorporated by Royal Charter can apply for an Order in Council to be made to protect the name of the association and any uniform with distinctive markings or badges used by the association.

Where such an Order has been made, use of the uniform, badge or marking without the permission of the association is prohibited. The associations that enjoy the protection of such an Order are the St John Ambulance, the

Royal British Legion, the Royal Life-Saving Society, the Scouts, the Girl Guides and the NSPCC. Therefore, any advertisement involving the reproduction of a uniform or badges belonging to one of these associations will require the consent of the relevant organisation.

Under the Uniform Act 1896, which is still in force today, it is unlawful for any person who is not serving in the forces to wear any military uniform without the permission of the Crown. There is, however, an exemption for the wearing of uniforms or dress as part of a stage play, music hall or circus, or in the course of bona fide military representation. This exemption is likely to cover most advertising uses. However, it should be noted that any civilian contravening the Act, or who, while wearing a uniform or any mark distinctive to a regiment, brings contempt on the uniform or emblem, will be liable to a fine.

The Police Act 1996 states that any person who, with the intent to deceive, impersonates a member of the police force or special constable will be guilty of an offence. The same applies to anyone who wears a police uniform in circumstances that would be likely to give the appearance so nearly resembling a police officer as to deceive. The offence requires an intention to deceive, and therefore use of uniforms within an advertisement is unlikely to fall foul of this section. However, when using uniforms in public (for example for filming) it is suggested that it would be prudent to inform the local police station.

Agencies are generally urged, when re-creating a police or other emergency service uniform, to create a generic copy of the uniform which does not feature an identifying police force (or other) badge or logo.

In 2007, Historic Royal Palaces (who employ the Yeoman Warders, also known as 'Beefeaters', who are retired military personnel) twice unsuccessfully complained about light-hearted depictions of pretend Beefeaters in advertising, on the basis that it implied the endorsement of the advertised services by the Tower of London and its Yeoman Warders. One was an Aer Lingus ad where the Beefeater's hat was replaced with an Irish souvenir hat with the caption 'someone's had a good time in Dublin'; the other was for Norwich Union with a caption to the effect that the bank will replace your keys if you lose them. The ASA felt that it was clear that the public would not consider the image to be of a real Yeoman Warder, and that they were only used light-heartedly to illustrate the concepts of flights between London and Dublin, and the yeomen's 'lock and key' for the Tower. Thus, the public would not take the Yeoman Warders (or Historic Royal Palaces) to be endorsing the advertised services.

Courtesy of the Ministry of Defence, UK

Notes

1 [2007] EWHC 1372 (Ch); [2007] FSR 36
2 Section 62 Copyright Designs and Patents Act 1988

PART FOUR
Industry issues:
Key challenges
for certain business
sectors

Alcohol   18

**PAUL JORDAN, SALLY DUNSTAN AND
ANDY BUTCHER**

BRISTOWS

Introduction

The level of alcohol advertising regulation in the UK continues to be contentious, with pressure on industry producers to ensure responsible messaging amid widespread concerns about binge drinking, anti-social behaviour, health impacts and the effect of alcohol advertising on young people. Nevertheless, calls to tighten restrictions must be seen in the context of high levels of industry compliance[1] with the self-regulatory codes, which contain strict rules on alcohol advertising in the UK, the ASA's continuous efforts to monitor and enforce those rules and a trend towards a reduction in alcohol consumption.

CAP, BCAP and Portman Codes

The UK Code for Non-Broadcast Advertising, Sales Promotion and Direct Marketing (CAP Code) and the UK Code for Broadcast Advertising (BCAP Code) both include specific provisions dealing with alcohol advertising. These were updated and strengthened in 2005, and again in 2009.

These Code rules apply alongside the Portman Code of Practice on the Naming, Packaging and Promotion of Alcoholic Drinks (Portman Code) launched in 1996 by the Portman Group and presently in its fifth edition.[2] The Portman Code is also a self-regulatory code which is consistent with the CAP and BCAP Codes and applies to all alcohol marketing primarily targeted to the UK and not otherwise regulated by the ASA or Ofcom. As well as below-the-line material such as labelling and point-of-sale materials, it covers websites and other digital media,[3] press releases, brand names, product descriptors, sponsorship, advertorials, branded merchandise, sampling and other promotional activities. Signatories to the Portman Code, which include producers, retailers, wholesalers, importers and industry bodies, agree to be bound by its terms, but it is applicable to all companies in the industry. It only applies to wholesaler- or retailer-led promotions if such entities are also producers promoting their own beverage products, or are engaging in a co-promotion with a producer. The Portman Group operates a free advisory service to enable advertisers to check compliance.

Anyone may submit a complaint under the Portman Code or raise an issue, and each will be considered by an independent complaints panel. All decisions are published on the Portman Group's website and in an annual report.

Other relevant rules

Legislation governs the naming of alcoholic beverages and the description of the type of beverage, including the term 'spirits'[4] and related terms and denominations,[5] the labelling and advertising of Scotch whisky,[6] the use of the terms 'wine' and 'liqueur' and references to various levels of alcohol, as discussed further below.[7] Certain terms are protected as geographical indications, such as Champagne (see Chapter 2). Further, names of alcoholic beverages have been protected under the common law action of passing off (see Chapter 4). For example, a drink named VODKAT (in combination with its packaging) was held to have misrepresented to consumers that the product consisted of vodka, when it contained only a vodka blend.[8] In respect of on-trade promotions, the British Beer and Pub Association has published 'Point of Sale Promotions: Standards for the Management of Responsible Drinks Promotions, including Happy Hours' and may investigate breaches by its member signatories.

The Code provisions

Alcoholic drinks

Alcoholic drinks are defined for the purposes of the CAP and BCAP Codes as drinks containing more than 0.5 per cent alcohol by volume (ABV).

Beverages marketed as low-alcohol drinks cannot contain more than 1.2 per cent ABV.[9] The alcohol rules apply to low-alcohol drinks, unless an exception applies; however, there will be no exception if the advertising for such products could be considered to promote a stronger alcoholic drink, or does not clearly state the drink's low-alcohol content. The rules also apply to soft drinks promoted as mixers.

The Portman Code applies to drinks above 0.5 per cent ABV sold in the off-trade to the final consumer; however, the spirit of the Portman Code will apply to any beverages that share the same branding as, or are a variant of, a drink that is subject to it. Drinks sold in the on-trade are covered if served as part of a producer-led, approved or supported co-promotional activity, including products in any form that are marketed primarily as an alcoholic drink (even if solid or frozen).[10]

General principles

The principles outlined in rule 18 of the CAP code, rule 19 of the BCAP code and rule 3.2 of the Portman Code aim to ensure that marketing communications both for alcoholic drinks and featuring alcoholic drinks are not targeted at individuals under 18 and do not encourage irresponsible drinking, reflecting marketers' general responsibility to consumers and society under rule 1.3 of the CAP Code and 1.2 of the BCAP Code. These provisions are summarised below.

The general prohibitions under the CAP and BCAP Codes on misleading advertising also apply. Complaints about misleading claims as to a beverage's country of origin are common, particularly as many beers with a heritage associated with a particular country are now brewed elsewhere.[11]

Irresponsible and immoderate drinking

Advertisements must not feature, imply, condone or encourage irresponsible, immoderate or excessive drinking in respect of the amount consumed and the manner in which the consumption is portrayed.[12] In that regard:

- Irresponsible drinking references may include drinking games, downing drinks excessively quickly and pub crawls. If a drink is traditionally consumed as a shot, the advert will be considered in the context of whether the consumption is reckless or irresponsible.[13]

- An excessive amount of alcohol (by reference to the Department of Health's guidelines)[14] cannot be dispensed per person, nor should drinks be shown as being poured over people or into their mouths. A promotion whereby each drink consumed gave entry into a prize draw was found by the ASA to encourage excessive use of alcohol.[15]

- The purchase of repeat rounds should not be shown in television advertising, although an advert could show someone buying a drink for each group member.[16]
- Adverts for nights out, implying excessive consumption, will breach the Codes.

Alcohol should not be shown being served in an irresponsible manner,[17] in relation to the size and number of measures and the way in which they are poured. Irresponsible servings may include the provision of cheap, all-inclusive drinks.[18] Further, the name of the drink (such as 'slammer'), the use of large, shared containers (such as goldfish bowls) and the nature of un-resealable packaging may breach the Portman Code, depending on the amount of alcohol in such a package. Servings must comply with Department of Health guidelines.[19] Any promotion involving multiple purchases should make it clear that the alcohol is for shared consumption.

There are also a number of mandatory conditions with which retailers must comply following Orders made under the Licensing Act 2003,[20] to ensure that age verification processes are in place, banning irresponsible promotions, banning the dispensing of alcohol directly into customers' mouths, and requiring the availability of free tap water and small measures.

Social success

While advertising can show drinking in a social context, it must not claim or imply that alcohol (or the selection of a particular brand) can enhance confidence or popularity,[21] be key to the success of a personal relationship or social event,[22] or imply that refusal is a sign of weakness or unpopularity.[23]

However, alcohol can be shown as thirst-quenching or being enjoyed responsibly within social settings, particularly if the success of an event or its participants is established before any reference to drinking, and alcohol is incidental.[24] The strapline 'Good times. They're out there'[25] was acceptable as it did not, in context, imply that drinking alcohol was key to the event.

Marketing cannot imply that alcohol might be indispensable or take priority in life, or that drinking can overcome boredom, loneliness or other problems, or make an individual a better person.[26] While a person could be shown drinking alone, the advert must not suggest that this is acceptable on a regular basis. The phrase 'Wednesday. I'm declaring war on mid-week boredom'[27] was found by the ASA to be unacceptable.[28]

Seduction and sexual success

Advertisements cannot link alcohol with seduction, sexual activity or sexual success, imply that alcohol can enhance attractiveness[29] or remove inhibitions, hint at promiscuity or use sexual innuendo. However, this does not preclude linking alcohol with glamour, romance or mild flirtation, provided that there is no sexual implication.

An advert for Belvedere vodka featuring a man with two women who appeared to be attracted to him, and a half-empty bottle, was found by the ASA to link the product to sexual success.[30] In contrast, a cinema advertisement for Estrella Damm beer was found to be acceptable as it showed a couple forming a romantic relationship over time, without any link between alcohol and seduction.[31]

Therapeutic or enhancing qualities and nutritional claims

(See Chapter 19 on food and nutrition and health claims.)

Alcohol cannot be portrayed as having therapeutic qualities, being capable of changing mood, physical condition or behaviour, being a source of nourishment, or being necessary to maintain a normal lifestyle.[32] Advertisements must not imply that alcohol can enhance mental or physical capabilities, or contribute to professional or sporting achievements. While an advert can imply that smart and physically fit people choose a particular alcohol brand, and can feature sports people or a sports event, it cannot imply that a sports-person's prowess has been enhanced by alcohol.

Factual information about product contents may be given, but the communications (and product names) must not make any health, fitness or weight-control claims other than nutrition claims referring to 'low alcohol', 'reduced alcohol' or 'reduced energy' (and any claim likely to have the same meaning for the consumer).[33] Other claims are not permitted (including 'reduced sugar' or 'reduced/low carbohydrate'). A reference to 'only' in con-junction with a reference to calorie or carbohydrate count may be a prohibited low-energy claim. A reference to 'light' may be permitted if it is clear that it refers to a reduction in alcohol content, or to flavour or colour.

In making a comparison between two of the advertiser's products or the advertiser's product and a competitor product, the difference in the compared quality (such as calorie count) must be significant in order not to mislead consumers (at least 30 per cent in the case of reduced energy claims).[34]

Claims such as 'energising' or brand names indicating a stimulating effect are usually unacceptable also. A calming or sedative effect cannot be claimed, although it may be suggested that alcohol can help people in a 'normal' (and not anxious) state relax.[35] Direct claims of health benefits are never acceptable, such as claims as to the contribution of beer to a healthy diet and heart health.[36] These provisions apply in addition to specific regulations on health and nutrition claims, and labelling requirements.[37]

Alcohol content

Marketing communications may give factual information about the alcoholic strength of a drink. They may also make a comparison with the alcoholic strength of another product, provided the comparison is with a similar beverage in the same category (eg wine or beer) and with a higher strength. They cannot imply that alcohol content, or an intoxicating effect, should be a reason for selection, although low-alcohol drinks may be presented as preferable (in the case of the Portman Code, provided the drink is below the average strength for similar beverages).[38] A relatively high alcoholic strength (eg 'world's strongest beer'[39]) should not be given undue emphasis.[40]

The Portman Code requires the alcoholic nature of the drink to be communicated on its packaging with absolute clarity.[41] If the packaging shape and/or design is unusual for the type of drink (eg a sachet featuring images of fruit called 'Shotpak'), the drink designation must be more prominent.

Unsafe or daring activities

Advertising must not portray drinking alcohol as a challenge or link alcohol with brave, tough or daring people or behaviour (even if such people are not drinking at the time). Advertisements featuring free runners,[42] and surfing and driving in difficult conditions,[43] have been found to have breached the Codes.

Further, communications must not show, imply, encourage or refer to aggression or unruly, irresponsible or anti-social behaviour[44] or link alcohol to illicit drugs.[45] Playful behaviour may be acceptable, so long as it is not childish or loutish.

Alcohol must not be linked with driving, or activities or locations in which drinking would be unsafe or unwise. An advert featuring a bullfighter was found to have linked alcohol with a dangerous sport.[46,47] Sponsorship of activities which may be dangerous after alcohol consumption, such as motor or yacht racing, is not in itself in breach of the Portman Code, although the associated messaging should be carefully considered.

Advertisements should not feature alcohol being drunk by anyone in their working environment, except in exceptional circumstances – celebratory drinks post-work may be acceptable.[48]

Marketing should also not imply that sporting or physical activities have been undertaken after alcohol consumption,[49] particularly swimming. An advertisement depicting people dancing on a beach holding beer bottles and then jumping into the waves was found to imply that the characters had been drinking before swimming at night, a potentially unsafe activity.[50]

Sales promotions

Alcohol sales promotions are permitted, so long as they do not imply, condone or encourage excessive consumption of alcohol.[51] If a promotion refers to multiple purchases, it should not imply that those purchases are for individual consumption, nor encourage consumers to exceed Department of Health drinking guidelines. The promotion must continue for long enough to allow consumers to participate without drinking excessively.[52] If alcohol is offered as a gift or prize, the promotion must prominently state that it is not open to under-18s.[53] (See below for restrictions that apply to promotions in Scotland.)

Alcohol and minors

General principles

Concerns about the impact of alcohol advertising on young people have driven much of the regulation and reform. The style, content and context of the advertising, and the media in which it appears, are all relevant. The list below sets out some general principles, though readers should note that there are subtle, but important differences between the rules for broadcast and non-broadcast advertising, only some of which are set out here. Generally, advertisements for alcohol must not:

- Be likely to appeal (or, in the case of television advertising, strongly appeal, and in the case of radio advertising, be targeted) particularly to people under 18, especially by reflecting youth culture. Under-18s should not comprise more than 25% of participants, audience or spectators at sponsored events.[54] (See 'Non-broadcast media' below.)

- Feature or portray real or fictitious characters who are likely to appeal particularly to under-18s in a way that might encourage them to drink, or whose example may be followed.

- Show people drinking or playing a significant role who are behaving in an adolescent or juvenile manner;[55] slapstick humour and practical jokes may be considered irresponsible.

- Show people drinking or playing a significant role who are or seem to be under 25, in particular, celebrities (especially video bloggers). While they may be shown, for example, in the context of family celebrations, they must be obviously not drinking.[56] The rules are stricter for broadcast advertising, in which children must not be featured, unless in the context of a family socialising responsibly, and in an incidental role.

- Exploit the immature, or those who are mentally or socially vulnerable.[57]

Particular caution should be used when including celebrities, sports, cartoons (especially featuring colourful characters[58] rather than adult satirical references,[59]) or animals; music, dance or fashion mostly associated with under-18s (for instance by referring to celebrities from *The X-Factor*[60]); and themes, jokes, behaviour and language associated with youth culture (including references to challenging authority and the generation gap). Care should also be taken with associated merchandise, particularly gifts with purchase promotions.

Non-broadcast media

No medium should be used where more than 25 per cent of its audience is under 18.[61] As such, the expansion of digital advertising causes challenges for the industry. Facebook promotions (where fewer than 25 per cent of users are under 18) have been acceptable, so long as appropriate age-gating is used, both for original and shared posts.[62] The Portman Code digital media guidance[63] stipulates that e-mail marketing must only be sent to persons who have affirmed that they are over 18. Similarly, age affirmation gating, requiring users to input their date of birth, should be used to deter under-18s from accessing a brand website. YouTube advertisements should only be served to logged-in users over 18.

The Portman Code guidance stipulates that the audience of any third-party websites which are to carry alcohol marketing should be carefully assessed by reference to syndicated audience data, independent demographic surveys and the site's own registered user databases.

The Outdoor Media Centre's Charter of Best Practice prohibits alcohol advertising within 100 m of a school front gate.

Alcohol may be advertised in cinemas before a film issued with a certificate confirming it is acceptable for under-18s, if more than 25 per cent of its audience is likely to be over 18.

Broadcast advertising and scheduling

Television advertising must obtain Clearcast clearance in order to be broadcast. Radio advertisements for alcohol advertising must be pre-cleared by Radiocentre before being broadcast as 'special category' advertisements.[64]

Product placement of alcoholic drinks in television programmes is not permitted under the Ofcom Broadcasting Code.[65]

Rule 32 of the BCAP Code strictly controls the placement of alcohol advertising (including programme sponsorship) on television and radio. Programmes commissioned for, principally directed at or particularly likely to appeal to audiences aged under 18 must not carry advertising[66] for drinks containing 1.2 per cent ABV or more.[67]

A drink containing less than 1.2 per cent ABV, if presented as a low-alcohol or no-alcohol version, cannot be advertised in or adjacent to a programme commissioned for, principally directed at or likely to appeal particularly to persons under 16.[68]

It is usually straightforward to identify a programme commissioned for or principally directed at children, owing to its content. However, identifying programmes likely to appeal particularly to children is more difficult and a number of considerations are taken into account,[69] including programme content, scheduling, the channel profile and audience indexing. BCAP Guidance on Scheduling and Audience Indexing states that programmes with an index of 120 or above (meaning that children aged within a relevant age bracket – so for alcohol advertising, 10–15 years old – are 20 per cent overrepresented in the programme audience compared to the audience as a whole) are considered as particularly appealing to children. If there is a pattern of a programme exceeding the 120 index score throughout episodes in a series, even if the average is below 120, scheduling restrictions are likely to be necessary. Broadcasters must exercise 'responsible judgment', and operate systems capable of avoiding unsuitable juxtapositions between advertising and programmes.[70]

Pricing and promotion of alcoholic drinks in Scotland

The Licensing (Scotland) Act 2005 (the '2005 Act') prohibits 'irresponsible drinks promotions' in licensed premises in Scotland, and defines eight different types of drinks promotion that are deemed irresponsible. A number of these 'irresponsible drinks promotions' are only prohibited in relation to consumption of alcohol *on* the premises. Prior to the Alcohol etc (Scotland) Act 2010 (the '2010 Act') coming into force in October 2011, one example of an 'irresponsible drinks promotion' prohibited for on-sales was any promotion involving 'the supply of an alcoholic drink free of charge or at a reduced price on the purchase of one or more drinks (whether or not alcoholic drinks)'. However, since October 2011, this prohibition also applies to off-sales, meaning that alcohol promotions such as 'buy one, get one free' and 'three for the price of two' are prohibited in Scottish supermarkets and off-licences. Therefore, an alcohol sales promotion that is lawful in supermarkets in England, Wales and Northern Ireland may be prohibited in Scottish supermarkets.

In addition to 'buy one, get one free' and 'three for the price of two' offers, the 2010 Act also prohibits Scottish retailers from selling alcoholic drinks packaged together at a lower per-drink price than that at which they can be purchased individually in the same shop.

The CAP and BCAP Codes require that marketing communications neither materially mislead nor imply that a product can be legally sold if it cannot. Therefore, advertisements for certain alcohol sales promotions will breach the Codes if targeted at a Scottish audience, even if compliant in the rest of the UK. To address this difficulty, CAP and BCAP advise that where such an ad is likely to be seen by Scotland-based consumers, it should specify that the promotion is not available in Scotland.

In May 2012, the Scottish Parliament passed the Alcohol (Minimum Pricing) (Scotland) Act 2012, giving the Scottish government the power to set a minimum price per unit for alcohol sold in Scotland. This legislation has not yet come into force due to a legal challenge brought by The Scotch Whisky Association (and other interested parties). The Court of Session in Scotland, which is hearing the challenge, has made a reference for a preliminary ruling to the Court of Justice of the European Union (CJEU), asking whether the legislation is compatible with EU law, and in particular, the law on free movement of goods.

In 2015, pressure was brought to bear on alcohol advertising in Scotland by way of the Alcohol (Licensing, Public Health and Criminal Justice) (Scotland) Bill, which proposes numerous restrictions on alcohol advertising. At the time of writing, the Bill has not progressed.

Summary

Pressure on alcohol advertising in the UK seems to grow every year, despite the numerous content and scheduling rules in the self-regulatory codes and the willingness of the ASA to enforce against those few ads that cross the line. In terms of pressure in the future, a public consultation on the Directive 2010/13/EU on Audiovisual Media Services (AVMS Directive) was undertaken in 2015, with a review due in 2016, looking at its effectiveness, efficiency and relevance. Among other issues, the existing EU alcohol advertising rules are under review, with the consultation looking at whether they should be changed, tightened or made more flexible. With continued pressure on regulators to ensure that stringent advertising rules are in place, we may see further, stricter changes ahead.

Notes

1 The Compliance Report of the ASA's Alcohol Advertising Survey 2009, covering all media within the remit of the Codes from 1 to 24 December 2009, found that of the 307 alcohol ads surveyed, 99.7% complied with the advertising codes.

2 See www.portmangroup.co.uk

3 Detailed guidance is provided in the Portman Code's publication 'Responsible Marketing of Alcoholic Drinks in Digital Media'.

4 Alcoholic Liquor Duties Act 1979

5 Spirits Drinks Regulations 2008

6 Scotch Whisky Regulations 2009

7 Food Labelling Regulations 1996; also see the Common Agricultural Policy (Wine) Regulations 1996.

8 *Diageo North America Inc. v. Intercontinental Brands (ICB) Ltd* [2010] EWHC 17 (Ch)

9 Rule 18, CAP Code; this is consistent with The Food Labelling Regulations 1996, Regulation 42(1) and Schedule 8 Part I, which provide that any description or implication of 'low alcohol' shall not be applied unless the drink is no more than 1.2% ABV.

10 Portman Code rule 2.5

11 See ASA adjudication on Heineken UK ad for Kronenbourg, 4 June 2014 – https://www.asa.org.uk/Rulings/Adjudications/2014/6/Heineken-UK-Ltd/SHP_ADJ_248899.aspx

12 Cap Code rule 18.1; Portman Code rule 3.2(f) and (g); BCAP Code rule 19.2

13 Mast-Jaegermeister UK Ltd, ASA adjudication, 30 July 2014

14 See http://www.nhs.uk/change4life/Pages/alcohol-lower-risk-guidelines-units.aspx and https://www.cap.org.uk/Advice-Training-on-the-rules/Advice-Online-Database/Alcohol-Sales-promotions.aspx

15 Hold Fast Entertainment Limited, ASA adjudication, 27 August 2014

16 BCAP Code rule 19.2

17 CAP Code rule 18.11; BCAP Code rule 19.12

18 Sirowek S.L t/a Stoke Travel, ASA adjudication, 10 October 2012

19 See http://www.nhs.uk/change4life/Pages/alcohol-lower-risk-guidelines-units. aspx and https://www.cap.org.uk/Advice-Training-on-the-rules/Advice-Online-Database/Alcohol-Sales-promotions.aspx

20 Licensing Act 2003 (Mandatory Licensing Conditions) Order 2010; Licensing Act 2003 (Mandatory Licensing Conditions) (Amendment) Order 2014

21 CAP Code rule 18.2; BCAP Code rule 19.3, Portman Code rule 3.2(e)

22 CAP Code rule 18.3

23 BCAP Code rule 19.4

24 See for instance Wells & Young Brewing Company Limited, ASA adjudication, 3 October 2012.

25 InBev UK Ltd, ASA adjudication, 6 January 2010

26 CAP Code rule 18.6; BCAP Code rule 19.7

27 Diageo Great Britain Ltd, ASA adjudication, 23 July 2014

28 Hi-Spirits Ltd, ASA adjudication, 17 July 2013

29 CAP Code rule 18.5; BCAP Code rule 19.6; Portman Code 3.2(d)

30 Moet Hennessy UK Ltd, ASA adjudication, 17 December 2008

31 Wells & Youngs Brewing Company Ltd, ASA adjudication, 17 November 2010

32 CAP Code rule 18.7; BCAP Code rule 19.8; Portman Code rule 3.2(j)

33 CAP Code rule 18.17; BCAP Code rule 19.18

34 BCAP Help Note: Health, Diet and Nutritional Claims in Radio Alcohol Advertisements

35 CAP AdviceOnline article: Alcohol: Therapeutic claims

36 ASA adjudications in George Gale & Co Ltd, 26 February 2003 and Coors Brewers Ltd, 10 March 2004

37 Regulation (EC) 1924/2006 on Nutrition and Health Claims made on Foods; Food Information Regulation No 1169/2011; Food Labelling Regulation 1996; Food Information Regulations 2014

38 Portman Code rule 3.2(a)

39 Brewmeister Ltd, ASA adjudication, 24 September 2014

40 CAP Code rule 18.9; BCAP Code rule 19.10

41 Portman Code rule 3.1

42 Cell Drinks, ASA adjudication, 3 August 2011

43 Mast-Jagermeister UK Ltd, ASA adjudication, 30 July 2014

44 CAP Code rule 18.4; BCAP Code rule 19.5; Portman Code 3.2(b)

45 CAP Code rule 18.8; BCAP Code rule 19.9; Portman Code 3.2(c)

46 Scottish Courage Ltd, ASA adjudication, 27 July 2005

47 Bacardi-Martini Ltd, ASA adjudication, 19 January 2005

48 CAP Code rule 18.13; BCAP Code rule 19.14

49 CAP Code rule 18.12; BCAP Code rule 19.13

50 Wells & Young Brewing Company Ltd, ASA adjudication, 30 November 2011

51 CAP Code rule 18.10; BCAP Code rule 19.11

52 Fuller Smith & Turner plc, ASA adjudication, 4 July 2001

53 EMAP Elan Ltd, ASA adjudication, 6 September 2006

54 Portman Group's Code of Practice on Alcohol Sponsorship (First Edition), Section 3

55 CAP Code rule 18.14; BCAP Code rules 19.15 and 19.16; Portman Code rule 3.2(h)

56 CAP Code rule 18.16; BCAP Code rule 19.17; Portman Code rule 3.2(i)

57 CAP Code rule 18.1

58 Diageo Great Britain Ltd t/a Parrot Bay, ASA adjudication, 15 October 2014

59 Cobra Beer Ltd, ASA adjudication, 24 September 2008

60 Maxxium UK Ltd, ASA adjudication, 12 December 2012

61 CAP Code rule 18.15

62 Hold Fast Entertainment Limited, ASA adjudication, 27 August 2014

63 Portman Code – Responsible Marketing of Alcoholic Drinks in Digital Media

64 Rule 19.1 of the BCAP Code

65 Rule 9.13

66 Rule 32.2, BCAP Code

67 Rule 32.2.1, BCAP Code

68 Rule 32.4.7, BCAP Code

69 See for detailed guidance BCAP's Guidance Note, *Scheduling and Audience Indexing: identifying programmes likely to appeal particularly to children and young people.*

70 Rule 32.1, BCAP Code

The advertising of food

Nutrition and health claims

REBECCA CHONG AND RICHARD LINDSAY

Introduction

The food industry is governed by a complex and evolving network of laws and regulations.

This chapter will first outline the legal framework for making nutrition and health claims, focusing on the main EU Regulation governing this area, and then explore to what extent the relevant sections of the UK Code of Advertising, Sales Promotion and Direct Marketing (CAP Code) and UK Code of Broadcast Advertising (BCAP Code) reflect the law and how the Codes have been interpreted.

The law and misleading advertising

If an advertising claim – whether or not it is a claim about food – is misleading, it will fall foul of the Consumer Protection from Unfair Trading Regulations 2008 (CPRs) which protect consumers against misleading business practices. If it is a claim about food, however, it could also be misleading under Section 15(2) of the Food Safety Act 1990, which states that: 'Any person who publishes, or is a party to the publication of, an advertisement... which

(a) falsely describes any food; or (b) is likely to mislead as to the nature or substance or quality of any food, shall be guilty of an offence.'

Further, under Article 16 of the General Food Law Regulation 178/2002: 'the advertising... of food or feed, including their shape, appearance or packaging, the packaging materials used, the manner in which they are arranged and the setting in which they are displayed, and the information which is made available about them through whatever medium, shall not mislead consumers'.

Breach of the provisions under the Food Safety Act and the General Food Law Regulation could result in imprisonment and/or a fine.

EC Regulation 1924/2006 on Nutrition and Health Claims made on Foods

In addition to ensuring that an advertising claim is not misleading, advertisers may only make a claim about nutrition or health in relation to advertising food if certain criteria have been met.

These criteria are set out in Regulation (EC) No 1924/2006 on Nutrition and Health Claims made on Foods (the '2006 Regulation'). The 2006 Regulation applies only to voluntary – as opposed to legally mandatory – nutrition and health claims made in commercial communications, including advertising, aimed at the final consumer.[1]

'Claim' is broadly defined under the 2006 Regulation as: 'any message or representation, which is not mandatory under Community or national legislation, including pictorial, graphic or symbolic representation, in any form, which states, suggests or implies that a food has particular characteristics'.[2]

It follows that even a trade mark or brand name may amount to a claim and, when the 2006 Regulation came into force, some brand-owners faced the possibility that they might no longer be able to use their trade marks in their advertising if the marks amounted to unauthorised claims. Could the trade mark SLIM FAST, for example, be construed as a claim regarding rate of weight loss?[3] However, in cases where a trade mark or brand name amounts to an unauthorised claim, brand-owners will be able to exploit a grace period which permits use of any trade mark or brand name that existed before 1 January 2005 until 19 January 2022.[4] Reliance on the grace period is subject to the trade mark or brand name in question being accompanied by a nutrition or health claim that is compliant with the 2006 Regulation (compliance is explored in detail below).[5]

The key articles of the 2006 Regulation stipulate that all nutrition and health claims must meet a general set of principles,[6] a general set of conditions,[7] and that they must have scientific substantiation[8] (the 'General Criteria').

It is important for advertisers to establish whether a claim they are making is a nutrition or a health claim because, in addition to meeting the General Criteria, the 2006 Regulation provides different additional criteria for both types.

EC Regulation 1924/2006 and nutrition claims

A nutrition claim is a claim that 'states, suggests or implies that a food has particular, beneficial, nutritional properties'.[9] For example, 'high in fibre'.

A nutrition claim can only be made if – in addition to meeting the General Criteria – it is listed as a permitted claim in the 2006 Regulation Annex (later amended by Regulation 1047/2012), and meets the stipulated conditions of use for that claim.[10] (Permitted nutrition claims may also be found in the EU Register of nutrition and health claims (the 'EU Register').)

It is not essential to use a permitted nutrition claim exactly as it appears in its approved form in the Annex. Provided a claim conveys the same meaning to consumers as that of a relevant, permitted nutrition claim, it may be used and will be subject to the same conditions of use as the permitted claim.[11]

Comparative nutrition claims

There are special provisions within the 2006 Regulation as to how to make comparative nutrition claims, and making such claims can be particularly tricky. In addition to ensuring that the claim is one of the four – 'energy reduced', 'increased [name of nutrient]', 'reduced [name of nutrient]', 'light/lite' – comparative nutrition claims listed in the Annex, a comparison may only be made between foods of the same category, taking into account a range of foods for that category. Also, the food against which the advertised food is being compared must not have a composition that allows it to bear a nutrition claim.[12] For example, it is acceptable to state that 'olive oil is lower in saturated fat than butter' because low in saturated fat claims are not allowed in relation to butter. Further, the advertiser is required to state the quantity of foods being compared and the difference in quantity of the nutrient and/or energy value (as relevant).[13]

EC Regulation 1924/2006 and health claims

A health claim is a claim that 'states, suggests or implies that a relation-ship exists between a food category, a food or one of its constituents and health'.[14] For example, 'contains calcium for normal bone growth and development'.

A health claim can only be made if – in addition to meeting the General Criteria – it is either authorised under the 2006 Regulation and included in the list of authorised health claims under the 2006 Regulation[15] (a list of authorised health claims was established by Regulation No 432/2012), or is an 'on-hold claim' (see below). In addition, certain information (such as quantity of the food and pattern of consumption to achieve the benefit claimed) must be included in any labelling, or, where labelling does not exist, in the presentation and advertising of the product.[16]

As with permitted nutrition claims, the full list of authorised health claims may be found on the EU Register. Non-authorised health claims are also included on the EU Register, together with the reasons why they were not authorised. (To all intents and purposes, there is no material difference between 'authorised' as used in relation to health claims and 'permitted' as used in relation to nutrition claims.)

An 'on-hold' health claim is a claim that is still under consideration by the European Commission. These claims are not on the EU Register. A large number of health claims that relate to botanical substances have been put on hold because the European Commission is still deciding how to address the conflict between the 2006 Regulation and the Traditional Herbal Medicinal Products Directive (2004/24/EC). On-hold claims may be used while they are still under consideration, subject to compliance with the General Criteria and the specific conditions that apply to health claims under Article 10 of the 2006 Regulation, as well as other relevant national legislation or provisions.

As with permitted nutrition claims, it is not essential to use an authorised health claim exactly as it appears in its approved form on the EU Register. Provided a claim conveys the same meaning to consumers as that of a relevant, authorised, health claim, it may be used and will be subject to the same con-ditions of use as the authorised claim.[17]

It is possible to make general, non-specific claims about the benefits of a nutrient or food for overall health, but only if it is accompanied by a specific authorised health claim.[18] For example, a claim that a food is 'vitally important to support your body' would be regarded as a general health claim and would need to be accompanied by a specific authorised health claim in order to be used.

There are a number of specifically prohibited health claims, including: claims that suggest that health could be affected by not consuming a food; claims that refer to a rate or amount of weight loss; and claims that refer to recommendations of individual doctors, health professionals, or associations other than national medical associations and health-related charities. In addition, while it is possible to make a *nutrition* claim about an alcoholic drink that contains more than 1.2 per cent by volume of alcohol provided that the claim refers to a reduction in the alcohol or energy content,[19] making a *health* claim about an alcoholic drink that contains more than 1.2 per cent by volume of alcohol is prohibited without exception.[20]

EC Regulation 1924/2006 and nutrient profiles

The term 'nutrient profile', as used in the 2006 Regulation, refers to the nutrient composition of a food or diet. The European Commission's objective in deciding to establish nutrient profiles was to prevent consumers being misled about the nutritional composition of food. A food would need to meet specific nutrient profiles in order for an authorised health or permitted nutrition claim to be made about it.

However, although nutrient profiles were meant to have been established by 19 January 2009,[21] we are still waiting. The European Commission explained in May 2015 that it was: 'not in a position to provide a definitive timeframe regarding their adoption and... As part of its reflections, the Commission is aware that the regulation foresees the possibility to exempt certain food from the obligation to comply with nutrient profiles.'[22]

In October 2015, the European Commission presented a roadmap proposal evaluating the 2006 Regulation with regard to the two outstanding issues of nutrient profiles and on-hold health claims made on plants and botanicals. It is anticipated that there will be a final report at the end of 2017 which may provide a resolution on both of these issues.[23]

The advertising Codes and the Food Rules

Introduction

Section 15 of the CAP Code and Section 13 of the BCAP Code (the 'Food Rules') contain the self-regulatory rules for making nutrition and health claims about food in non-broadcast and broadcast advertising, respectively.

The Food Rules broadly reflect the 2006 Regulation regarding nutrition and health claims – hence this section does not provide a comprehensive review of those rules – and each contains a general rule that only permitted nutrition and authorised health claims may be made.[24]

An example of this general rule with regard to a health claim is demonstrated in an Advertising Standards Authority (ASA) adjudication concerning a TV advertisement by Jane Plan Ltd,[25] in which the ASA upheld three complaints that the company had made unauthorised health claims. The advertisement was for a diet plan called Jane Plan, which included home delivery of meals. The complaints suggested that the advertiser's use of the statements 'lose weight the easy way' and 'the thing that really makes Jane Plan successful is that it works' amounted to unauthorised health claims which were likely to be regarded as claims regarding weight loss, specifically prohibited under the BCAP Code.[26] The advertiser argued that Section 13 of the BCAP Code ought not to apply on the basis that the claims were not about food as such but were about the plan as a whole. However, (in addition to upholding a complaint that the advertiser had made a misleading claim regarding being the one of the UK's leading diet companies), the ASA decided that, as the ad featured food and placed emphasis on the food element of the plan, consumers were likely to draw a connection between the claims and the food. As such, it found that these were unauthorised food claims and in breach of the BCAP Code.

There will be instances in which it is not commercially efficacious to adopt the exact wording used in authorised claims, and, following the position under the 2006 Regulation (as discussed earlier), the Food Rules expressly state that a health claim that would have the same meaning to the consumer as an authorised health claim may be used in marketing communications.[27] While this is not also expressly stated in relation to nutrition claims, the same approach ought to apply.

The Department of Health has issued guidance on how to reword authorised health claims,[28] and it is clear that where rewording is implemented, it should be used to aid consumer understanding. In an ASA adjudication concerning a magazine advertisement for Pharma Nord's Omega 7 Sea buckthorn oil, it was found that the claim that Vitamin A 'maintains normal structure and function of the... female reproductive tract' did not have the same meaning as the authorised health claim that 'Vitamin A contributes to the maintenance of normal mucous membrane' and that it amounted to an exaggeration of the authorised health claim.[29]

The Food Rules and comparative nutrition claims

As noted earlier, making comparative nutrition claims can be particularly tricky because there are only four types of claim that are acceptable and there are complex restrictions on how they may be made. This section, therefore, considers those types of claim, rather than taking a broader look at the Food Rules and nutrition claims generally. Unsurprisingly, comparative nutrition claims have been the subject of a number of adjudications by the ASA.

The Food Rules echo the 2006 Regulation and state that: 'Comparative nutrition claims must compare the difference in the claimed nutrient to a range of foods of the same category which do not have the composition that allows them to bear a nutrition claim.'[30]

'Foods of the same category' are foods that are similar in terms of nutritional content. In an ASA ruling on PharmaCare (Europe) Ltd, the ASA found that 'breakfast foods' was not a sufficiently narrow category for making comparative nutrition claims because the description depended on the occasion on which the foods were consumed as opposed to the specific food category. As such, oats, milk and eggs were not in the same food category as chia and flax seeds for the purpose of making a comparison.[31]

Alternatives or substitutes are likely to be considered foods in the same category. In a 2014 ASA adjudication on an ad for Quorn, the ASA stated that it was acceptable for a comparison to be made between beef mince and Quorn, the latter being an alternative to meat.[32]

Since a comparison must be made with a 'range of foods', a comparison with one food is insufficient unless that one food is considered to be representative of the relevant category.[33] In an ASA adjudication on an ASDA store e-mail promoting SMA Toddler Milk, the ASA said that the conditions for comparison had not been met because cow's milk alone was not representative of the relevant food category; a comparative claim for SMA Toddler Milk would need to be made against a range of foods in the category that included other toddler milks.[34]

As noted above, for comparative claims against foods in the same category, only those foods for which a nutrition claim cannot be made may be used as a comparator. In an ASA adjudication about an ad for Birds Eye frozen vegetables, the ASA said that a claim which compared fresh and frozen vegetables was not compliant because the comparator, fresh vegetables, could bear a nutrition claim, in particular regarding vitamin C.[35] In the ASA adjudication mentioned above about a TV ad promoting Quorn, the ASA found that a comparison regarding fat content could be made between Quorn and beef mince because the packs of lean beef mince against which the comparison was made were not able to bear a 'low saturated fat' claim.

Courtesy of Quorn

The Food Rules and health claims

Complaints to the ASA in relation to health claims commonly concern the clarity with which health claims are made.

Again echoing the 2006 Regulation, general statements about the benefits of a nutrient or a food for health are not acceptable unless they are accompanied by a specific, authorised health claim.[36] In an ASA adjudication concerning an ad for a health supplement called 'Thrive Plus Boost', a number of claims made about the product, including: 'designed to... energize your system with each serving', 'detox & cleansing support', 'enhanced energy levels', 'Neutraceutical', 'phytonutrient dense beverage' and 'Thrive' and 'Boost' (particularly when used in conjunction with 'plus' and '+'), all amounted to general health claims, but, since they were not accompanied by any specific authorised health claims, were in breach of the Food Rules.[37]

It must also be clear to which relevant food or nutrient a health claim applies; it is important not to imply that the claim relates to the food or product as a whole if it relates only to a component of the food or product. In an ASA adjudication concerning a poster advertising Lucozade Sport that used the tagline 'HYDRATES AND FUELS YOU BETTER THAN WATER', the ASA said that health claims could only be made for the nutrient, substance, food, or food category for which they had been authorised and not for the product itself. The poster ad did not provide any explanation as to how Lucozade Sport provided the claimed health benefits. Consumers would not necessarily understand that the benefits would arise as a result of the product being a carbohydrate–electrolyte solution.[38]

On-hold health claims

As mentioned above, it is possible to use on-hold claims, but, just as authorised health claims have to reflect the actual claim listed on the EU Register, on-hold claims must reflect the particular claim that has been submitted. In an ASA adjudication concerning a national press ad and a website for Promensil MENOPAUSE, it was noted that the on-hold health claim on which the advertiser was trying to rely was for 'red clover', generally. But the health claim in the ad was for 'Red Clover isoflavones to help you stay comfortable during the menopause'. Since the health claim in the ad referred specifically to red clover isoflavones and not just red clover, it did not properly reflect the on-hold claim and was found to be in breach of the Code.[39]

On-hold claims are assessed in the same way as authorised health claims under the Food Rules, so exaggerated claims are also unacceptable. In the same adjudication, the ASA acknowledged that the on-hold claim on which the advertiser relied related to how red clover 'helps to maintain a calm and comfortable menopause/helps women coping with the telltale signs associated with menopause such as hot flushes, sweating, restlessness and irritability'. But wording in the ads including: 'over 15 years of Scientific Research on effectiveness', 'guarantees the optimum level (80mg) of active ingredients, which really does make a difference', and 'recommended... to women who opt for a natural menopause' went beyond the wording of the on-hold claim.

Summary

This chapter covers only some of the key areas of the law and regulation of nutrition and health claims. Although these types of claim are prevalent, the rules are complex and advertisers and their agencies should take great care when preparing their campaigns. As noted above, complaints to the ASA are not uncommon and the sanctions for breaching the 2006 Regulation can be draconian.

Notes

1 Regulation 1924/2006, Article 1(2)

2 Regulation 1924/2006, Article 2(2)(1)

3 'EU Health Food Claims Law Begins to Bite', BBC News, 7 July 2010

4 Regulation 1924/2006, Article 28(2)

5 Regulation 1924/2006, Article 1(3)

6 Regulation 1924/2006, Article 3

7 Regulation 1924/2006, Article 5

8 Regulation 1924/2006, Article 6

9 Regulation 1924/2006, Article 2(4)

10 Regulation 1924/2006, Article 8

11 Regulation 1924/2006, recital 21

12 Regulation 1924/2006, Article 9(2)

13 Regulation 1924/2006, Article 9(1)

14 Regulation 1924/2006, Article 2(5)

15 Regulation 1924/2006, Article 10(1)

16 Regulation 1924/2006, Article 10(2)

17 Regulation 432/2012, recital 9

18 Regulation 1924/2006, Article 10(3)

19 Regulation 1924/2006, Article 4(3)

20 Regulation 1924/2006, Article 4(3)

21 Regulation 1924/2006, Article 4

22 Parliamentary Questions E-005223-15, Answer given by Mr Andriukaitis on behalf of the Commission, 26 May 2015

23 Department of Health Bulletin, Update from the European Commission's Working Group Meeting on Health Claims, 9 November 2015

24 CAP Code 15.1.1, BCAP Code 13.4

25 ASA ruling on Jane Plan Ltd, 9 September 2015

26 BCAP Code, 13.4, 13.4.2, 13.6, 13.6.5

27 BCAP 13.4, CAP 15.1.1

28 'General Principles on Flexibility of Wording for Health Claims', January 2013

29 ASA ruling on Pharma Nord (UK) Ltd, 16 September 2015

30 CAP 15.3 and BCAP 13.5.1

31 ASA ruling on PharmaCare (Europe) Ltd, 11 June 2014

32 ASA ruling on Marlow Foods Ltd, 23 April 2014

33 CAP 15.3.1 and BCAP 13.5.2

34 ASA ruling on ASDA Stores Ltd, 15 October 2014

35 ASA ruling on Birds Eye Ltd, 17 August 2011

36 CAP 15.2, BCAP 13.4.3

37 ASA ruling on Le-Vel Brands LLC, 15 July 2015

38 ASA ruling on GlaxoSmithKline UK Ltd, 8 January 2014

39 ASA ruling on PharmaCare (Europe) Ltd, 27 January 2016

The advertising of food   20

Children

REBECCA CHONG AND RICHARD LINDSAY

Introduction

In addition to reflecting the law on nutrition and health claims and ensuring that consumers are provided with accurate and clear information about food, Section 15 of the CAP Code and Section 13 of the BCAP Code (the 'Food Rules', as discussed in the previous chapter) are designed to ensure that advertising does not encourage unhealthy eating or poor nutritional habits among children.

This chapter will focus on how the Food Rules (and associated rules) under the CAP and BCAP Codes restrict the extent to which food advertising is permitted to influence the dietary habits of the consumer, in particular the advertising of food to children.

Healthy eating

The basic principle of the CAP and BCAP Codes that all advertising must be prepared with a sense of responsibility[1] is indicative of a self-regulatory system designed to ensure that advertising does not have a negative impact on consumers and society. With regard to the advertising of food, this general principle is supported by the Food Rules, which state that advertising must not condone or encourage excessive consumption of food[2] and not disparage good dietary practice[3] (wording reflecting the 2006 Regulation[4] – see previous chapter on nutrition and health claims). They also prohibit marketing communications that would discourage people from adopting a balanced and varied diet.

As children may be more impressionable and vulnerable than adults, the CAP and BCAP Codes provide specific rules governing advertising directed at children.[5] The Food Rules additionally place particular emphasis on restricting the advertising of food to children in response to concerns over poor childhood diet. The BCAP Code states that advertisements must avoid anything likely to condone or encourage poor nutritional habits or an unhealthy lifestyle, especially in children,[6] and in the CAP Code the same point is made specifically in relation to children.[7]

The Food Rules go further by controlling how, if at all, advertisers are permitted to use marketing techniques, such as promotional offers and the use of licensed characters and celebrities, in advertising to children.

HFSS products and the distinction between TV broadcast versus radio and non-broadcast rules

Promotional offers

The Food Rules state that any advertising that contains a promotional offer must be used or prepared with a due sense of responsibility.[9] Further, except in relation to advertising for fresh fruit and vegetables, the use of promotional offers in non-broadcast advertising for 'food products' – references to 'food' includes drinks – targeted directly at pre-school or primary school children is prohibited.[10] For radio ads, the rule is identical, but 'food products' includes soft drinks (not all drinks).

For television broadcasting, however, the equivalent Food Rules specifically focus on prohibiting the promotion of 'HFSS products', defined as food or drink products[11] assessed as high in fat, salt or sugar by a nutrient profiling model developed by the Food Standards Agency (now under the remit of the Department of Health).[12] No such categorisation applies to non-broadcast or radio ads though, at the time of writing, CAP have published a consultation proposing to align the two codes and introduce restrictions in non-broadcast ads for HFSS products targeted at or likely to appeal particularly to children.

Where not expressly prohibited, the use of promotional offers is still subject to a number of restrictions. The Food Rules also state, for example, that advertising featuring a promotional offer that is linked to a food product of interest to children must avoid creating a sense of urgency or encouraging the purchase of an excessive quantity for irresponsible consumption,[13] and must not encourage children to eat more than they otherwise would.[14] Where an advertisement concerns a collection-based promotion, it must not seem to urge children or their parents to buy excessive quantities of food.[15]

Further, advertising must not encourage children to eat or drink a product only to take advantage of an offer. The product must be offered on its merits.[16] There is an exception to this rule for non-broadcast promotions for fresh fruit or vegetables.[17]

Licensed characters and celebrities

As with promotional offers, use of licensed characters and celebrities popular with children must be used with a due sense of responsibility,[18] and use is subject to similar restrictions. (The rules do not apply to equity brand characters – ie characters designed by/for the particular brand.)

The Food Rules state that except in relation to advertising for fresh fruit and vegetables, the use of licensed characters and celebrities in non-broadcast food advertising – and again, 'food' includes drinks – targeted directly at pre-school or primary school children is prohibited.[19] The ASA found that a Scooby Doo section on a Swizzels Matlow website which contained images and information about Scooby Doo-branded products – which were not fresh fruit or vegetables – and two child-friendly Scooby Doo-themed games, was aimed at primary school children and therefore in breach of the CAP Code as it contained a licensed character.[20]

For radio ads, the rule is identical to that for non-broadcast, but again expressly refers to soft drinks as well as food products.[21]

And for television broadcasting, the equivalent Food Rules make the same distinction as with promotional offers and specifically prohibit the use of licensed characters and celebrities for HFSS product ads rather than food products (or food products and soft drinks) generally.[22]

Pester power and emotive advertising

The Food Rules contain a specific restriction against television and non-broadcast advertising that directly advises or asks children to buy or ask others to make enquiries or purchases for them.[23] Further, advertising must not appeal to children's emotions or imply that the advertised product confers superiority,[24] and use of high-pressure or hard-sell techniques[25] to children is also prohibited. The rules for television advertising specifically prohibit the encouragement of children to 'pester' or 'make a nuisance' of themselves[26] and state that ads must not imply that children will be inferior to others, disloyal or will have let someone down by not purchasing or consuming the product.[27]

While the same restrictions on exploiting emotions are not expressly stated in the BCAP Code in relation to radio advertising, considering the spirit of the Code it is unlikely that radio advertising for food that directly advises children to buy or ask others to make purchases for them, or which otherwise cajoles or exploits the emotional vulnerability of a child, would be acceptable.

Nutrition and health claims and children's health

The Food Rules for non-broadcast and radio advertising allow claims that refer to children's development and health if those claims are authorised by the European Commission.[28]

The television broadcasting rules are more prescriptive. The same claims are allowed in respect of non-HFSS product ads as in non-broadcast and radio advertising, but the rules specifically prohibit the use of any health and nutrition claims in HFSS product ads targeted directly at pre-school or primary school children.[29]

Scheduling of HFSS advertising on TV

In addition to the restrictions on the content of advertising discussed above, television advertising of HFSS foods to children aged under 16 is subject to additional restrictions as to how and when ads are placed. HFSS ads must not be scheduled in or adjacent to programmes commissioned for, principally directed at, or likely to appeal particularly to audiences below the age of 16.[30] As BCAP's guidance on Scheduling and Audience Indexing explains:[31] 'In practice, it is usually straightforward for broadcasters to identify a programme commissioned for or principally directed at a particular age group… Identifying programmes that appeal particularly to children or children and young people is more complicated.'

So, while it should be simple enough for broadcasters to identify programmes commissioned for or principally directed at children under 16, they use audience indexing to identify whether a programme is likely to appeal particularly to that age group. Audience indexing is a predictive tool which determines what proportion of a particular category of viewers is watching a programme relative to the proportion of the audience as a whole. Programmes that score above 120 on the index are deemed to have particular appeal to the under-16 age group.

Stricter rules for advertising to children?

The EU Pledge

Concern over the extent to which advertisers are permitted to advertise food, in particular to children, is not a recent issue. In 2007, the EU Pledge[32] was launched to demonstrate a commitment to socially responsible food advertising to children.

The Pledge is a voluntary initiative, but a number of major food and drinks companies have signed up. Its two original main commitments were: (i) no advertising to children under 12, except for products that meet certain nutritional requirements; and (ii) no communication related to products in primary schools, except where specifically requested by or agreed with the school for educational purposes. By the end of 2011, signatories accounted for more than 80 per cent of marketing spend in the EU.

At the end of 2014, the Pledge signatories announced plans to extend its scope with effect from 31 December 2016 to include radio, cinema, DVD/CD-ROM, direct marketing, product placement, interactive games, and mobile and SMS marketing, in addition to TV, print, third-party internet and company-owned websites. Under an enhanced commitment intended to take effect from the same date, they will also either: (i) only advertise products to children under the age of 12 years that meet the common EU Pledge Nutrition Criteria; or (ii) not advertise their products at all to children under the age of 12 years. They also agree not to engage in food or beverage product marketing communications to children in primary schools.

Summary

There is a significant amount of pressure on the advertising industry to change the way it advertises food and drink, particularly to children, even though the CAP and BCAP Codes already include strict rules governing the advertising of food and drink. As noted above, there are some obvious differences between the rules for TV broadcast and non-broadcast and radio ads; most obviously, neither the CAP Code nor the rules for radio ads categorise HFSS products and there are no targeting restrictions for non-broadcast ads equivalent to those for TV ads. CAP's consultation on aligning the codes could have significant ramifications for non-broadcast advertising of food and drink to children. Further, the government's new obesity strategy is yet to be published and may contain further restrictions.

Notes

1 CAP 1.3, BCAP 1.2

2 CAP 15.4, BCAP 13.3

3 CAP 15.12, BCAP 13.5

4 Recital (18)

5 CAP 5, BCAP 5

6 BCAP 13.2

7 CAP 15.11

8 ASA ruling on Nestlé UK Ltd, 23 December 2015

9 CAP 15.13, BCAP 13.9, BCAP 13.13

10 CAP 15.14, BCAP 13.13

11 BCAP 13.9

12 Nutrient Profiling Technical Guidance, Department of Health, January 2011

13 CAP 15.14.2, BCAP 13.9.1, 13.13

14 CAP 15.14.3, BCAP 13.9.4

15 CAP 15.14.4, BCAP 13.9.3, 13.13

16 CAP 15.14.1, BCAP 13.9.2, 13.13

17 CAP 15.14.1

18 CAP 15.15, BCAP 13.10, BCAP 13.14

19 CAP 15.15

20 ASA ruling on Swizzels Matlow Ltd, 29 August 2012

21 BCAP 13.14

22 BCAP 13.10

23 CAP 15.16, BCAP 13.12

24 CAP 15.16.1, BCAP 13.12.3

25 CAP 15.16.2, BCAP 13.12.4

26 BCAP 13.12.1

27 BCAP 13.12.2

28 CAP 15.17, BCAP 13.15

29 BCAP 13.11

30 BCAP 32.5.1

31 Advertising Guidance Note no. 4: BCAP, Scheduling and Audience Indexing: identifying television programmes likely to appeal particularly to children and young people

32 http://www.eu-pledge.eu

Gambling 21

DAVID ZEFFMAN

OLSWANG

Introduction

The advertising of gambling in the United Kingdom is tightly regulated. The primary legislative requirements are set out in the Gambling Act 2005 (the 'Act') but several other sources of regulation must be taken into account when developing advertising for gambling services.

The overarching principles set out in the Act underpin much of the regulation relating to gambling advertising. They can be recognised in each of the relevant pieces of regulation in some form and comprise:

1 preventing gambling from being a source of crime or disorder, being associated with crime or disorder or being used to support crime;

2 ensuring that gambling is conducted in a fair and open way; and

3 protecting children and other vulnerable persons from being harmed or exploited by gambling.

While the spirit of these principles can be seen throughout the regulatory framework, the Act contains very few specific details in relation to advertising. Responsibility for devising specific requirements for advertising in this sector has fallen to the Gambling Commission (as the regulator of licensed operators), which publishes the Licence Conditions and Codes of Practice attached to gambling licences, and to the Committee of Advertising Practice (CAP) and the Advertising Standards Authority (ASA). In addition, industry groups have established and subscribed to a number of self-regulatory codes that set out standards with which they agree to comply.

What is gambling?

Under the Act, gambling includes 'gaming, betting and participating in a lottery'. In this chapter we address gaming and betting. Lotteries are treated differently from gaming and betting and are addressed in Chapter 13.

'Gaming' is defined as 'playing a game of chance for a prize'. This captures traditional casino games (such as poker or roulette) as well as bingo. It can also capture new games that result in a prize of money or money's worth being paid out to the winner.

'Betting' is defined as 'making or accepting a bet on:

1 the outcome of a race, competition or other event or process;

2 the likelihood of anything occurring or not occurring; or

3 whether anything is or is not true.'

Much of what constitutes betting is very familiar, bets on the Grand National or the Champions League Final being obvious candidates, but betting on more unusual events is also common and can provide publicity opportunities for bookmakers (Paddy Power's Oscar Pistorius advert being an example of the publicity (positive or negative) that can be garnered by offering odds on unusual events – see Chapter 5).

The Gambling Act: who can advertise?

At the end of 2014, the Act was amended by the Gambling (Licensing and Advertising) Act 2014. The amendments changed the categories of those able to advertise facilities for gambling in Great Britain, with a distinction between those offering remote facilities (eg online poker or a bookmaking app) or non-remote facilities (eg a casino or a betting shop).

Those who advertise gambling facilities in Great Britain other than those permitted to be advertised will commit a criminal offence.

Remote gambling

Remote gambling facilities may only be advertised in Great Britain by holders of a remote gambling licence issued by the Gambling Commission. The licence allows advertising by both remote means (e-mail, banner-ads etc) and non-remote means (such as perimeter advertising at sports events).

There is an exception to this rule which may allow advertising of remote gambling facilities in Great Britain without a licence, though it should be approached with caution. If an unlicensed, remote gambling operator wants to advertise its facilities in Great Britain but does not have customers there (which can happen where, for example, the operator is targeting an audience in a foreign country by sponsoring sports teams in Great Britain with a global audience, such as a Premier League football team), and it employs effective geo-blocking mechanisms which ensure that people in Great Britain are not able to access its remote gambling facilities, then that operator could lawfully advertise in Great Britain without a remote gambling licence. In practice, such advertising is unlikely to be common as there are many parties in the chain (in our example, they could include the Premier League football club and the television broadcaster), who will each need to be confident that they would not commit an offence by carrying the advertising. Many online publishers, including Google and Microsoft, operate a blanket policy that they will not publish gambling adverts unless the relevant operator is licensed.

Non-remote gambling

The restrictions on non-remote facilities distinguish between those that are located within, and those that are located outside, Great Britain. If the non-remote facilities are located within Great Britain (for example, a betting shop), the operator must hold an operating licence. If the non-remote facilities are located outside Great Britain (for example, a Las Vegas casino), those facilities may be advertised without a licence.

The Gambling Commission maintains a register of its licensees which can be searched online.

The Licence Conditions and Codes of Practice

Published by the Gambling Commission and governing advertising by all gambling licence holders, the Licence Conditions and Codes of Practice are regularly updated and increasingly address specific concerns which the Gambling Commission has raised in relation to gambling advertising.

In particular, the Licence Conditions and Codes of Practice require that licensees:

- undertake advertising in a socially responsible manner;

- comply with the UK Code of Advertising, Sales Promotion and Direct Marketing (CAP Code) and UK Code of Broadcast Advertising (BCAP Code) (and apply the rules set out therein to any media not specifically covered by the Codes);

- have regard to the CAP and BCAP guidance notes relevant to gambling advertising (currently the 'Guidance on the rules for gambling advertisements');

- comply with any relevant industry advertising codes, including the Gambling Industry Code for Socially Responsible Advertising (see below);

- do not show anyone who is, or appears to be, under 25 (there is an exception to this rule where the advertising material appears at the point of sale (including online) and the person shown is the subject of the bet and shown in the context of the bet (eg taking part in the sport and not gambling)); and

- do not show anyone behaving in an adolescent, juvenile or loutish way.

In light of the high volumes of complaints received by the ASA and widespread concerns, the Licence Conditions and Codes of Practice specifically address 'free bet', 'bonus' and similar promotional offers, requiring that:

- adverts state significant limitations and qualifications (which must not contradict the headline claim);

- if time or space is limited, consumers are given as much information about significant conditions as practicable and are directed to an easily accessible alternative source where all the significant conditions of the promotion are prominently stated (it must be possible for participants to retain or access these conditions easily throughout the term of the promotion); and

- any terms and conditions relating to a consumer's understanding of a free bet offer, and the commitments that they have to make in order to take advantage of such an offer, should be stated in the advert itself. If time or space makes this impossible, significant conditions should be displayed no further than one click away from the advert.

The CAP and BCAP Codes

In addition to the general requirements covering all advertising in the CAP and BCAP Codes, Section 16 of the CAP Code and Section 17 of the BCAP Code specifically address gambling advertising. The intention of these specific rules is to ensure that marketing of gambling products is socially responsible and, in particular, has regard to the need to protect those under 18 and other vulnerable persons from being harmed or exploited by advertising featuring or promoting gambling.

These gambling-specific sections of the Codes set out comprehensive, stringent requirements for gambling adverts and, among other matters, require that advertising must not:

- portray, condone or encourage gambling behaviour that is socially irresponsible or could lead to financial, social or emotional harm;
- exploit the susceptibilities, aspirations, credulity, inexperience or lack of knowledge of children, young persons or other vulnerable persons;
- suggest that gambling can provide an escape from personal, professional or educational problems such as loneliness or depression;
- suggest that gambling can be a solution to financial concerns, an alternative to employment or a way to achieve financial security;
- portray gambling as indispensable or as taking priority in life, for example over family, friends or professional or educational commitments;
- suggest that gambling can enhance personal qualities, for example that it can improve self-image or self-esteem, or is a way to gain control, superiority, recognition or admiration;
- suggest peer pressure to gamble nor disparage abstention;
- link gambling to seduction, sexual success or enhanced attractiveness;
- portray gambling in a context of toughness or link it to resilience or recklessness;
- suggest gambling is a rite of passage;
- suggest that solitary gambling is preferable to social gambling;
- be likely to be of particular appeal to children or young persons, especially by reflecting or being associated with youth culture;
- exploit cultural beliefs or traditions about gambling or luck; or
- condone or encourage criminal or anti-social behaviour.

While not addressed by the CAP or BCAP Codes, it should be noted that product placement (when a company pays a programme maker to include its products or brands in a programme) is not permitted for gambling products in television programmes, despite the product placement laws being relaxed in 2011. Product placement of gambling products is, however, allowed in programmes included in on-demand services, subject to compliance with the various conditions set by the Authority for Television On Demand.

The ASA, the UK's independent regulator of advertising across all media, enforces the CAP and BCAP Codes. ASA rulings are a useful barometer of areas of public and regulatory focus, with common themes being discernible when particular types of advertising practice are under close scrutiny (for example, free bets and bonuses). In addition, they can be a helpful means of determining where the regulator will draw the line (though there is scope for inconsistency between rulings).

Lessons from previous ASA rulings

1. Do not feature children or other images or elements that are likely to particularly appeal to children (including children's toys). Adverts around the time of the royal birth featuring teddy bears and children were banned (17 June 2015). A separate campaign was banned for the heavy focus on fairy-tale-like elements and use of cartoon imagery (27 May 2015).

2. If elements that may be (but are not necessarily) of particular appeal to children are to be used, ensure that tight scheduling restrictions are in place in order to avoid young audiences (27 May 2015).

3. Ensure that any significant terms, including qualifications (such as wagering requirements and restrictions on withdrawals), are shown in close proximity to any offer (7 January 2015).

4. Do not make 'money-back' claims if the promotion actually means that customers get a free bet and not a cash refund (3 September 2014).

5. Use expressions like 'risk free' with care. Too many qualifications, which together contradict the headline claim, are likely to be found to be misleading (7 January 2015).

▶

> **6** As a minimum, ensure that adverts for offers such as bonuses and free bets that are published on a medium with only limited space include a statement that terms and conditions apply and that these terms and conditions are only one click away (7 January 2015).
>
> **7** As with advertising in other sectors, avoid images that are likely to cause offence, such as those associated with religion (6 August 2014 and 27 August 2014) or that could be seen as demeaning to women (28 May 2014).

Gambling industry codes

Self-regulation is an important part of the regulatory landscape for gambling operators. In addition to the CAP and BCAP Codes, the primary code is the Gambling Industry Code for Socially Responsible Advertising (the 'Industry Code'). While Section 47 of the Industry Code states that it 'cannot be made mandatory', the Licence Conditions and Codes of Practice provide that licensees should follow the Industry Code as good practice.

The Industry Code

The Industry Code sets out social responsibility standards for gambling operators and is supplemental to, and reiterates some of the provisions of, the CAP and BCAP Codes.

The following general principles are set out in the Industry Code:

- Advertisements should comply with the CAP and BCAP Codes.
- Advertisements must be legal and not misleading.
- Advertisements should be socially responsible, as described in the CAP and BCAP Codes.
- Care must be taken not to exploit children and other vulnerable people.
- Advertisements should not specifically or intentionally target those under 18 by the selection of media, style of presentation, content or context in which they appear.

The above are already familiar principles from the Licence Conditions and Codes of Practice and the CAP and BCAP Codes. In addition, the Industry

Code sets out more specific requirements in relation to social responsibility messaging, the television watershed and sports sponsorship. Specifically:

- The website address www.gambleaware.co.uk should be included on all advertising, if feasible and practical.

- Operators are encouraged to include additional 'educational messaging' within adverts (examples of which include 'Don't let the game play you', 'Know your limit and play within it' and 'Please play responsibly').

- Gambling products other than bingo should not be advertised on television before 9.00 pm (with the exception of sports betting around televised sporting events).

- Operators should not allow their logos or other promotional material to appear on merchandising designed for use by children (such as football shirts).

With effect from 20 February 2016, a series of amendments to the Industry Code came into effect, namely:

- the removal from pre-watershed television advertising of sign-up offers targeted at new customers;

- a restriction on pre-watershed television advertising making reference to other gambling products that would not normally qualify for pre-9.00 pm exemption;

- a requirement to have socially responsible gambling messages at the end of all television and radio adverts;

- a requirement that operators make the www.gambleaware.co.uk website address more prominent in print and broadcast adverts, and that reference is made to it in all television sponsorship; and

- a requirement that print and television adverts must also include messaging to make it clear that the product being promoted is only suitable for those aged 18 or over.

The Senet Group and other industry codes

In response to increased scrutiny of the industry and the potential for further legislation, some operators have increased their commitment to social responsibility by subscribing to additional self-regulatory codes.

The most prominent new group is the Senet Group, an independent body comprising William Hill, Ladbrokes, Coral, Paddy Power and Scotbet. The Senet Group has two primary functions: to promote responsible gambling (which it does through jointly funded advertising campaigns), and to hold its members to the advertising commitments set out below:

- A voluntary TV advertising ban on sign-up offers (free bets and free money) before 9 pm.
- Withdraw all advertising of gaming machines from betting shop windows.
- Dedicate 20 per cent of shop window advertising to responsible gambling messages.

The number of self-regulatory codes and subscribers to them is likely to continue to increase.

Enforcement

As noted above, the ASA is responsible for investigating breaches of the CAP and BCAP Codes and imposing sanctions on non-compliant advertisers. Complaints are made directly to the ASA and, where sanctions are imposed, these generally require advertisers to withdraw or amend offending adverts. The ASA's rulings are published on their website and often attract press coverage, bringing negative publicity to the advertiser.

Repeated or serious breaches of the CAP or BCAP Codes are likely to come to the attention of the Gambling Commission, and, for very severe breaches, there is a risk that a licensee would have its licence revoked. Broadcasters may be referred to Ofcom.

Northern Ireland

Gaming advertising in Northern Ireland is subject to a different regime and is more limited than that in the rest of the UK. In particular, the Betting, Gaming, Lotteries and Amusements (Northern Ireland) Order 1985 prohibits any person: 'inviting the public to subscribe any money or money's worth to be used in gaming whether in Northern Ireland or elsewhere, or to apply for information about facilities for subscribing any money or money's worth to be so used'.

This does not mean that all gaming advertising is banned, but the advertising of both remote and non-remote gaming facilities must not invite people to subscribe money. Inviting participation, however, is not banned.

As a consequence of the above, care should be taken to ensure that gaming advertising published in Northern Ireland goes no further than describing the services and games available. Customers should not be invited to play for money and incentives for play should be avoided. References to 'free welcome bonus' or 'play for free' should also be avoided as they are potentially indirect invitations to subscribe for money.

The above does not apply to betting, which may be advertised in Northern Ireland – subject to the same restrictions set out in the rest of this chapter.

Pressures on the industry

The coming into force of the Act in September 2007 brought with it greater freedom for gambling operators to advertise their services, and advertising volumes have increased significantly since that time, with advertisements on television in particular becoming ever more common. However, the increased visibility of gambling advertising appears to have heightened public awareness of the issues related to it, in turn pressurising regulators to apply ever greater scrutiny to the sector.

The landscape of the gambling industry has changed dramatically in the past decade, with the continuing rise of remote gambling and utilisation of social media and new mobile technologies in particular providing new opportunities for operators. This, together with the passage of the Gambling

(Licensing and Advertising) Act 2014, the increased volume and diversification of gambling advertising and concerns about the effect on problem gambling of gaming machines in betting shops, led the Department for Culture, Media & Sport to call for a re-examination of the regulatory framework in May 2014. While the various reviews since undertaken by the regulators suggest overall satisfaction with the advertising regulatory regime, problem areas were identified (such as in relation to promotional offers), and concern relating to the impact of gambling advertising on children in particular was prevalent. It is in this context that operators continue to face pressure from the public, regulators and government, and the industry still finds itself labelled controversial and in need of an especially watchful eye from regulators.

With the industry very much in the cross-hairs of regulators, gambling operators and advertising agencies must tread carefully when developing advertising for gambling services and ensure compliance with the framework described in this chapter. With heightened scrutiny comes greater risk of any failings being identified, which in turn could lead to examples being made of non-compliant operators and further calls for stricter regulation. Operators would be wise to bear this in mind when attempting to capture a share of an increasingly competitive market.

Political advertising

22

PAUL HERBERT

GOODMAN DERRICK LLP

Introduction

This chapter examines the complexities of political advertising and the different treatment accorded to it under the law and the self-regulatory codes. Of particular relevance is the ban on the broadcasting of political advertising, which is so broad in scope as to extend far beyond politics in the conventional sense and encompass social advocacy.

Political advertising: TV and radio

Political advertising – the definition of which is explained below – has always been prohibited in TV and radio. The rationale is based on widespread acceptance 'of the perception that that the power and pervasiveness of broadcast media over other media was such that it could give an unfair advantage to those who could afford to promote their political views over the air waves over those who could not, and, as a result, unfairly distort the democratic process'.[1]

The ban is now enshrined in Sections 319 and 321 of The Communications Act 2003 (CA 2003).

S.319(2) requires: 'that advertising that contravenes the prohibition on political advertising set out in s321(2) is not included in television or radio services.'

S.321(2): For the purposes of s319(2) an advertisement contravenes the prohibition on political advertising if it is:

a   an advertisement which is inserted by or on behalf of a body whose objects are wholly or mainly of a political nature;

b   an advertisement which is directed towards a political end; or

c   an advertisement which has a connection with an industrial dispute.

Already it will be apparent that the ban is broad in its application, but there is more:

S.321(3): For the purposes of this section objects of a political nature and political ends include each of the following:

a   influencing the outcome of elections or referenda, whether in the United Kingdom or elsewhere;

b   bringing about changes of the law in the whole or a part of the United Kingdom or elsewhere or otherwise influencing the legislative process in any country or territory;

c   influencing the policies or decisions of local regional or national governments whether in the United Kingdom or elsewhere;

d   influencing the policies or decisions of persons on whom political functions are conferred by or under the law of the United Kingdom or of a country or territory outside of the United Kingdom;

e   influencing the policies or decisions of persons on whom functions are conferred by or under international agreements;

f   influencing public opinion on a matter which in the United Kingdom is a matter of public controversy; and

g   promoting the interests of a party or other group of persons organised in the United Kingdom or elsewhere for political ends.

Notably, Section 321(7) excludes two categories of activity from the ambit of the ban: (a) advertisement[s] of a public service nature inserted by or on behalf of a government department; or (b) a party-political or referendum campaign broadcast....

So, there are three key elements to this regime. First, the definition of what is 'political', thereby falling within the ban's remit for advertising purposes, is very broad indeed. It is certainly capable of including social advocacy exercised by the likes of single-interest or larger, more established groups. Typically, these types of group seek to influence public opinion on matters as diverse as politics, policy, religion, morals, conservation and so on.

Why should the prohibition extend to social advocacy? The argument is that the causes that social advocacy groups might represent and the messages they might wish to convey may fall within the scope of what many would consider 'political'. Much blurring can occur at the margins, especially if a group's aim is to seek a change in law or policy.

> I instance those who... supported the ban on hunting with dogs with donations to one party; those who regard abortion or civil partnerships as necessary rights or as sins; ... interest groups who may seek to identify the religious affiliations or beliefs of politicians as a basis for their non-selection as candidates... Those who campaign for an end to what they see as abuses of animals, whether in research, circuses, sport or clothing and those who take a different view may promote their views as seeking legislative change or as alterations to public attitudes. They may argue that the MPs who support their legislative aim or policies should be returned at the next election or de-selected if they do not; they may simply invite public debate and commercial boycotts... This... shows that there is no discernible distinction in practice which can be drawn between one so-called political party or group and another so-called social advocacy group. (Ouseley J in the High Court in the ADi case – see below)

Second, Section 321(2) prohibits advertising on behalf of a body whose objects are political, irrespective of the nature or content of the advertising. This is a particularly controversial feature of the prohibition and has resulted in many broadcast advertisements being declined for transmission whose content could not be described as political in any sense of the word. This was another point at issue in the ADi case:

The width of the statutory prohibition is remarkable. It would appear, for example, to withhold from ADi, or from any organisation whose objects were wholly or mainly to bring about changes in the law, the ability to place for broadcasting an advertisement with no political content whatever, eg, to attend a car boot sale... Moreover, a good deal of commercial advertising is likely to be objectionable to the principles of some section of the viewing public. For example, the broadcasting of an advertisement encouraging people to patronise some particular zoo or circus would be likely to offend ADi and its supporters; the broadcasting of an advertisement encouraging people to eat burgers of various sorts would be likely to offend organisations that disagree with the manner in which beef cattle are reared or slaughtered or both... Why should these organisations not counter the broadcasting of advertisements that offend their principles with the broadcasting of their own advertisements promoting their principles? (Lord Scott in the House of Lords)

Third, Section 321(7) excludes two categories of activity from the ambit of the ban: it permits public service announcements on behalf of government departments and party-political and election broadcasts by political parties. An example of how this limb has been interpreted is discussed in the 'Bedtime Stories' example below.

Although the ban is reproduced in the UK Code of Broadcast Advertising (BCAP Code), Ofcom has retained jurisdiction for adjudicating on alleged breaches. Thus, complaints are handled by Ofcom rather than the ASA. The prohibition is reflected in Section 7 of the BCAP Code, which more or less replicates the statutory definitions, including the exemptions under Section 321(7): likewise, in Section 7 of Clearcast's Notes of Guidance. Rule 7.1 of the BCAP Code also specifically requires any radio advertising that might fall under this prohibition to be centrally cleared through Radiocentre Copy Clearance, whose Copy Guidelines also provide guidance on the subject.

Application of the ban

Here are some examples of how the ban has been interpreted and applied by Ofcom.

Regulatory decisions

The Make Poverty History (MPH) Campaign

Transmitted by various broadcasters on 31 March 2005 (Ofcom Broadcast Bulletin 43, 12/9/2005)

MPH is a body representing around 300 charities, celebrities and other organisations. It was set up in 2004 for the purpose of campaigning for the elimination of poverty in developing countries. In December 2004, the BACC (whose role has been taken over by Clearcast) cleared an advertisement for MPH featuring a number of celebrities saying that 'Somebody dies avoidably through poverty every three seconds.' A caption stated 'Make Poverty History' and directed viewers to the MPH website, which encouraged viewers to lobby government directly to make this a high priority on their political agenda.

There were two questions for Ofcom: first, whether MPH was a body whose objects were wholly or mainly political and as such was prohibited from advertising under Section 321 CA 2003; and second, whether the MPH advertisements, by signposting viewers to the MPH website, were directed towards a political end in breach of Section 321(2)(b) CA 2003 in that they sought to influence government policy and decision making.

Ofcom determined that influencing policies relating to trade debt and aid could not reasonably be described as objectives that are *not* political in nature. Also, there was no escaping the fact that MPH had expressly characterised itself as an organisation that seeks to achieve important changes to the policies of the UK government and those of other Western governments. In relation to the second issue, although this was by now academic, Ofcom concluded that the relevant sections of CA 2003 were deliberately worded very widely so that, even if the content of an advertisement is not in itself political, it might nevertheless be an advertisement 'directed towards' a political end. The use of the word 'towards' clearly implies that if the advertisement has political objectives then the advertisement is caught.

Premier Christian Radio: advertisements for *The Politics Programme*

April and May 2008 (Broadcast Bulletin 115 11/08/2008)

On 30 April 2008, Premier Christian Radio transmitted an advertisement promoting *The Politics Programme*, a show scheduled for broadcast subsequently on Revelation TV and Genesis TV. It stated:

> Alan Craig, the Christian People Alliance and Christian Party's candidate
> for London Mayor, has seen ITV force him to rewrite comments in his party
> election broadcast about a radical Muslim group. Join me, George Hargreaves,
> on *The Politics Programme* on Genesis TV and Revelation TV on 30 April at
> 9 pm when we ask the question: 'Has the Christian People Alliance and
> Christian Party's Mayoral candidate Alan Craig been a victim of political
> censorship gone bad and political correctness gone mad?

The broadcaster said it considered that the advertisement was not directed to a political end but was rather advertising a television debate. It did not give a political view but asked the question that was to be debated in the programme. Listeners were not invited to react in a particular way, which they would have if the advert had been directed towards a political end.

Ofcom, however, considered that the advertisement showed undue partiality in relation to the London Mayoral election. While the advertisement did not call on listeners to vote for any particular candidate, it implicitly promoted the candidacy of Alan Craig. Not only did it specifically refer to him, but it clearly implied that he had in some way been a victim of unjust treatment. It was also worded in such a way as to leave listeners with a one-sided view of ITV's decision to instruct Alan Craig to rewrite his party election broadcast as being some form of censorship. It was therefore in breach.

Marie Stopes International (MSI)

Channel 4 May and June 2010 (Broadcast Bulletin 166 27/09/2010)

MSI is a registered charity providing services in the fields of sexual health, sterilisation and pregnancy, including advice about the provision of abortions. Its advertisement showed three women in everyday settings – a bus stop, a park, a café – and each time, a caption appeared with a name and the words '– is late': 'Jenny Evans is late', 'Kate Simmons is late' and 'Shareen Butler is late'. The voiceover then said: 'If you are late for your period you could be pregnant. If you are pregnant and not sure what to do, Marie Stopes International can help.' Several listeners complained to the effect that because abortion in the UK is a matter of continuing political debate and controversy and MSI actively campaigns to change abortion law, the advertisement could be regarded as being part of this wider campaign and therefore as political.

Ofcom considered first whether MSI is a body whose objects are wholly or mainly of a political nature. It pointed out that MSI is a registered charity and that the large majority of its activities and objectives could not be described as political in nature. Its main purpose was in the area of family planning services. Therefore, Ofcom concluded that MSI was not a body whose objects were wholly or mainly of a political nature.

Was the advertisement directed towards a political end? In this context it would depend on whether the advertisement was seeking to bring about changes of law or influencing the legislative process or influencing public opinion on a matter of public controversy. Ofcom did not consider these objectives could reasonably be ascribed to the content of the advertisement.

It is interesting to compare and contrast this decision to the decision arrived at in the Make Poverty History case. MSI clearly fell on the other side of the line from MPH in terms of its objectives, though, to readers, the rationale for that finding may be unclear. Notably, the MSI decision makes no reference to the earlier MPH decision. There is nothing sinister about this; Ofcom tends not to operate on a system of precedent like our courts, preferring to look at each case entirely on its own merits.

Bedtime Stories' advertisement for Act on CO_2

Various broadcasters, October 2009 (Broadcast Bulletin 167 11/10/2010)

Act on CO_2 was a joint initiative of three government departments intended to co-ordinate government efforts to reduce businesses' and individuals' carbon footprints produced through work and daily life. The advertisement showed a father reading his young daughter a bedtime story warning of the dangers caused by the excessive levels of CO_2 caused by human activity.

Ofcom received over 500 complaints. Many pointed to the political purpose of the advertisement, in some cases describing it as government propaganda. Others referred to the prohibition on issue campaigning and exhibiting partiality and influencing the viewers' willingness to vote for a political party promoting these policies.

Ofcom noted that Act on CO_2 was a cross-departmental campaign intended to raise the public's awareness of the wider context on which the UK government's policy of reducing carbon dioxide emissions is based. That was potentially an issue of a public service nature. Ofcom also noted that the advertisement imparted some information about actions that viewers could take to conserve energy, albeit that information was limited. However, on balance, Ofcom decided that the advertisement was of a public service nature and fell within the exception in Section 321(7)(a) CA 2003.

The above examples represent a selection of adjudications in respect of potentially 'political' adverts that were actually aired. Yet they represent a fraction of the total number of ads submitted for broadcast but which have been declined by BACC or Clearcast owing to concerns about compliance with Section 7 of the BCAP Code. Thus, great care is required in relation to ads by animal charities, especially those that campaign against animal cruelty; ethical farming practices, even when these are espoused by the large supermarkets; and, of course, issues concerning global warming and climate change (unless published on behalf of government departments as with the Act on CO_2 Campaign).

There have been no recorded breaches of Section 7 of the BCAP Code by national television or radio broadcasters since 2010. The majority that have been recorded in Ofcom's Broadcast Bulletins concern local radio advertisements that have not been submitted to the Radiocentre for clearance as required under s7.1 (because the advertisers did not consider them to be political) and advertisements on minority TV channels that do not use Clearcast's clearance services.

Legal challenges

The wide scope of the ban has created much resentment among the charitable and non-governmental organisation sectors, many of whose activities are caught by the ban and yet who could hardly be described as political in the usual sense of the word. This has led to several legal challenges over whether the ban is actually lawful (see for instance *R* v. *Radio Authority, ex parte Bull & Another* (1997 2 All ER 561) and *London Christian Radio* v. *The RACC and the Secretary of State for Culture Media and Sport* (2012 EWHC 1043), both of which failed).

More recently, Animal Defenders International (ADi) took their challenge all the way to the European Court of Human Rights in Strasbourg (ECtHR).

The ADi case

© Animal Defenders International

'My Mate's a Primate' campaign, courtesy of Animal Defenders International

ADi is a non-governmental organisation which campaigns against the use of animals in commerce, science and leisure. In 2005, it launched a campaign called 'My Mate's a Primate' which was directed against the keeping and exhibition of primates and their use in television advertising. As part of the campaign, ADi sought to broadcast a 30-second TV advertisement which opened with an image of an animal's cage in which a girl in chains gradually emerged from the shadows. The screen then went blank and three messages were relayed in sequence: 'a chimp has the mental age of a four-year-old'; 'although we share 98% of our genetic make-up they are still caged and abused to entertain us'; and 'to find out more and how you can help to stop it please order your £10 educational information pack'. In the final shot, a chimpanzee was shown in the same position as that of the girl.[2] The proposed advertisement was submitted to the BACC for clearance, but the BACC declined to clear it for broadcast on the grounds that ADi's objectives were wholly or mainly of a political nature – campaigning for changes in the law or policy to protect animals. ADi issued proceedings for judicial review of this decision on the grounds that the prohibition on political advertising was incompatible with its right to freedom of expression under Article 10 of the European Convention of Human Rights. Both the High Court (in December 2006 – [2006] EWHC 3069) and the Supreme Court (March 2008 – [2008] UKHL 15) rejected ADi's claim. In September 2008, ADi lodged an application with the ECtHR.

In its judgment delivered in April 2013, the Grand Chamber held by the slenderest of majorities – 9 votes to 8 – that the UK's ban did not violate Article 10 as it did not amount to a disproportionate interference with ADI's right of freedom of expression. Therefore, the ban survives. However, the narrowness of the Court's decision, and the robustness of the minority opinions, suggest that another challenge is entirely possible.

Political advertising: non-broadcast

The UK Code of Advertising, Sales Promotion and Direct Marketing (CAP Code) Remit

All forms of political advertising are permitted in non-broadcast media, with political advertising, in the conventional sense, being specifically exempt from the remit of the CAP Code. This is explained in the Code's Introduction and in rule 7.1: '7.1 – Claims in marketing communications, whenever published or distributed, whose principal function is to influence voters in a local, regional, national or international election or referendum are exempt from the Code.'

As CAP's AdviceOnline note on Political Advertising clarifies, the intention of rule 7.1 is 'to exempt types of advertisement, not types of advertiser'. The ASA and the CAP Executive interpret this rule: 'as excluding from the Code ads, whether party-political or not, that seem to have as their main purpose the influencing of voters in elections or referenda of a political but not necessarily party-political, governmental or legal nature'.

It follows, then, that while party-political and similar types of political adverts the principal function of which is to influence voters, as defined in rule 7.1, are exempt from the Code, all other types of 'political' advertising in the much broader sense, regardless of the complexion of the advertiser, are subject to it.

Rule 7.2 of the CAP Code says: 'Marketing communications by central or local government, as distinct from those concerning party policy, are subject to the Code.'

CAP's AdviceOnline note explains: 'Marcoms that are placed by charitable or commercial organisations that seek to lobby or raise awareness of a "political" subject by, for example, urging readers to write to their MPs, too, are subject to the Code.'

So, 'political' advertising, in a much broader sense than just seeking to influence voters, is also permitted in non-broadcast media, but is not exempt from the CAP Code and must comply with it. Indeed, one of the reasons that the broadcast prohibition was upheld in the ADi litigation was that it did not preclude the advertiser from securing publication of its message on all non-broadcast platforms.

Causes and ideas under the CAP Code

The advertising of causes and ideas covers a broad spectrum, including the likes of environmental campaigns, government health and safety campaigns, and marketing by charities and other pressure groups.[3] With the introduction of CAP's Online Remit Extension in 2011, the CAP Code continued to apply to any online advertising in paid-for space (such as banners and pop-ups) but was extended 'to advertisements and other marketing communications by or from companies, organisations or sole traders on their own websites, or in other non-paid-for space online under their control, that are directly connected with the supply or transfer of goods, services, opportunities and gifts, or which consist of direct solicitations of donations as part of their own fund-raising activities'.

Marketing communications for causes and ideas are not generally concerned with the supply or transfer of goods, services, opportunities or gifts, of course. But some do solicit donations and those are subject to the CAP Code, even if appearing in non-paid-for space.

Since 14 October 2014, the remit of the CAP Code regarding the marketing of causes and ideas has changed in the offline environment. Before this date, the Introduction to the Code made clear that the Code applied to all advertisements in a wide range of offline media. The Code does not define 'advertisement', but offline ads for causes and ideas would have been included, whether in paid-for or non-paid-for space and whether or not they solicited donations. With the recent change, though, the Code no longer applies to: 'marketing communications for causes and ideas in non-paid-for space, except where they contain a direct solicitation for donations as part of the marketer's own fund-raising activities'. So the rules are basically the same for online and offline communications. Any offline ads in paid-for space will be subject to the Code, as will any offline ads in non-paid-for space that solicit donations.

Summary

The area of political advertising is one of the more erudite subjects which fall to be considered in a work of this nature. In the broadcast context it raises important, and it would appear, finely balanced arguments about freedom of expression. More generally, identifying and understanding what is and isn't 'political' for CAP/BCAP Code purposes can be very challenging for those involved in the creative and compliance processes.

At the time of writing, we are witnessing in the United States the quadrennial race for the party Presidential nominees as a precursor to the November 2016 Presidential Election. TV 'Attack Ads' are an oft-used weapon in the armouries of the various candidates and their protagonists. They are, of course, absolutely prohibited in the UK. Supporters of the ban would have us look no further than the US experience to understand its rationale. However, tangible concerns remain about the breadth of the ban and its impact on otherwise legitimate campaigning and social advocacy.

Notes

1 R *(on the application of ADi)* v. *Secretary of State for Culture, Media & Sport* [2006] EWHC 3069

2 Animal Defenders International (2005) *My Mate's a Primate* [Video] https://www.youtube.com/watch?v=qON_lFQE4HY

3 See CAP Regulatory Statement on Marketing of Causes and Ideas, 2014

Smoking and vaping

23

**DAN SMITH, MATHILDA DAVIDSON
AND GEORGE SEVIER**

Introduction

Smoking led to some of the UK's most iconic advertising. But that is in the increasingly distant past and, in this country, the whole idea of tobacco advertising now seems anachronistic.

While electronic cigarettes – 'vaping' – are enjoying a (perhaps short-lived) moment in the advertising spotlight, public health and anti-smoking messages are now just about the only place you are likely to see tobacco smoking in UK advertising.

Tobacco

Most forms of tobacco promotion were banned by the Tobacco Advertising and Promotion Act 2002 (TAPA 2002). Since then, legislation has further limited the ability of tobacco companies to promote their products.

With each new restriction, tobacco companies have sought to reassign their marketing budgets to the limited media or marketing activities still available to them. For example, they have looked to maximise the branding impact and effectiveness of product packaging. However, with the advent of plain packaging (considered below), it appears that, in the UK at least, the promotion of tobacco to the public is effectively extinct.

The ban: legislation on tobacco advertising and promotion in the UK

Non-broadcast media

The TAPA 2002 introduced a complete ban on the advertising and promotion of tobacco products in non-broadcast media.[1] The ban is broadly defined and includes a prohibition on any advertisement that has the purpose or effect of promoting a tobacco product[2] – so it would cover an advert for a *non-tobacco* product which, nevertheless, has the effect of promoting a tobacco product.

Offences are committed by all those involved in the publication of the advert, not just the advertiser.[3] This includes the agencies involved in creating or placing the advert and the proprietor or editor of the publication (whether in print or digital media). There are narrow defences, which are unlikely to be of widespread comfort, where a person did not know, and had no reason to suspect, that the purpose of the advert was to promote a tobacco product, and where they could not reasonably have foreseen that that would be the effect of the advert.[4]

Sponsorship

The TAPA 2002 also bans sponsorship of cultural and sporting events where the purpose or effect of the arrangement is to promote a tobacco product.[5] The days of the Embassy World Snooker Championship are now long gone. Tobacco companies may continue to donate money to support events but not in return for branding or marketing rights, for example.

Point of sale

Following the TAPA 2002, some limited marketing activity was still allowed at the point of sale. However, subsequent restrictions culminated in a ban on the display of tobacco products, first in large stores and then, since 6 April 2015, in all stores, across the whole of the UK.[6]

Brand sharing

The TAPA 2002 also introduced a ban on brand sharing,[7] but this was effected under separate regulations.[8]

These regulations state that the use, in a non-tobacco advertisement, of any feature that is the same as, or likely to be mistaken for, a feature connected to a tobacco product, is prohibited if the purpose or effect of using

'1982 McLaren MP4', courtesy of Dave Hamster (Flickr, CC BY 2.0)

that feature is to promote tobacco products. So, using branding familiar from cigarette packaging to promote clothing would be banned where that branding also served to promote the cigarettes.

There is an exception for companies that used features connected to tobacco products for non-tobacco advertising prior to September 2002. Dunhill, which was involved in the luxury goods business before that date, can therefore continue to promote its menswear collection.

Sampling and vouchers

With limited exceptions for trade, the TAPA 2002 also bans businesses from giving away products or vouchers that have the purpose or effect of promoting tobacco products.[9] Most obviously, this prevents businesses from giving away cigarettes, but it is also the reason why, for example, tobacco products are invariably excluded from supermarket loyalty schemes.

Broadcast advertising

The TAPA 2002 does not cover tobacco advertising on television or radio as this was already banned under the Broadcasting Acts of 1990 and 1996 (following the European Union 'Television without frontiers' Directive in 1989).[10]

Are any tobacco promotions still permitted in the UK?

Exclusions from the TAPA 2002

The TAPA 2002 includes a number of exclusions, which allow some (very limited) scope to continue promotional activities.

Trade marketing

The promotion of tobacco products is permitted in business-to-business communications, where both parties work within the tobacco trade, and in publications circulated solely within the tobacco industry.[11] The exclusion only applies where the materials are specifically directed to those making purchase decisions regarding tobacco products (together with more senior people in the business).

Response to requests for information

A tobacco manufacturer is entitled to respond to requests for information about tobacco products from consumers.[12] It would, therefore, be legal to send a brand magazine to a customer who has requested one. However, it is only permitted to send the information once, and no further promotional material may be sent out unless a further request is made.[13]

Publications where an EEA state is not the principal market

Advertising can be carried in publications, printed outside the European Economic Area (EEA), for which all or part of an EEA state (or states) is not the principal market.[14] This exemption does not include in-flight magazines. It does apply to digital media, but only where the publisher does not carry out business in an EEA state and the publication is not intended to be accessed principally by persons in one or more EEA states.[15]

Specialist tobacconists

Certain tobacco advertisements are permitted in specialist tobacconists[16] so long as they are not for cigarettes or hand-rolling tobacco, are not visible from outside the premises and include a health warning/health information meeting specified requirements.

Digital media

Digital media marketing is included in the ban under Section 2(3) of the TAPA 2002. UK (and EEA) tobacco companies are not permitted to carry product advertising on their websites.

An exception exists for e-commerce – the supply of information to an individual will not be a banned tobacco advertisement where a website provides a means of purchasing tobacco products *and* the information is only made available *after* the individual has initiated the purchase.[17]

Other activities

PR

Although consumer-focused public relations activity is banned, the tobacco companies continue to invest in corporate PR and social responsibility initiatives. They still put their corporate name to events – for example, British American Tobacco currently sponsors the London Symphony Orchestra – but cannot do so for the purpose of promoting their tobacco products (or in a way that would have that as its effect).

The tobacco companies have also been heavily involved in campaigning against new regulatory proposals, notably plain packaging, and have used advertising to get their message across.

Packaging

Faced with the narrowing scope for marketing in the UK, the tobacco companies invested heavily in branding and packaging. However, even that avenue is about to be closed down. After a series of U-turns, in March 2015 Parliament voted in favour of standardised or plain packaging. From May 2016, packaging manufactured for the UK market must be plain and the sale of plain packs will be mandatory from May 2017.[18]

The Standardised Packaging of Tobacco Products Regulations 2015 contain an extensive list of requirements for plain packaging and will apply to both cigarettes and rolling tobacco. The packaging must be in a prescribed colour (Pantone 448C, which resembles a drab brown) and in a matt finish.[19] Text stating the brand and variant names of the product will be permitted, but this text cannot include any character that is not alphabetic, numeric or an ampersand.[20] The text must be in a prescribed location, font and text size.[21] Tobacco companies will be permitted to print their contact details on the packaging, but again this must adhere to detailed requirements regarding location, font and text size.[22]

Sanctions for breach of the TAPA 2002

Breach of the TAPA 2002 is a criminal offence, enforced by local Trading Standards officers.[23] The ultimate sanction is imprisonment and/or unlimited fines for serious breaches.[24] Advertisers and agencies should bear this point in mind: individuals within the organisations can be held *criminally* liable if they are involved in the creation or publication of any tobacco advertising in contravention of the Act.

Incidental smoking in advertising and smoking paraphernalia

Self-regulatory code rules and relevant guidance

The UK Code of Advertising, Sales Promotion and Direct Marketing (CAP Code) reflects UK legislation and prohibits the advertising of tobacco products.[25] The UK Code of Broadcast Advertising (BCAP Code) includes all tobacco products as a prohibited category for broadcast advertising.[26] The BCAP Code also:

- provides that advertising must not promote smoking or the use of tobacco products;[27]

- deals specifically with brand sharing, restricting the advertising of non-tobacco products that share a name, emblem or other feature with a tobacco product;[28] and

- prohibits any references to tobacco or smoking in adverts of particular interest to children or teenagers, except in the context of an anti-smoking or anti-drugs message.[29]

Within those rules, it is, in theory, permissible for advertising (which is not tobacco advertising) to show or refer to smoking. However, complaints are frequently made in respect of advertising that depicts smoking, in particular by anti-smoking lobby groups.

Clearcast guidance (in relation to broadcast advertising) states that Clearcast will normally reject any advertising that shows smoking, cigarettes or other tobacco products. It states that shots of smoking or smoking paraphernalia may be allowed in very limited circumstances, such as in health-related public service or smoking prevention advertisements. While incidental smoking images in clips from films made before the dangers of smoking were widely known may be acceptable, it is not possible to get around the rules by creating a period film – it is the date when the film is made that matters.

Rolling papers and filters may not be advertised in broadcast media.[30] They may be advertised in non-broadcast media but are subject to stringent CAP Code rules[31] which provide, among other things, that advertising must not encourage people to start smoking or to increase their level of smoking and must not glamorise smoking in any way (or link it to a long list of attributes or benefits). The rules further dictate that advertisements must not appeal to people under the age of 18 and must not condone the use of illegal drugs. They place controls on the age of people appearing in ads and the media where those ads can be placed.

ASA adjudications

The ASA has ruled on a number of complaints relating to smoking and ancillary products; some examples are set out below. E-cigarettes are considered later in this chapter.

The 'Best Spots to Smoke' smartphone app

A poster and website advertised a smartphone app, listing and reviewing the 'best spots to smoke by location or event'.

Following complaints, the ASA decided[32] that the adverts did not promote tobacco products (rather they promoted a service, albeit one offered by a tobacco company). However, it found that text such as 'how nice it is when you can smoke in a comfortable smoke spot!', and a link to a video that featured people smoking, presented smoking in a positive light. Further, the overall impression given by the adverts served to normalise and condone smoking, which is an unsafe practice. The regulator therefore ruled that the adverts were harmful and irresponsible and in breach of the relevant CAP Code rules.

The mobile phone case with built-in cigarette lighter

In another example, a sponsored ad on Facebook for a mobile phone case with an inbuilt cigarette lighter featured a close-up image of a cigarette being lit. Text stated 'TAG SOMEONE WHO CAN USE THIS'.[33] There is no general prohibition on advertising cigarette lighters and the ad did not encourage non-smokers to start smoking, or existing smokers to continue. However, the ASA considered that the overall impression of the ad was that it normalised and condoned smoking and presented it in an appealing manner, which was irresponsible.

The infant cigar smoker

Complaints were upheld by the ASA against an advert featuring an image of a toddler smoking a cigar with the text: 'You Wouldn't Let Your Child Smoke. Like smoking, eating meat increases the risk of heart disease and cancer. Go vegan!' However, the child smoking was not the cause for complaint; rather it was considered misleading to liken the risks associated with eating meat to the risks of smoking.[34]

The 'Twist and Burn' rolling paper ad

In 2003, the ASA upheld a complaint against Imperial Tobacco whose magazine advertisement for Rizla cigarette papers featured the phrase 'twist and burn', alongside an image of a Rizla packet twisted at one end. The regulator considered that the words 'twist and burn', with a packet 'twisted in the manner of a cannabis joint', were likely to be interpreted by readers as 'an allusion to the culture of cannabis use'.

Anti-smoking advertising and smoking cessation aids

Anti-smoking advertising

Like any other advertising claims, claims in government anti-smoking campaigns must not be misleading and must be substantiated by appropriate evidence. Anti-smoking advertising by the Department of Health has, in the past, been challenged by Forest (The Freedom Organisation for the Right to Enjoy Smoking Tobacco), in particular as to whether claims about smoking being a cause of cancer can be substantiated. The ASA rejected a complaint from Forest about an advert showing a growth on a cigarette which grew in size as a man smoked the cigarette. The ASA said that peer-reviewed scientific papers supported the claim that smokers experienced higher genetic mutation rates.[35]

Smoking cessation aids

CAP guidance indicates that marketers offering treatment to help smokers stop smoking should hold proof if they claim or imply that smokers will not have to make an effort to overcome their addiction. Relevant product advertising therefore typically includes wording such as 'Willpower required'.

Complaints are likely to be upheld by the ASA where advertising suggests that a method or product makes it quick or easy to stop smoking if there is an implication that the method or product, rather than the smoker's desire to stop, is the key to success. However, the use of the word 'effective' has been permitted, for example in: 'For the truly committed, hypnosis could be an effective way to help you give up smoking'.[36] There is a need for robust substantiation to support claims, potentially consisting of rigorous and objective trials on people. Claims based on alternative remedies may be particularly problematic.

Anti-smoking products may be regulated by the Medicines and Healthcare Products Regulatory Agency (MHRA), as products treating addiction or its symptoms are considered to be medicinal products. Where that is the case, a marketing authorisation must be held.[37]

Electronic cigarette advertising

The regulatory regime

Before 2014, there were no specific rules governing the advertising of electronic cigarettes in the UK. Regulation instead fell within the ambit of the specific CAP and BCAP Code rules (see above), together with the Codes' general provisions, including rules on misleadingness, health claims and harm and offence.

Initially, there were fears that even mentioning the word 'cigarette' in a TV advert might contravene the BCAP Code rules on the promotion of smoking. This led to some bizarre advertising, which did not show the product or even mention that it was an electronic cigarette. The ASA subsequently upheld complaints that the advertising omitted material information about the products.[38] To clear up the confusion and provide specific regulation of a fast-growing market for advertising, CAP launched a consultation and new rules specific to e-cigarette advertising came into force on 10 November 2014.[39] At the time of writing, these rules may soon change again as a result of the Tobacco Products Directive 2014/40/EU (TPD 2014).

The TPD 2014 and UK implementing legislation

The TPD 2014 establishes a new regulatory regime for electronic cigarettes which will, in practice, draw a distinction between medicinal electronic cigarettes and consumer electronic cigarettes. Medicinal electronic cigarettes (which claim or imply they can be used for cutting down, quitting or reducing the harm caused by smoking tobacco) fall outside the TPD 2014[40] and will be regulated as medicinal products. As such, it will be possible to advertise them to the public only if they are authorised on a non-prescription basis. Consumer electronic cigarettes will be subject to significant restrictions on advertising. The definition of electronic cigarettes in the TPD 2014 is limited to electronic cigarettes and accessories that 'can be used for consumption of nicotine-containing vapour',[41] meaning that electronic cigarettes that can only be used to inhale nicotine-free vapour are not subject to these restrictions.

The UK government has, at the time of writing, published draft regulations to implement the TPD 2014 in the UK.[42] It has taken what it refers to as 'a minimal approach' and suggested that it has no intention of going beyond the requirements of the TPD 2014.[43] Once finalised, the new rules will come into effect from 20 May 2016.

The proposed rules cover only e-cigarettes and accessories that can be used to consume nicotine-vapour. They include a ban on advertising any such consumer e-cigarettes or accessories on TV (including on-demand TV) or radio, in newspapers, magazines and periodicals (except certain limited trade press) or via sponsorship impacting on more than one European country. Guidance refers to a ban on 'Internet display advertising, e-mail and text message advertising',[44] but the draft regulations[45] appear to go further, so the impact on manufacturers' own websites is, as yet, unclear. The draft UK rules do not currently prohibit domestic advertising such as billboards, posters and leaflets.

The UK government has made clear that the proposed new rules would not prevent public health campaigns or 'stop smoking' messaging as these 'are not commercial communications'.[46]

A tougher line in Scotland?

There are currently no plans to introduce national rules in England, Wales and Northern Ireland that would exceed the requirements of the TPD 2014.[47] However, the Scottish Parliament is currently considering enabling legislation that, if passed, would give the Scottish government the ability to pass additional measures (which could include the regulation of electronic cigarettes that can be used to inhale nicotine-free vapour only and/or the regulation of 'domestic advertising' of electronic cigarettes).

The CAP and BCAP Code rules

CAP has said it will review the specific Code rules on e-cigarette advertising once it is clear how the TPD 2014 will be implemented in the UK. However, at the time of writing, the following rules continue to apply.

The definition of 'electronic cigarette'

The CAP and BCAP Codes define an electronic cigarette as: 'any product intended for inhalation of vapour via a mouth piece, or any component of that product, including but not limited to cartridges, tanks or e-liquids'. This is broader than the definition in the TPD 2014, and it remains to be seen how CAP will approach e-cigarettes that can be used only for the inhalation of nicotine-free vapour, once the new UK legislation is in force.

The rules

The Code rules cover marketing communications for, and which refer to, electronic cigarettes and related products, including e-shisha and e-hookah products, whether or not they contain nicotine. The rules are strict and clearly inspired by the approach to alcohol in the Codes.

Ads for electronic cigarettes must:

- be socially responsible;

- contain nothing that promotes any design, imagery or logo style that might reasonably be associated in the audience's mind with a tobacco brand;

- contain nothing that promotes the use of a tobacco product or shows the use of a tobacco product in a positive light;

- make clear that the product is an electronic cigarette and not a tobacco product;

- not contain health or medicinal claims unless the product is authorised for those purposes by the MHRA – electronic cigarettes may be presented as an alternative to tobacco but marketers must do nothing to undermine the message that quitting tobacco use is the best option for health;

- not use health professionals to endorse electronic cigarettes;

- state clearly if the product contains nicotine;

- not encourage non-smokers or non-nicotine-users to use electronic cigarettes;

- not be likely to appeal particularly to people under 18, eg by reflecting or being associated with youth culture, featuring characters likely to appeal particularly to people under 18 or showing people, using electronic cigarettes or playing a significant role, behaving in an adolescent or juvenile manner;

- not feature people using electronic cigarettes or playing a significant role who are, or who seem to be, under 25;

- in the case of non-broadcast communications, not be directed at people under 18 through the selection of media or the context in which they appear (no medium should be used to advertise electronic cigarettes if more than 25% of its audience is under 18 years of age); and

- in the case of radio ads, be centrally cleared in advance.

ASA rulings on e-cigarette advertising

Following the introduction of the specific Code rules in 2014, the ASA has issued a number of adjudications on e-cigarette ads. These have tended to concern glamorising, and therefore indirectly promoting, the act of smoking and appeal to under-18s. Other issues arising in complaints prior to the new rules – for instance, claiming that e-cigarettes are safer than tobacco smoking without having the necessary substantiating evidence – are equally likely to be problematic under the new regime.

'Sultry' vaping

In 2014, two TV ads for VIP electronic cigarettes featured a woman using an electronic cigarette and exhaling vapour.[48] It was no surprise that the ads attracted complaints. The ASA held that they created a strong association with traditional tobacco smoking and presented it as the central focus of the ads, in a sultry and glamorous way. They therefore indirectly promoted the use of tobacco products in breach of the Code rules.

A later 2015 adjudication[49] dealt with complaints in relation to a TV ad showing a couple smoking electronic cigarettes. The ASA held that, while it was clear that the products shown were electronic cigarettes, the ad created a strong association with traditional tobacco smoking and presented it 'in a sultry and glamorous, and therefore in a positive way'. The regulator again also concluded that the ad indirectly promoted the use of tobacco products.

Appeal to under-18s

In February 2015, the ASA declined to uphold complaints concerning a poster and magazine ad for E-Lites electronic cigarettes.[50] The ASA held that, despite the product resembling a cigarette, clear clarifying text meant that it was sufficiently clear that it was not a tobacco product. In addition, the ASA found that the use of a fashionably but formally dressed model over the age of 25 would not have particular appeal to people under 18.

By contrast, in June 2015, a number of different complaints were upheld in relation to ads for Hubbly Bubbly electronic cigarettes.[51] The ASA found that a banner ad failed to make clear that some of the products in the Hubbly Bubbly range contained nicotine, in breach of Code rules. Ads featuring young-looking models and naming celebrities such Zayn Malik and Cheryl Fernandez-Versini were likely to appeal particularly to under-18s. In addition, a YouTube video, using music, venue and a staccato cutting style to give the impression of a rave scene, included a number of participants who appeared to be under 25. The ASA considered that the overall impression of the ad was of a cool scene in which electronic cigarettes featured prominently, and that, in combination with the youthful appearance of the participants, made it likely to appeal particularly to those aged under 18.

Appeal to non-smokers

A TV ad for KiK showed a group of adults using and discussing e-cigarettes. One man in the group said: 'I used to smoke normal cigarettes, but after I quit I tried these. I actually prefer them.'

The ASA considered[52] that 'the vast majority of the dialogue positioned the product as one of interest to current smokers'. However, the use of the words 'but after I quit' implied that the man concerned was a non-smoker who had then taken up e-cigarettes. That was found to be irresponsible and in breach of the Code rule on encouraging non-smokers to use e-cigarettes.

Summary

Most major tobacco companies now have at least one electronic cigarette brand in their product portfolios and e-cigarettes are fast becoming a major contributor to overall advertising spend. But it is not clear how long this can last. The implementation of the TPD 2014 in the UK could mean that, in a few years, e-cigarette advertising to the public (at least in certain media) seems every bit as much of a historical oddity as tobacco advertising does today.

Notes

1 Tobacco Advertising and Promotion Act 2002, Section 2(1)

2 Tobacco Advertising and Promotion Act 2002, Section 1

3 Tobacco Advertising and Promotion Act 2002, Section 2(2)

4 Tobacco Advertising and Promotion Act 2002, Section 5(1)&(2)

5 Tobacco Advertising and Promotion Act 2002, Section 10(1)

6 The Health Act 2009, Section 21

7 Tobacco Advertising and Promotion Act 2002, Section 11(1) and the Tobacco Advertising and Promotion (Brandsharing) Regulations 2004

8 Tobacco Advertising and Promotion (Brandsharing) Regulations 2004, which came into force on 31 July 2005

9 Tobacco Advertising and Promotion Act 2002, Section 9(1)

10 'Television without frontiers' Directive, 1989, Article 13

11 Tobacco Advertising and Promotion Act 2002, Section 4(1)(a)

12 Tobacco Advertising and Promotion Act 2002, Section 4(1)(b)

13 Tobacco Advertising and Promotion Act 2002 – Explanatory Notes

14 Tobacco Advertising and Promotion Act 2002, Section 4(1)(c)

15 Tobacco Advertising and Promotion Act 2002, Section 4(1)(d)

16 Tobacco Advertising and Promotion Act 2002, Section 6(A1) and The Tobacco Advertising and Promotion (Specialist Tobacconists) (England) Regulations 2010

17 Tobacco Advertising and Promotion Act 2002, Section 4(1A)

18 The Children and Families Act 2014, Section 94(3) and The Standardised Packaging of Tobacco Products Regulations 2015

19 The Standardised Packaging of Tobacco Products Regulations 2015, Section 3(2)

20 The Standardised Packaging of Tobacco Products Regulations 2015, Schedule 1, Section 1(2)(a)

21 The Standardised Packaging of Tobacco Products Regulations 2015, Schedule 1, Section 1

22 The Standardised Packaging of Tobacco Products Regulations 2015, Schedule 1, Section 3

23 Tobacco Advertising and Promotion Act 2002, Section 13

24 Tobacco Advertising and Promotion Act 2002, Section 16

25 CAP Code rule 21.1

26 BCAP Code rule 10.1.3

27 BCAP Code rule 10.3

28 BCAP Code rule 10.4

29 BCAP Code rule 10.5

30 BCAP Code rule 10.1.3

31 CAP Code rule 21

32 ASA adjudication – Imperial Tobacco Ltd t/a Smoke Spots, 12 November 2014

33 ASA adjudication – Imperial Lightercase Inc, 11 March 2015

34 ASA adjudication – People for the Ethical Treatment of Animals (PETA) Foundation, 7 August 2013

35 ASA adjudication – Department of Health, 30 July 2014

36 ASA adjudication – EasyStop, 17 October 2001

37 CAP Code rule 12.11

38 ASA adjudication – Zulu Ventures Ltd trading as Sky Cig, 25 September 2013

39 Section 22 of the Non-Broadcast Code and Section 33 of the Broadcast Code

40 Directive 2014/40/EU, Article 20(1)

41 Directive 2014/40/EU, Article 2(16)

42 Draft Tobacco and Related Products Regulations 2016, with additional implementing measures proposed via the BCAP Code, Ofcom Broadcast Code and amendments to the Communications Act 2003

43 Guidance: Article 20(5), Tobacco Products Directive: proposals for UK law, 11 December 2015

44 Ibid.

45 As circulated to interested parties by the Department of Health, 23 November 2015

46 Guidance: Article 20(5), Tobacco Products Directive: proposals for UK law, 11 December 2015

47 Ibid.

48 ASA adjudications – Must Have Ltd t/a VIP Electronic Cigarettes, 26 February and 24 December 2014

49 ASA adjudication – Mirage Cigarettes Limited, 29 April 2015

50 ASA adjudication – Zandera Limited, 25 February 2015

51 ASA adjudication – Hubbly Bubbly Ltd, 10 June 2015

52 ASA adjudication – Vape Nation Ltd, 24 December 2014

PART FIVE
Business affairs

Client/agency contracts

24

JO FARMER

LEWIS SILKIN

ISBA/IPA Creative Services contract template of suggested terms

Introduction

The most important legal relationships that any agency enters into are the contracts with its clients. These govern both the income derived from the client and everything else that can make the difference between a profitable piece of business or an over-serviced account. If done well, the client/agency contract provides a road map for the relationship from cradle to grave, preventing the uncertainty that flows from not having a contractual relationship clearly documented.

Why does this matter? When the relationship is going well, it probably doesn't. While there is sufficient goodwill between the parties, any ambiguities can usually be resolved amicably enough. The problem comes when there is a dispute between the parties, or one party wishes to bring the relationship to an end. Where there is no written contract, problems can easily arise. For example, there can be disputes over who owns the intellectual property rights in the work that the agency has created or over the period of notice that should be given for the relationship to end.

Since 1998, the IPA and ISBA (Incorporated Society of British Advertisers) have been encouraging their respective members to complete signed, written client/agency contracts based on the ISBA/IPA template of suggested terms. In 2015, the IPA and ISBA launched a new model template of suggested terms for client/agency creative services appointments (which we refer to below as the ISBA/IPA Suggested Terms).

In this chapter, we explore the most important clauses (and the clauses that are most often negotiated and/or disputed) in client/agency creative services contracts, with reference to the new ISBA/IPA Suggested Terms.

The ISBA/IPA Suggested Terms

The new ISBA/IPA Suggested Terms adopt a modular approach to the sorts of services commissioned from agencies. This means that the different types of services typically offered by a marketing communications agency (from creative to social media, PR to app development) can easily be added to the client/agency agreement throughout the life cycle of the relationship.

In addition, the ISBA/IPA Suggested Terms recognise that relationships may be retainer based – the document for which ISBA and the IPA have called the 'Retainer Plus' version – or project based – the document for which ISBA and the IPA have called the 'Project Plus' version. Common also is a hybrid of the two (ie a retainer model with a number of separate projects outside the scope of the retainer being agreed from time to time). This hybrid model is also catered for in the Retainer Plus version.

Term of the appointment: retainers

For agencies being appointed on the Retainer Plus model, it may be crucial to agree an initial fixed period during which neither party can terminate the agreement 'without cause' on notice. This is to ensure that the agency has the chance to bed the relationship down and so that it can recover its expenditure in preparing to work for the client. Most creative and planning work is carried out at the beginning of the relationship, whereas fees are usually spread over the course of a year or more. If the client terminates the contract a few months into the relationship, then the agency is unlikely to have been properly remunerated for its initial work and can be left out of pocket.

The notice period must be considered in conjunction with the term. While some clients may argue that agencies should not be given the right to terminate the client/agency contract at all, most should be more reasonable and will acknowledge that both parties should have the right to terminate the agreement on reasonable notice. The question of what is reasonable depends on the circumstances and the size of the account, but it is not uncommon to see notice periods of between three to six months in retainer contracts. Ideally, the notice period should be long enough to give the agency the chance to redeploy its staff and try to find new business to replace the exiting client.

The 'Effective Date' or 'Commencement Date' specified in the contract should be the date on which the agency starts to provide its services, which can be a date in the past (ie if the parties have not been able to sign the contract in time before the agency started the services) or future. If this date has already passed, it means that the contract is deemed to have come into effect on that date. By contrast, the date on the front cover of the contract, at the top of the first page and next to the signatory blocks, gives the date of the contract itself rather than the date it came (or comes) into effect, and should be the date on which the parties sign the contract (or if signed on different dates, the date of the later signature). The contract should never be backdated (or for that matter, post-dated).

Term of the agreement: projects

The term of the agreement and notice period for termination of the Project Plus agreement is likely to be less important to agencies than it is with retainer appointments. This is because the Project Plus client/agency contract operates as a framework within which to agree projects, but there is no overall commitment or obligation on the client to use the agency. Therefore, at any point in time, you could have an ongoing agreement, but no active or ongoing projects (and therefore no fees coming into the agency).

However, there can be a great deal of uncertainty over the client's ability to cancel individual projects that are already under way or have been agreed. Clients might argue that they need the flexibility to be able to cancel projects if, for example, there are budgetary changes, or they want to change strategic direction. While it may be understandable that the client needs some flexibility, agencies must consider what would happen if projects can be cancelled on a moment's notice, meaning that the agency, which may have already incurred or committed to significant costs, also loses a stream of anticipated revenue without any chance to redeploy staff assigned to the project.

The new ISBA/IPA Suggested Terms try to address this uncertainty in a balanced way, and give drafting options for the parties to consider. The ISBA/IPA Suggested Terms clarify that clients can cancel projects at any time, but will still be liable to pay agency fees up to the date of cancellation of that project and costs incurred by the agency. The parties can then choose from the drafting options as to how to define what level of further fees will be payable to the agency to compensate it for the loss of revenue it would have earned had the contracted project not been cancelled. Depending on the option agreed, the client could pay: (i) the agency's fees during a specified project notice period; or (ii) particular cancellation fees as set out in a Scope of Work (which may increase depending on when the client cancels the project); or (iii) the entire project fee, regardless of the fact that it has been cancelled, because that is the fee that was contractually agreed by the parties.

Exclusivity and non-compete

A non-compete clause is a clause whereby the agency agrees not to provide services to a competitor of the client. An exclusivity clause is a clause whereby the client agrees not to use any other agency to provide similar services. Exclusivity clauses are less common these days in creative services appointments, but non-compete clauses are part and parcel of most client/agency contracts – though that is not to say that they are always reasonable in their scope and duration.

Agencies should enter into non-compete clauses with caution, and should weigh up the benefits of entering into a wide non-compete clause with a particular client against the risk of the agency being locked out of working with other brands in a particular sector. Where agencies accept a non-compete obligation, a few golden rules apply:

Who is a 'competitor'?

The client's view of who their competitors are may be very different (and broader) than the agency's. This is particularly true with brands that offer a wide range of different products and services. As ever with contracts, certainty and clarity are crucial, and so the client/agency contract should include a clear definition of 'Competitor'. This might be by describing the client's sector in words, or by reference to a list of named competitors. Listing named competitors, together with the particular industry sector, will be preferable to the agency for absolute certainty, but it may not be flexible enough for the client to allow for future entrants to their industry. Agencies should also ensure that any non-compete clause allows them to continue working for existing clients.

For how long should the non-compete last?

For retainer appointments, it may be appropriate for the non-compete to last for the term of the agreement. For project appointments, however, it would be unreasonable to expect agencies to accept a non-compete locking it out of working for other organisations in the client's sector for the duration of the framework agreement. Where work is on a project-by-project basis, but the agency is no longer providing services and receiving fees from the client because there are no projects in operation at any particular time, the agency should not be prevented from obtaining work from other, competing clients. The solution to this may be to state that the non-compete only lasts for the length of the particular project, or for as long as the fees in respect of all projects exceed a specified amount.

Who should the non-compete bind?

If the agency is prepared to agree to a non-compete, then, in an ideal world, it might stipulate that it only restricts staff who work on the client's account from working on competitor accounts (perhaps with some information barriers in place to stop sensitive client information from being leaked within the agency to staff working on competitor accounts). If this is not acceptable to the client, and if the agency is prepared to agree to an agency-wide non-compete, then it should ensure that the obligation covers only the agency itself, rather than extending to any agency group members or affiliates.

Remuneration and third-party costs

It may be obvious, but remuneration is one of the most important clauses in a contract. The client is entitled to expect that the remuneration set out in the contract will cover everything that falls within the ambit of the contract, while on the other hand, the agency should be entitled to ask for additional remuneration if the client wants to vary the terms of the contract by adding further services, projects, accounts or territories.

The ISBA/IPA Suggested Terms include some possible remuneration options, but that is all they are: options. The manner in which an agency structures its fees, commission and/or payment by results will vary, and every contract must be considered separately.

Different clients will take differing positions on payment terms, which is a matter for clients and agencies to negotiate on a case-by-case basis. However, payment terms should be no greater than 30 days without good reason, and when accepting client payment terms, agencies should take care to ensure that the client's preferred timescale does not affect any third-party payment terms. For example, if a third party, such as a production company, needs an instalment for campaign costs paid up front before starting work on the production (which is typical in the industry), then the agency should not be adversely affected by the client's payment terms, and should not be expected to fund the payment to the production company unless it is in receipt of funds from the client. A common way to deal with this issue is to specify in the client/agency contract that the agency can demand (and be paid) so-called 'rush payments' where third parties demand payment on a faster turnaround than the client's normal payment terms usually allow.

Third-party contracts

In the UK, it is industry standard practice for an advertising agency to contract as 'principal' in its own name with third parties such as production companies, talent, research companies and other suppliers. This means that the agency enters into such third-party contracts in its own name, not as 'agent' on behalf of clients. If anything goes wrong between the agency and its suppliers, then it is the agency who will be liable to the supplier, not the client. The supplier can sue the agency for breach of contract, even if the breach of contract was caused by something that the client did (or didn't) do. The classic example of this is where an agency negotiates music usage rights for a TV commercial on behalf of a client, and enters into licences with third-party rights holders. If the client then breaches those usage rights (for example, by using the music outside of the territories specified in the licence), then the rights holder will be able to sue the agency for breach of the licence. Contrast this with the position in the United States, where the industry standard practice is for agencies to contract with third parties as 'agent' on behalf of clients, rather than as principal.

As a result of this UK practice, the client/agency contract needs to specify what happens if a client causes the agency to breach the terms of any third-party contract that the agency has entered into as principal but on the client's behalf. In the ISBA/IPA Suggested Terms, there is a provision specifying that the client will indemnify the agency against any losses arising from any such act or omission by the client. However, in order to take advantage of this protection, the agency needs to ensure that the client has been notified of any significant contract terms or restrictions in such third-party contracts.

Warranties

It is customary for agencies to give clients the benefit of warranties and undertakings (ie contractual promises as to an existing or future state of affairs) in relation to specific aspects of the services and deliverables in the client/agency contract.

A common warranty sought by clients is a warranty that the deliverables being created by the agency do not infringe third-party intellectual property rights. In the new ISBA/IPA Suggested Terms it is suggested that agencies restrict such a warranty to infringement of copyright only. This is because other intellectual property rights (such as patents and trade marks) operate differently from copyright in that the risk of infringement of such rights is not necessarily within an agency's control. For example, an agency could independently develop a tagline for a client without having copied it from anyone else, but it may still infringe a third-party trade mark somewhere in the world. This is because trade marks are protected by registration on a territory-by-territory basis, and the first person to register a particular trade mark will obtain a monopoly on using it. It is therefore entirely possible for an agency to innocently infringe a third-party trade mark by creating something similar, without realising. The only way of countering this risk would be to conduct trade mark searches everywhere in the world, which would be prohibitively expensive for most advertising campaigns.

Another common warranty sought by clients is that the advertising complies with all applicable laws. It is recommended that agencies narrow any such warranty to compliance with directly applicable advertising laws and regulations in the UK only (rather than any laws and regulations anywhere in the world). It is also recommended that the client remains responsible for its own products and services, and for any materials provided by the client (or by predecessor agencies). Finally, if the client operates in a specialist sector (such as pharmaceuticals, consumer credit, banking, gambling, etc), then the agency may wish to stipulate that the client is responsible for compliance with laws and regulations particular to its sector.

Limitation of liability

This clause is also one of the most important in a client contract. Without it, an agency has no financial cap on its overall liability to the client should things go wrong. The absence of such a clause might also invalidate the agency's insurance.

There are complex laws that govern the enforceability and extent of limitation of liability clauses which, in the event of ambiguity, are generally interpreted on a presumption against the party seeking to rely on them, so they need to be drafted carefully. Agencies ought to ensure that:

- The limit on liability for direct losses is set at a level lower than the agency's professional indemnity (PI) insurance cover. For particularly large accounts, this may mean that the agency ought to set the liability cap by reference to a specific monetary amount rather than multiple of the fees, in order to give the agency certainty that the financial cap is lower than the PI insurance cover.

- They exclude liability for indirect or consequential loss and loss of profit (actual or anticipated), loss of goodwill, loss of anticipated savings and other similar special losses. In practice, there can be considerable debate about whether particular losses such as those listed here are direct or indirect, but to ensure compatibility with the agency's PI insurance, it should usually exclude losses of these types.

Copyright and other intellectual property rights

The intellectual property clauses in client/agency contracts tend to be among the most heavily negotiated clauses of the contract, and there is no standard approach as to how to deal with them.

Intellectual property rights in creative materials, computer software and code, and proprietary methodology may well be the agency's greatest asset – in addition to its staff. From a client's perspective, it will want to ensure that it has the right to use creative assets that have been paid for.

There are many different ways that a client and agency could agree to deal with ownership and use of intellectual property rights in creative materials. The ISBA IPA Suggested Terms offer optional drafting for two of the most common scenarios:

1 The agency assigning (ie transferring outright) to the client the intellectual property rights in the materials it creates specifically for a particular project, subject to payment of fees.

2 The agency retaining ownership of, but licensing to the client, the intellectual property rights in the materials it creates specifically for a particular project, for a specific period of time, in agreed territories and media. This licensing approach is one that agencies could explore where they are being remunerated on the basis of how successful the advertising is. However, in order for this licensing model to be attractive to clients (who are often used to owning intellectual property rights outright), the agency may need to demonstrate that it is sharing the risk of the advertising not being successful. So, the agency will, in all likelihood, need to show that the upfront fees for *licensing* the intellectual property rights in the creative materials are lower than if the agency had *assigned* them.

There are numerous other options for dealing with intellectual property rights, but the two optional clauses in the ISBA/IPA Suggested Terms are probably the most common.

When negotiating intellectual property rights clauses, agencies should bear the following in mind:

1 If possible, resist a client's demands for an automatic assignment to the client of all intellectual property rights in materials produced by the agency *on creation*, and instead ensure that all assignments of intellectual property rights – if the agency is prepared to consider assignment in the first place – are subject to payment of the agency's fees. This can be a hotly negotiated clause, with the agency not wanting to give up ownership of its intellectual property until it has been paid, but the client not wanting to be prevented from using the creative materials before it pays for them (particularly in case there is a genuine dispute with the agency over what fees are payable for the creative work).

2 Ensure that the agency is not contractually promising to assign intellectual property rights in materials that the agency may not own or otherwise have the right to assign (eg rights of talent appearing in advertising, music rights, photography and other third-party materials). The ISBA/IPA Suggested Terms deal with this issue by stating that the agency must obtain a licence from third parties in order that the client can use their materials for the purposes set out in a Scope of Work.

3 Consider whether there are any underlying proprietary intellectual property rights belonging to the agency which are not appropriate to assign to the client. For example, are there any methods, processes, know-how or other proprietary tools or software that the agency uses when creating the materials for the client, which the agency needs to be able to use with other clients across its business? If so, the agency should ensure that such proprietary intellectual property is carved out from any assignment of rights to the client.

4 Explore whether the agency should only be assigning the intellectual property rights in creative materials that are *approved* by the client for further development and inclusion in their advertising, or to put it another way, whether the assignment of rights should exclude materials or ideas that are *rejected* by the client. However, from the client's perspective, it may want to own rejected ideas so that it can return to develop them at a later date if it chooses to do so.

Audit

If the agency can enter into a contract with no audit provisions at all, then there is no obvious reason why it should not do so. Preparing for an audit is a time-consuming and disruptive exercise that is unlikely to yield any benefit for the agency.

If a client insists on including audit provisions, then the agency should seek to protect itself from the worst excesses of some of the more over-zealous audits. In the ISBA/IPA Suggested Terms, there are provisions dealing with the purpose of the audit (ie to check contract compliance, not for fee negotiation), the amount of notice an agency should expect from a client wishing to conduct an audit, confirmation that any independent auditor is paid on a time-spent rather than money-saved basis, as well as provisions detailing when audits can take place (ideally during normal office hours only) and what records the audits can cover.

TUPE

The Transfer of Undertaking (Protection of Employment) Regulations 2006 (TUPE) operate so as to automatically transfer an employee's contract of employment (unless they object), on the same terms and conditions, from an incumbent agency to a successor agency when the incumbent agency's client/agency contract ends. TUPE may also apply to situations where the client decides to bring the services in-house. The general effect of TUPE is to transfer any employees who are dedicated to working on the client account, together with any relevant liabilities, such as unpaid bonuses, holiday pay, grievance claims, etc in relation to those employees, to a successor agency (or the client, as the case may be).

Often, one of the primary reasons that a client may wish to change agency is to obtain 'new blood' and fresh thinking on the account. In these circumstances, the last thing the client wants is to end up with the same staff working on the account, which is the effect of TUPE. It is, therefore, not unusual to find in clients' standard contracts attempts to mitigate the effects of TUPE by requiring the agency to give indemnities protecting the client and any successor agency from unfair dismissal or discrimination claims over which the agency has no control. Depending on the size of the account, such a clause could prove to be financially disastrous for an agency losing a piece of business, and agencies should exercise caution before accepting such a clause.

The parties cannot contract out of TUPE. It is a statutory employee right and as such overrides anything to the contrary in a contract. There is no point in the contract saying: 'The parties agree that TUPE does not apply.'

In view of the duties and potential liabilities imposed by TUPE, the ISBA/IPA Suggested Terms seek to strike a fair balance between the parties. In essence, they aim to ensure that: (i) once a new client/agency agreement begins, the client is responsible for TUPE-related liabilities arising prior to its commencement – because the new agency will have had no involvement with the relevant individuals prior to that date; (ii) on termination of the client/agency agreement, the outgoing agency will be responsible for TUPE-related liabilities that have arisen during the term of the agreement – because the outgoing agency will have been the employer of the relevant individuals during that period; and (iii) the client will be responsible for TUPE-related liabilities arising after the termination of the client/agency agreement – because the outgoing agency will have no involvement with the relevant individuals after that date.

Further information regarding the IPA/ISBA TUPE Protocol and a practical guide to handling TUPE transfers can be found by IPA members on the IPA website at www.ipa.co.uk. Agencies are always encouraged to seek legal advice in this area.

Summary

Since the first ISBA/IPA client/agency model terms were created, far more agencies get their agreements with clients signed. Agencies have, by and large, learnt that they can demonstrate greater professionalism and confidence if they have carefully tailored agreements ready to provide to clients prior to starting work on a new account. New business directors, finance directors and those appointed to negotiate terms, including agency in-house lawyers, should be familiar with standard contract terms to protect their agencies from unreasonable obligations and liabilities and to manage risk. The new ISBA/IPA Suggested Terms offer structured building blocks from which to negotiate client/agency contracts and can be adapted to fit a wide range of disciplines and types of appointment with relative ease.

Pitching 25

INDIA FORSYTH AND RICHARD LINDSAY

Introduction

Owing to the nature of the pitch process in advertising, agencies face a range of commercial challenges that few other industries have to consider prior to being awarded work.

As well as standard confidentiality concerns relating to fees, rates and staff, agencies also hand over their 'stock' – their valuable ideas and advice – to prospective clients in advance of the award of work, and consequently run the risk of these being used at a later date without their consent or involvement.

It is, therefore, essential that agencies are aware of the legal issues involved in the pitch process and how best to deal with them in order to protect their businesses and avoid disputes in the future.

This chapter provides a summary of the resources available to IPA member agencies to assist with pitch practice and an overview of some of the key issues to consider during the pitch process.

Resources for IPA member agencies

The IPA has developed a New Business Pitch Pack which is available to its members.[1]

The Pitch Pack includes a recommended Pitch Protocol and a template recommended Pitch Agreement/NDA endorsed by ISBA. It also includes access to the IPA's Pitch Protection Scheme. Both the Pitch Agreement and Pitch Protection Scheme are discussed in further detail below.

The IPA has also worked with ISBA to create a joint industry website, www.thegoodpitch.com, which serves as a hub for information and resources on recommended industry best practice in pitching.

Pitch Agreement/NDA

This standard document is available to IPA members via the New Business Pitch Pack web page and the IPA Legal & Public Affairs Department website page.[2] From a legal perspective, the two key areas covered in a pitch agreement should be intellectual property and confidentiality.

Intellectual property

As discussed in Chapter 1, under English law, copyright arises automatically for qualifying works, and first belongs to the creator of the work, which would normally be the agency in a pitch situation. Transfer of ownership of copyright technically requires an assignment in writing, signed by the assignor. A licence to use copyright does not have the same strict requirements.

Agencies should carefully check the terms of any proposed pitch agreement supplied by the potential client. The aim is to ensure that it does not contain an assignment of copyright in content created by the agency for the pitch (unless the agency is actually willing to assign its rights – which is rare). If there is no assignment, the agency should also check the terms of any licence allowing the client to use content created by the agency for the pitch. The licence terms should be limited to allowing use solely for the purposes of considering the pitch and nothing more without the agency's express approval.

Where a fee is payable to the agency for participating in the pitch, the agency should ensure that the pitch agreement makes clear that the fee is for working on the pitch rather than as payment for an assignment of rights (unless the agency has agreed that with the potential client).

Confidentiality

In a pitch situation, confidential information will usually be exchanged, and it is in the interests of each party that such information is protected.

Some of the information exchanged will be obviously identifiable as confidential. For example, the client may need to disclose the product or service that it wishes to advertise, its wider marketing plans and budget considerations. The agency may need to disclose information about its fees, staff and creative executions or strategic documents. Perhaps less obvious is that the ideas that may be shared by the agency at pitch stage should also be treated as the agency's confidential information. It is vital for the agency that this is made clear. Copyright will protect only the execution of ideas, not the ideas themselves.

An obligation to treat information as confidential can arise through circumstances, where the information is clearly of a confidential nature and the situation implies such an obligation. However, it can be dangerous to rely on this in a commercial context such as pitching. It is far safer to include appropriate confidentiality provisions in a pitch agreement so that there is little chance of confusion and a subsequent dispute.

The IPA template Pitch Agreement/NDA endorsed by ISBA enables both parties to retain ownership of their own intellectual property and confidential information, enabling the other party to use them only in relation to the evaluation of the pitch.

Pitch Protection Scheme

It is good practice for agencies to ensure that all ideas and materials they create for pitches are protected. One method of doing so is to place materials, including the recording of ideas, into some sort of formal repository. The aim is to enable the agency to be able to prove what they created and when should a dispute arise regarding the ownership of a copyright work or an idea that they presented to a potential client in a pitch scenario.

The IPA's own scheme allows IPA member agencies to record the details of the pitch, a summary of the ideas presented and key materials shared with the potential client. A registration certificate is then provided to the agency. Agencies need not use the IPA's scheme. Any process by which agencies can demonstrate their ownership of their ideas and copyright works should help.

Other considerations

Copyright/confidentiality notices

A further, simple method by which agencies can protect their rights is to use a copyright and/or confidentiality notice on all materials provided to potential clients.

As with a pitch protection scheme, a copyright and/or confidentiality notice does not convey any legal protection in its own right. Rather, it is a useful tool by which agencies can put others on notice that they claim ownership of the rights in the materials to which the notice is fixed. For this reason, it is good practice for agencies to use copyright/confidentiality notices on their pitching materials, as a minimum.

An example of a notice is set out below. The wording should, of course, be tailored to the particular pitch situation and the agency's requirements.

All information, including all concepts and ideas, contained in this document has been created by, and belongs to, [AGENCY]. All such information is strictly confidential and may not be used for any purpose without the written agreement of [AGENCY]. Copyright ©[AGENCY] [YEAR]. All rights reserved.

Internal policies/procedures

Agencies should also consider maintaining a document such as an internal policy so that staff know to follow a particular procedure to help protect their agency's work. Such a policy could, for example, explain how to deal with the retention of working drafts and how and where to record the date of creation of pieces of work and the names of those involved in their development. Thought should also be given as to how to keep track of the development of work produced on digital platforms. For example, staff may be required to download or print and file copies of work on a regular basis.

TUPE and the IPA Pitch Protocol

The advertising industry is particularly exposed to the effects of the Transfer of Undertakings (Protection of Employment) Regulations 2006 (TUPE).

As explained in Chapter 24, TUPE can lead to a situation whereby the agency that wins a pitch is required to take on the employees of the incumbent agency who were previously engaged in working on the business the successful agency has now won. This can have significant implications on the actual value of the new client's business to the successful agency. Pitching agencies should, therefore, ask the potential client at the earliest opportunity for full information about the likelihood and details of any such employee TUPE transfers. However, while the pitching agency will want information on staff (and any claims) it may inherit from the incumbent agency, clients generally know little about the terms on which an agency's staff work (and less about any outstanding claims). And, of course, the incumbent agency may not be keen to help a competitor. It is only after the pitch that TUPE requires the incumbent agency to provide the successful agency with certain information about any employees who are transferring under TUPE.

Agencies and advertiser clients are encouraged to use the IPA's Pitch Protocol, endorsed by ISBA, for just this reason.[3] Applying the Protocol involves the incumbent agency, and an agency that has been short-listed on a pitch, exchanging a simple letter. By doing so, they enter into an agreement on the terms set out in the Protocol. The key elements of the agreement involve the provision of information, co-operation over any TUPE transfers and the allocation of any responsibility for claims by staff following a TUPE transfer.

Summary

Pitches are often carried out under high pressure. It is easy to understand why agencies might not put the issues covered by this chapter at the top of their priority lists. Failing to deal with these issues can, however, lead to much greater difficulties at a later date, regardless of whether the pitch is won – and the agency might need to have difficult conversations with its new client – or lost, and the agency might face the possibility of seeing its ideas and/or copyright works used without its permission.

Agencies should aim for best practice in the pitch process and reap the benefits of being up front and dealing with matters in advance.

Notes

1 www.ipa.co.uk/Page/New-Business-Pitch-Pack

2 www.ipa.co.uk/Document/Client-Agency-Pre-Pitch-NDA

3 www.ipa.co.uk/document/tupe-voluntary-protocol-2006-updated-july-2014

Production of commercials

Agency/production company contracts

KIM KNOWLTON (Institute of Practitioners in Advertising)

AND STEVE DAVIES (Advertising Producers Association)

Introduction

The term 'commercial' nowadays includes all types of filmed content, be it advertising in the traditional sense or, for example, branded content, and regardless as to the medium on which the content is shown to the public, be it broadcast television or online.

The UK has an enviable reputation for producing commercials of the highest quality. Today, with ever-expanding platforms through which commercials may be viewed, this reputation continues to grow.

The actual procedure of making commercials is a complex one. Shooting a commercial can be one of the most expensive activities that an advertising agency will undertake on behalf of its client. Scripts and costs will vary, the process is complex, frequently conducted under time pressure, and it involves a considerable degree of artistic, and therefore largely subjective, input.

The UK production industry is among the finest and most professional in the world, and the combination of knowledgeable and experienced production company directors and producers and equally informed agency production departments has ensured the maintenance of the highest artistic and technical standards.

The job of the agency production department and the production company is to make an outstanding commercial for the agency's client.

The role of the contract between agency and production company is to facilitate this service and, in particular, to ensure clarity as to which of the agency and production company is responsible for each aspect of the production, which is the principal reason the documents are lengthy, as they also operate as a checklist so that nothing is overlooked.

The current industry standard contract, which comes in two parts, known as the PIBS (Production Insurance Briefing Specification – Part 1) and Contract Terms (Part 2), is endorsed by the Advertising Producers Association (APA), the Institute of Practitioners in Advertising (IPA) and the Incorporated Society of British Advertisers (ISBA). It was formally adopted in July 2003 and was subsequently updated and re-launched in the summer of 2004 (with some minor changes added from time-to-time since then).

What follows is commentary on the existing document as it stands today, taken from the previous edition of *Ad Law* without changes. At the time of writing, the IPA is working on an update of the PIBS and the Contract Terms.

The purpose of the contract

The 2004 contract breaks the process of making a commercial down into two separate, though related, parts:

- The Production and Insurance Specification (known as the 'PIBS') that sets out all the information specific to the production under consideration and assigns responsibilities between the agency and production company for the job. This forms Part 1 of the arrangement.

- The Production Contract (or Part 2 of the procedure) that sets out the terms that apply to every commercial produced under it.

Although Part 2 is entitled 'Contract', both Part 1 and Part 2 are contractual documents and the rights and obligations of the parties are defined by both documents taken together.

Although the advertising agency is working for a client in arranging and contracting for the production of a commercial, it is important to note that in this context, the agency is a principal in law. In consequence, the advertising agency is liable to the production company in respect of its contractual obligations as principal, rather than as an agent for the advertiser.

The production or commercials contract

Paradoxically, the contracting process is best explained by taking Part 2 of the contract first and then running through the contents of Part 1, the PIBS.

Part 2: the contract

This chapter will consider the most important clauses only.

Responsibilities (Clause 1)

This defines the commercials to be made by reference to the PIBS, the script and the cost estimate in order that the production company is clear about what film it is making and the agency is clear about what film it is getting. The production company will also produce a treatment for the script – an explanation of how it will bring it to life on the screen. This is not a contractual document but it assists in ensuring the parties share a vision of how the commercial will look.

Payment (Clause 5)

Production companies and agencies agree a fixed price for the production and contract in advance of the commercial being produced – and that sum is written into the contract.

It shows the production company's fee, referred to as the mark-up, which is a percentage of the costs of the production. The production company is then responsible for producing the commercial for that fixed price; it cannot invoice the agency for extra costs it incurs because, for example, an unforeseen problem arises. The contract provides exceptions; if the agency requires the production company to do additional work, for example by changing the script, or the agency defaults on its obligations, for example in providing actors, and such results in additional costs. Half the budget is payable no later than seven days before the shoot and the balance after the shoot as set out in the contract.

The position is different for 'fast track' productions (those defined as commercials which are to be completed within 21 days of the contract being signed), where 75 per cent of the budget is payable no later than seven days before the shoot.

Copyright and other rights (Clause 12)

It is essential that the agency ensures it obtains all the necessary rights needed to comply with its obligations to the client. Thus, provided the agency pays for the commercial, this agreement provides for the assignment of copyright in the commercial by the production company to the agency. Thus the agency can use the commercial and any image from it in any media, anywhere in the world.

However, there is an important exception for animation; the agency may use the commercial (or clips from it in any audiovisual media, anywhere in the world), but copyright in the animation remains with the production company. Thus if the agency wants to use a still from it, for example in some other advertising or in merchandising, it may only do so if it agrees a fee for such use with the production company. It is very important a client understands the restrictions that will always exist with using commercials indefinitely, whether because of animation rights, or artists' and models' performance rights.

The PIBS provides a shopping list for agencies so that they have the option of agreeing the price for a particular use of animation at the outset. They can agree that such fee is payable on first use. The clause also provides that agencies and production companies are responsible for obtaining copyright clearance on third-party material they include in the commercial.

Postponement or cancellation at agency's request (Clauses 13 and 14)

The agency may postpone production but must pay the production company the extra costs of making the commercial that result. Similarly, the agency may cancel the production of the commercial but it will then be obliged to pay the production company the costs it has incurred, plus producer's and director's fees and mark-up, in sums to be agreed.

Insurance (Clauses 16–18)

The insurance clause is very important. It may be that this clause needs amending if the client wishes to insure. The usual clause, however, provides that the agency indemnifies the production company and insures itself against specified items and vice versa.

If weather is unsuitable for filming a commercial on a planned shoot day and the shoot day has to be extended or another shoot day is required as a result, the extra day is referred to as a 'weather day'. The client is responsible for that additional cost. In contractual terms, the agency is responsible for paying that cost to the production company and the agency is entitled to recover that cost from the client. Weather day insurance is available. The premium will depend upon the type of weather to be insured against, that is, the definition of 'unsuitable' weather in respect of the commercial being shot and the likelihood of that weather occurring at that location at that time. However, weather insurance premiums are typically 30–40 per cent of the cost of a weather day, so it is not unusual for clients to opt not to buy cover and take the risk of having to pay for a weather day themselves. The production company is responsible for the additional cost of sets built outside prior to the commencement of the shoot if the agency asks and pays for the production company to insure against that. The production company is also responsible for additional costs as a result of it not being able to reach the location because of adverse weather.

Disputes procedure (Clause 23)

Under this contract, the agency and the production company agree that any dispute will be dealt with by mediation or arbitration, rather than going to court. The aim of this is for industry disputes to be determined by representatives of the industry who have a good understanding of it. Further, in most circumstances, mediation provides a quicker, cheaper and more flexible method of determining disputes. This issue is dealt with in a little more detail below.

Part 1: the Production and Insurance Briefing Specification (PIBS)

Moving on to consider the first part of the agreement, the PIBS records the details particular to the commercial being shot as part of the agreement between the agency and production company; it is as much part of the contract between them as Part 2 – the contract.

The PIBS is set out in such a way as to operate as a checklist to assist the parties in ensuring that every element of production of the commercial is attributed as a responsibility to either the agency or the production company.

The PIBS deals with the following:

Section A

This contains spaces to insert information as to duration of the commercial, formats required and critical dates.

Section B: insurance

The purpose of this clause is to ensure that all the different types of insurance that might be required are considered, and, if they are appropriate to the production, that it is made clear which elements the production company and the agency are responsible for, because the production insurance contains many elements and is best obtained from a specialist broker.

The section details the different areas that need to be insured:

- non-appearance insurance;
- employer's liability insurance and worker's compensation;
- commercial producers' indemnity insurance;
- personal accident insurance;
- negative insurance;
- vehicle insurance;
- all-risks loss or damage to agency props and wardrobe;
- weather insurance;
- special requirements insurance; and
- evidence of insurance in effect.

Section C: time-critical information

This clause provides an opportunity for the agency to identify whether the shoot could be postponed because of force majeure (rather than being cancelled).

Section D: animation

See Clause 12 of Part 2 (above) in respect of animation copyright.

Section E: agency approvals

Agencies should use this section to identify those elements of the production where the agency specifically requires approval before the production company proceeds.

Section F: currency/exchange rate fluctuations

This clause sets out the procedures for commercials being shot outside the UK. The method adopted is for the production company to identify what part of the quote they must pay out in foreign currency and what exchange rate was used. The production company fixes the exchange rate on the day the production is confirmed by forward buying the currency. The price agreed is varied to reflect the actual cost to the production company of forward buying the currency and that adjusted figure is inserted in Clause 5 of Part 2.

Section G: checklist

This section is a checklist of other items that may be required as part of producing the commercial, with the opportunity to say that they are inapplicable, or the responsibility of the agency or of the production company.

Section H: additional contractual requirements

Any additional terms specific to each case can be inserted in this section.

Section I: payments

It is important to set out clearly in this section when the price, agreed in Clause 5 of Part 2, is due to be paid. For overseas shoots, and other shoots that are front-end cost heavy, it is appropriate for the parties to consider accelerating payment of the second 50 per cent. For example, the parties could agree that half of the second 50 per cent (ie 25 per cent of the total fee) will be paid immediately following the last shoot day.

Section J: showreels

The agency commits to endeavour to get licences in favour of the production company to use the commercials to promote itself, in the same terms as the agency gets such rights for itself.

Section K

This section provides that the agency should issue the contract – part 2 to the production company by the day following verbal/written confirmation.

Disputes

Fortunately, disputes in commercials production are comparatively rare – but when they do crop up – even with the procedures outlined in the contract – they are time consuming and emotionally draining.

As such, invoking the formal dispute procedure is a step only usually taken as an 'action of last resort', when informal discussions have broken down and neither side can see a way forward.

The rationale of an industry disputes procedure

Given that the sums involved in production disputes are comparatively small in commercial law terms, it is clearly desirable to avoid recourse to the courts. In these circumstances, the procedure outlined in Clause 23 of the contract was designed to provide a totally confidential, fair and rapid means of resolving disagreements.

In the first instance, however, the IPA and APA will, if asked, investigate whether an informal intervention from them can help resolve the problem, and recent experience has shown this to be an effective means of resolving some potential disputes, by tackling the issue before the parties' positions become ingrained.

Recognising the need for administrative expertise in the actual process of mediation and arbitration, it was agreed to place the process of the arrangement into the hands of professional mediators/arbitrators, who would work alongside knowledgeable representatives of the industry to determine a fair and reasonable outcome. To this end, the Centre for Disputes Resolution (CEDR) has been appointed to carry out this role.

Mediation

In mediation, the parties are invited to work towards a mutually agreeable solution via a professional mediator. The respondent may decline to participate in mediation and proceed directly to arbitration, but a resolution achieved via this process can benefit the parties by reducing administration costs and avoiding the potentially damaging effects on commercial relationships by allocating blame. It is a confidential process, unlike court proceedings. However, should this route prove unfruitful, or if the respondent requires it, a dispute can move to formal arbitration.

Arbitration

Arbitration is more similar to court proceedings. The parties in the standard contract agree to CEDR appointing an arbitrator, who in turn administers the procedure to a strict timetable. Evidence of claims and defences are exchanged between the parties and they put their case at a hearing before a tribunal made up of a panel of mutually acceptable representatives from the film production industry, advertising agencies and advertisers (one per sector) under the chairmanship of the CEDR arbitrator.

Conclusion

As will be gathered from all the above, making a television commercial is a highly complex procedure, frequently conducted under considerable pressure. The Production Contract (Parts 1 and 2) acts as a bedrock on which the British advertising industry creates some of the most outstanding and effective television commercials made anywhere in the world.

By providing clarity and certainty in an environment driven by creativity, the contract's value to all parties is immense.

INDEX